BROKEN POTS, MENDING LIVES

The archaeology of Operation Nightingale

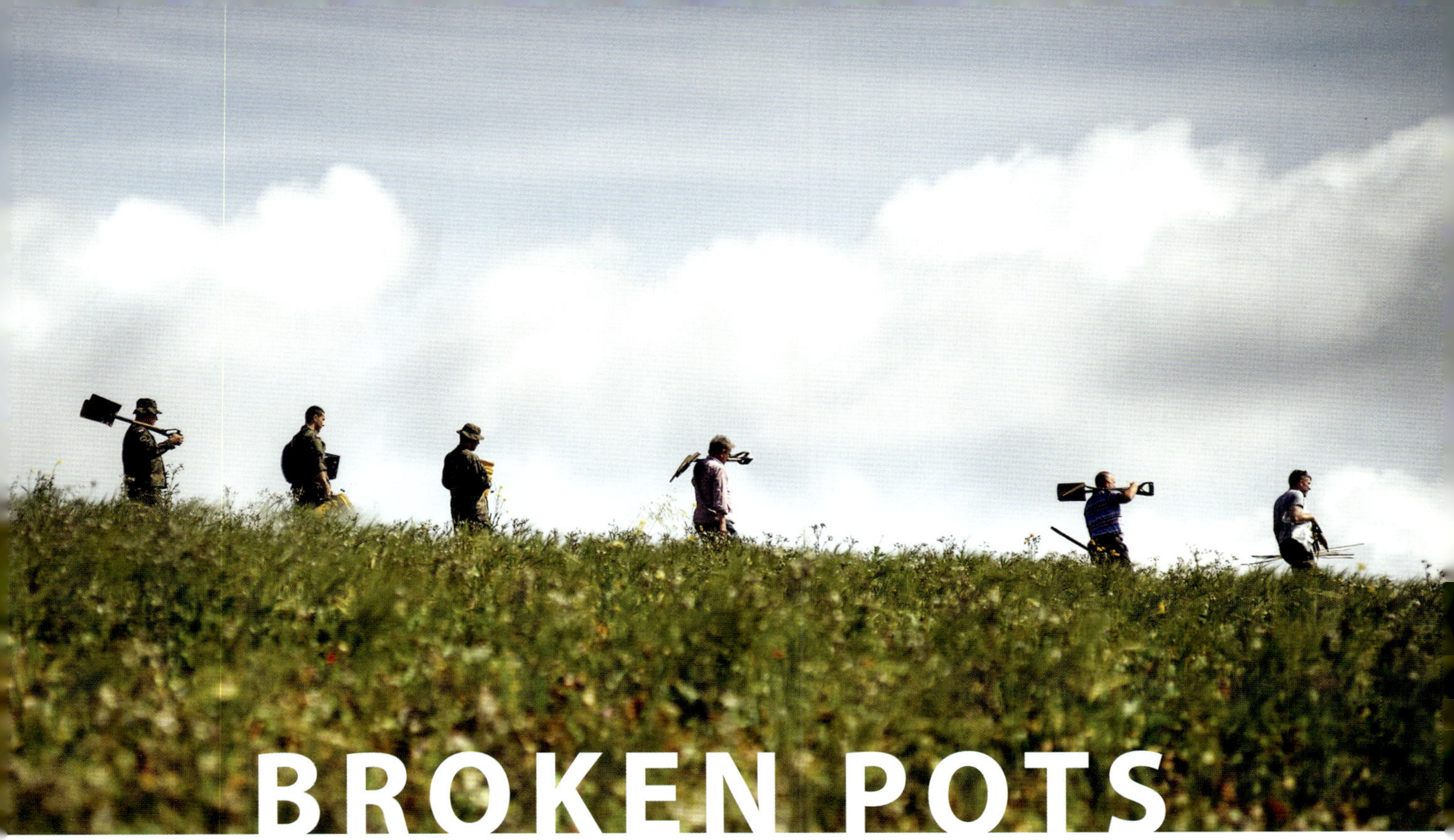

BROKEN POTS MENDING LIVES

The archaeology of Operation Nightingale

RICHARD OSGOOD

with contributions from

ALICE ROBERTS, RICHARD BENNETT AND HARVEY MILLS

Oxford & Philadelphia

Published in the United Kingdom in 2023 by
OXBOW BOOKS
The Old Music Hall, 106–108 Cowley Road, Oxford, OX4 1JE

Hardcover Edition: ISBN 978-1-78925-938-4
Digital Edition: ISBN 978-1-78925-939-1 (epub)

A CIP record for this book is available from the British Library

Printed and bound in the Czech Republic by FINIDR s.r.o.
Text layout by Frabjous Books

For a complete list of Oxbow titles, please contact:

UNITED KINGDOM
Oxbow Books
Telephone (0)1226 734350
Email: oxbow@oxbowbooks.com
www.oxbowbooks.com

UNITED STATES OF AMERICA
Oxbow Books
Telephone (610) 853-9131, Fax (610) 853-9146
Email: queries@casemateacademic.com
www.casemateacademic.com/oxbow

Oxbow Books is part of the Casemate Group

Contents

Acknowledgements

Were I to acknowledge everyone that has made Operation Nightingale possible then this would probably be the longest section of the entire book, such has been the generosity from so many people. You all know how much you have helped, contributed and assisted and thus do consider yourself thanked even if you are not listed below.

I have been incredibly self-indulgent with this work, examining only the projects for which I had a level of responsibility. Phil Abramson, Alex Sotheran and Guy Salkeld in my team within Defence Infrastructure Organisation, Ministry of Defence (and Martin Brown beforehand) have done just as much with their Operation Nightingale sites and could easily write a narrative to surpass the stories I have told – they are a dream to work with and essential to the success of the programme. Without the forbearance of our boss, Richard Brooks, however, none of this might happen – so thanks to him too.

At the start of Operation Nightingale, we were working largely with the Rifles Regiment – Nev Holmes, Becka Maciejewski and Mike Smith were to the fore with these efforts. Many other cap badges have also now assisted – from 17 Port and Maritime Regiment to the Royal Military Police. The Royal Air Force, Royal Artillery and others have provided superb logistic support on several projects. Surgeon Commodore Peter Buxton not only gave assistance from a military and medical perspective but also with his archaeological hat on too (how many other people can procure a mobile X-ray team for site!).

Giles Woodhouse, ex of the Mercian Regiment, Help for Heroes and now Wessex Archaeology gave me vital support at the start, not only with advice on logistics and wellbeing requirements but also continued support on projects and friendship too. His role at Help for Heroes was the reason behind arranging University placements at Winchester with Dr Paul Everill. It seems a very long time since I was sending 'Blueys', a form of letter on blue paper sent within the Ministry of Defence Post, about archaeology to Giles when he was in Afghanistan.

On some of the excavations, we have been indebted to the support of the military Training Safety Marshalls who looked out for us and made sure that military exercises taking place at the same time were aware of our work: Rob Chisnall, Kev Morris, Les French and Jeff Elson. The two former Marshalls also provided us with drone photography that made it to publication in the journal *Antiquity* too (Sean Davies and his 'cherry-picker' and Adam Stanford with pole-camera have been our other go-to aerial photographic methods).

Successive Commanders of Salisbury Plain from Mike Beard to Tim Jalland recognised the worth of the endeavours and did all they could to support the project – and the same can be said for the Commanders of the Bulford and Tidworth Garrison like Colonel Jamie Balls.

We have tried to spread the news of our work as far as we could and this would have been impossible without our television drive, from Sir Tony Robinson and Phil Harding *et al.* at *Time Team* to Alex Langlands and Raksha Dave at *Digging up Britain's Past* and, of course, Professor Alice Roberts and the *Digging for Britain* team. Other media folk such as Dr Cat Jarman, Julian Richards, Dan Snow and Mary-Ann Ochota should also take a bow at this point too. Mike Pitts with *British Archaeology* and Carly Hilts at *Current Archaeology* also performed wonders in ensuring our excavations featured in their excellent magazines. Dr Jessica Liu, Dr Isabel Burton, Dr Mark Roughley and Professor Caroline Wilkinson worked really hard to provide us with the faces from Rat Island and Bullecourt and make our skeletons into people once more.

Throughout the projects we have needed outlets to maintain the interest of the team; Butser Ancient Farm, the Ancient Technology Centre, Stonehenge, the Hawk Conservancy, the Wiltshire Heritage Museum, Salisbury Museum, Bullecourt 1917 – Jean et Denise Letaille Museum, Jo Hutchings and John and Liz Dymond of the Aldbourne Heritage Centre, Neil Stevens, Liverpool John Moores University and Cranfield Forensic Institute.

Professional archaeologists have volunteered their time on site and their expertise and knowledge behind the scenes too, from Wessex Archaeology to Cotswold Archaeology and Oxford Archaeology to Museum of London Archaeology; that they can see the worth is clear from the fact that several of our 'graduates' now work for them. This has also been augmented by the Council for British Archaeology, the Chartered Institute for Archaeologists, English Heritage, Cadw, Historic Environment Scotland, Department of Environment Northern Ireland and Historic England. Professor Simon James of the University of Leicester, Professor Carenza Lewis of the University of Lincoln, Dr David McOmish then of Historic England, Matt Nichol of Cotswold Archaeology, Briony Clifton of the National Trust, Dr Rich Madgwick of Cardiff University, Dave Murdie of Wessex Archaeology, Peter Masters of Cranfield Forensics Institute, David Sabin and Kerry Donaldson of Archaeological Surveys, Giselle Király of Wessex Archaeology and Dan Miles of Historic England have all been tireless in their support.

Our bomb disposal assistants, Dave Moutter, Mark Khan and Florian Douchatelle deserve very big credit in fulfilling a fairly crucial role on Risk Assessments on military sites.

Some of these projects have also benefitted from a degree of financial support beyond that provided by the Ministry of Defence – military charities feature large with this: Help for Heroes SSAFA, Combat Stress and the Royal British Legion. Furthermore, the National Lottery Heritage Fund, the Trusthouse Foundation and Len Kelly provided key funding.

A number of the projects added special heritage 'vignettes' that added heritage texture, engagement and excitement to the work: Caroline Nicolay and Pario Gallico for historic food, Ian Thackray with his smithing and others fitted this bill wonderfully. While the cast of the TV series *Band of Brothers* and the legend that is former Welsh Rugby Captain, Gareth Thomas, were wonderful for site morale. Our Anglo-Saxon (or early medieval) projects have benefitted hugely from the presence of Weorod – the early medieval historical re-enactment group – and expert input on some of the items was also given by Matt Bunker.

The hard work of our volunteer staff is crucial and sometimes does not get the praise it deserves. My thanks here in print to all of them. Some of the stalwarts of this operation are Briony Lalor, Roger Collins, Jayne O'Connell, Kathy Garland, Carlos Rocha, Janine Peck, Katie Marsden, Chris Brown, Sarah Ashbridge, Sarah Holloway, plus many others.

The team excavating Boles Barrow on a windswept Salisbury Plain in 2023. This monument is over 3500 years old. © Harvey Mills

From an individual point of view the programme could not have happened without the involvement of the wonderful archaeologist Phil Andrews of Wessex Archaeology. He is everything one could wish for in a site director: phenomenally knowledgeable, pragmatic, observant, patient, kind and incredibly conscientious. He also takes a lot of the administrative burden and we all love him dearly. Every wellbeing project needs a Phil.

Thanks also to Julie Gardiner and Ruth Sheppard at Oxbow Books/Casemate Publishers respectively for the idea of the book and subsequent encouragement and editing. I take any blame for the text of this book but hope, whatever shortcomings there are, it is alleviated by the wonderful photographs of Harvey Mills, the beautiful illustrations of Alice Roberts, and the insight of Dickie Bennett – three most valued friends of mine.

To Katherine and Ruth – for putting up with me disappearing, to cluttering the house with pottery, tools and much, much worse, ruining your intended evening television-watching, incorporating research into family holidays and even being begged to do last-minute map drawing – THANK YOU.

Finally – to all the men, women and families of the Armed Forces of those nations that have taken part in Operation Nightingale thus far – my salute. And see you in an excavation trench soon.

Richard Osgood
Winchester 2023
twitter: @richardhosgood
Instagram: richardhosgoodarchaeologist

Foreword

Alice Roberts

October 2021, and I'm driving down to Somerset to pick up my good friend, archaeologist Stuart Prior, before we head east to Hampshire, to Butser Ancient Farm. Butser is an astonishing place, where you find yourself confronting the past, physically engaging with it. There's a beautiful Roman villa, a Neolithic longhouse and a small hamlet of Iron Age roundhouses. It's a working farm too, with rare Manx Loaghtan sheep, an endangered breed of English goats and ancient crops. You step back in time as you enter.

But Butser was missing something in between the reconstruction of Neolithic and Iron Age buildings on site, and that was the Bronze Age. All the houses at Butser are based on real places, uncovered by archaeologists, with the buildings painstakingly reconstructed from actual plans. And it is usually just plans, at ground level, that is all we have to go on for such ancient structures. Imagining, and recreating, what they looked like above ground requires a combination of ethnographic comparisons, experimental archaeology and practical know-how.

A plan for a Bronze Age emerged on the eastern edge of Salisbury Plain, at Dunch Hill. The Plain is littered with Bronze Age burial mounds but Dunch Hill contained something very special and surprisingly rare: evidence of not just the dead, but of the living; a Bronze Age settlement. A team from Wessex Archaeology led an excavation on the site, with volunteers from Operation Nightingale joining them, uncovering the unmistakable traces of a roundhouse: dark shadows in the ground showing where its wooden posts once stood.

As well as digging the site, the veterans of Operation Nightingale followed up with reconstructing the roundhouse, following their plans precisely, at Butser. With the large timbers of the house plotted out, they were left wondering what the walls were made of: wattle and daub, turf or ground-up chalk? The build became an experiment, with different sections of wall built using various materials. And it featured in the ninth series of *Digging for Britain*, the BBC TV archaeology series, when Stuart, having joined the presenting team, visited the farm to catch up with the project.

I'd first come across Operation Nightingale through filming *Digging for Britain*; over many series, we have often visited their digs to help share their precious moments of discovery with a wide television audience. From the Bronze Age roundhouse at Dunch Hill, to Anglo-Saxon burials at Avon Camp and the graves of prisoners from the 18th-century prison hulks moored in Portsmouth Harbour, I've had the privilege of not only seeing some incredible archaeology but meeting some wonderful people. Among them are people whose stories fill the pages of this book, including Sean Cahill, digging an Anglo-Saxon site at Avon Camp;

Opposite: Participants discussing the recording of the graves at Avon Camp. © Harvey Mills

Richard Osgood and Professor Alice Roberts in the *Digging for Britain* studio with artefacts found on the Bullecourt Tank dig in 2018. © Rare Television Ltd

John Bennett, who would thatch the reconstructed Dunch Hill roundhouse at Butser Farm; and, of course, Richard Osgood, MOD archaeologist and co-founder of Operation Nightingale.

Operation Nightingale was born out of an idea that archaeology might help a few veterans suffering with physical or mental setbacks: that the practice of digging, the teamwork and camaraderie, the space it creates for contemplation could all be useful. It worked so well, that over the last ten years, hundreds of veterans have passed through its ranks.

The day that Stuart and I arrive at Butser Ancient Farm is a special one. The Bronze Age roundhouse was finished, the place was thronged with Operation Nightingale recruits and their families, and we would be officially opening the new house to the public. It was a joyful occasion. There were lots of familiar faces and lots of new people to meet. And running through it all, binding everyone together, a deep appreciation of the past and the incredible heritage lying in our landscapes, a connection with long-gone generations of ancestors, the pleasure of teamwork and community, and the healing power of archaeology.

The cast

A number of people, places and organisations will appear on more than one occasion in the pages of this book: military figures, archaeologists and various heritage organisations and professional archaeological companies. It might therefore be useful for the reader to have a list of these participants as they are what has made Operation Nightingale the success it has been. Where relevant, I have included the military unit of the veteran as it might be of interest too.

Phil Abramson. Phil works as one of the four archaeologists for the Defence Infrastructure Organisation, working in Catterick Garrison, Yorkshire in the North of England. Along with his colleague **Alex Sotheran**, Phil runs the Operation Nightingale projects in the north of Britain (and occasionally Wales and Cyprus!). He could wax lyrical about the effectiveness of these projects too.

Phil Andrews. Archaeologist with **Wessex Archaeology**. Phil is an incredibly experienced archaeologist and led much of the fieldwork on the Operation Nightingale projects that I have coordinated.

Paul Barnsley. Paul was in the Royal Regiment of Artillery in the British Army, joining us via the charity **Help for Heroes**. He served in, among other theatres, Bosnia, and has made several of the key discoveries of our programme. I share the curse of being a Bath rugby and Southampton football supporter with him.

Dickie Bennett. One of many 'Richards' on the Operation Nightingale project hence going by the 'moniker' of 'Dickie' to prevent confusion. Dickie was a British Royal Marine Commando, in 40 Commando among others and, again, joined us via **Help for Heroes**, coming to Barrow Clump with his daughter Molly. Dickie then went to the University of Exeter to study archaeology, gaining a First Class BA and also a Master's degree. He established Breaking Ground Heritage (BGH) to assist with recruitment of participants on our projects and to facilitate logistics; from this point he now also leads the vital wellbeing assessments and has published widely on this subject.

John Bennett. John is another of our ex-Navy participants, serving on various ships and submarines. Having joined us for work on the **Butser** roundhouse, John demonstrated that, had he not been a 'Matelot' he would have made a very fine thatcher. Not being put off by the experimental work, nor indeed the excavations on Rat Island and Avon Camp, as this book comes out John is undertaking an archaeology degree at the University of Winchester.

Martin Brown. Martin and I excavated together for many years on a First World War site in Ploegsteert in Belgium and he was in at the start of Operation Nightingale with his role working in the MOD archaeology team. Although not examined in this book, Martin directed the early years work of the Operation Nightingale digs at Caerwent in Wales with Professor Simon James in Leicester. He works for an archaeological consultancy, TetraTech, and often finds himself on MOD project work.

Chris Burdon. Chris was in the 1st Battalion, the Royal Regiment of Fusiliers, an Infantry Regiment of the British Army. He has a useful knack of making great finds as his work at Avon Camp with us revealed. He also made the best discovery at Dunch Hill – the Late Bronze Age pin – which was where we met him. Chris currently works for **English Heritage** at Stonehenge with his role including showing people around the world-famous stones; a tour he gave to Operation Nightingale participants.

Butser Ancient Farm. Founded by the archaeologist Dr Peter Reynolds in 1972, Butser Ancient Farm is an open-air experimental archaeology museum and research centre. There are Iron Age roundhouses, a Neolithic and Anglo-Saxon longhouse and a Roman villa all built using techniques and materials available in those times. The centre aims to provide important information on how these structures might have been built, what materials were needed and how long construction would have taken. Our project has contributed a Bronze Age roundhouse to the experimental village.

Sean Cahill. Sean is a veteran of the Royal Navy and was on HMS *Glamorgan* during the Falklands conflict of 1982. He joined Operation Nightingale with **Phil Abramson** and **Alex Sotheran** on a project in Otterburn – *Exercise Lidar Truth*. I first met Sean at Avon Camp where he ended up as the project 'poster boy' having been interviewed by **Alice Roberts** on BBC TV's ***Digging for Britain***. Sean has since embarked upon a degree course in archaeology at the University of Bradford, joining them on their fieldwork in the Orkney Isles, he also made some pretty special discoveries in his second season at Avon Camp

Tyler Christopher. Tyler joined us in the first year at Barrow Clump in 2012 having been an infantry soldier in 4th Battalion, the Rifles. I first met him when he was on a course at Lackham agricultural college and this clearly paid off as he now works as a farmer on his own holding in Wales. Tyler has also played sledge hockey for Great Britain and has a great passion for nature and wildlife.

Ken Cisson. Ken served with the 10th Mountain Division of the US Army, based at Fort Drum in New York State. He was one of the group of participants that joined our Operation Nightingale project at Chisenbury Midden on **Salisbury Plain**. Ken studied at State University New York, Oswego.

Briony Clifton. Briony is an archaeologist of many talents, having had a long association with the **Cranbourne Ancient Technology Centre** in Dorset, she was one of the first people to show the programme the value of 'experimental archaeology', making pottery with the team at East Chisenbury Midden on **Salisbury Plain**. This was followed by an art project to make clay sculptures on the trees nearby, something that proved really effective for mindfulness. Briony works as an archaeologist for the National Trust, her bailiwick being the Avebury and Stonehenge World Heritage Site region, which isn't too bad!

Kris Conlin. Kris was an infantryman with the British 2nd Battalion, the Princess of Wales's Royal Regiment. After his medical discharge from the army, Kris met up with **Giles Woodhouse** and embarked on the **Help for Heroes**/University of Winchester degree course and now has an archaeology degree. Since graduating he has worked for a variety of commercial archaeology companies in the UK, where he says, 'You will often find me on site hiding under a white hard hat happily digging away at the most complex feature I can find, content, happy and at home unravelling the past.' Kris joined us at Barrow Clump and also at the excavations at Barton Farm in Winchester where his Regimental forebears had encamped over 200 years before.

Ant Cook. An infantryman in the 1st Battalion of the Royal Welsh Regiment, Ant worked at Chisenbury Midden alongside the American team that came over to assist. Being a proud Welshman, he was an ideal team member for the excavations of Mametz Wood on the Somme. A great rugby fan, this dig enabled him to throw a rugby ball around with the captain of the Welsh Rugby Team, Gareth Thomas, in one of the more special 'added extras' that the programme has seen.

Elaine Corner. Elaine was in several military units but the one I most associate her with is the Royal Electrical and Mechanical Engineers. Thus, when she joined us on the Spitfire dig, it was perhaps no surprise that she ended up with lots of the mechanical components of the airframe in the finds tent. Following this she joined Step Together Volunteering, a charity that helped my work by providing team members for various excavations. Elaine was one of the joint leaders of our roundhouse build at **Butser Ancient Farm** in Hampshire, but when this was completed she told me that she had never actually done any of the excavation work. This we fixed with her participation at Avon Camp in the summer of 2022.

Peter Cosgrove. Peter was in the 2nd Royal Tank Regiment and has a real passion for history. He is one of the group's model builders, producing incredible results every time. As a 'tanky' (or 'tanker' in the US), his ethos was key to the success of the first year at Bullecourt in France and the subsequent design and build of our wooden tank. He also re-enacts tank crew from the First World War and this was perfect when our tank went on the road for the annual Chalke Valley History Festival near Salisbury, Wiltshire.

Cotswold Archaeology. Cotswold Archaeology is a commercial archaeological company in the UK, founded over 30 years ago and with offices in Andover, Cirencester, Milton Keynes and Suffolk. Cotswold ran our *Exercise Shallow Grave* dig.

Cranborne Ancient Technology Centre. This started life in 1985 as a school experimental project by Jake Keen to construct an Iron Age roundhouse. From this point it has expanded to enclose several such structures and a Viking Longhouse and Roman villa amongst other structures. The centre works to examine building, farming and craft techniques from the past.

Jackie Crutchfield. We first met Jackie while walking along a series of frontline combat trenches on the film set of the *1917* movie and she has been on lots of our field projects since then, working at Rat Island, Barrow Clump, Avon Camp, **Butser**, Flowers Barrow (with my colleague Guy) and others too. She has clearly got the bug! Jackie now works for the National Health Service in the UK.

Rob Cummings. Rob served in the 1st Battalion of the Scots Guards – among other operation tours, Rob was in the First Gulf War. Rob joined us on a history tour of Beacon Hill overlooking **Salisbury Plain** and joined us on excavations at Barrow Clump and Netheravon on the Plain and Barton Farm in Winchester. Rob was one of the first Winchester University cohort and he gained a 2:1 degree in Archaeology. He now works as a commercial archaeologist and we occasionally see his lovely finds on Facebook (most recently an Early Bronze Age flint barbed and tanged arrowhead).

Barry Cunliffe. Professor Sir Barry Cunliffe CBE is one of the best-known archaeologists in Britain; responsible for excavating such sites as Portchester Castle, Fishbourne Roman Palace, Danebury Hillfort and the Roman baths in Bath. I worked for Barry for eight years as his Research Assistant and cannot believe quite how much I learned from him. We still keep in touch and he is now one of the trustees of Breaking Ground Heritage.

Digging for Britain. This is a UK television programme on the BBC presented by Professor **Alice Roberts**, which follows archaeological fieldwork around the British Isles – often getting the field teams to film the work themselves. The programme began in 2010 and Operation Nightingale has contributed eleven excavations over this time – all of which feature in this book.

English Heritage. English Heritage is a charity that manages over 400 historic monuments, buildings and places. One of these is Stonehenge, right on the edge of the military training area of **Salisbury Plain**. The Operation Nightingale team have been fortunate to visit the centre of this monument on a couple of occasions.

David Errickson. David is a Senior lecturer in Archaeology and Anthropology at the Cranfield Forensic Institute, University of Cranfield in Bedfordshire, which has very close links with the Ministry of Defence, being in part located at the Defence Academy at Shrivenham. David is our go-to expert with **Nick Márquez-Grant** on human remains on the Rat Island project. He has also worked very closely with the Defense Prisoner of War/Missing in Action Accounting Agency (the DPAA) in the United States, leading programmes in Europe to recover their war dead from aviation crashes

Jeanette Flitney. Jeanette was an Officer in the Royal Logistics Corps and started with us at Barrow Clump; she is now a veteran of our work, lending a hand and her expertise on a vast number of the projects from the scientific studies of isotopes from the midden work at Cardiff through to our Spitfire dig. Perhaps her best discoveries are not even mentioned in this book as it was not one of my projects; a collection of gold Iron Age coins from a cave on land owned by the National Trust.

James Galvin. James is one of many of our participants who enjoys using a metal detector and he joined us at Bullecourt going over the spoil heaps as one of our licensed detectorists. A former infantryman in the Royal Anglian Regiment, James has also worked his skills at the *Band of Brothers* site. He can be spotted working as an extra in films and television programmes these days!

Scott Hawkes. Scott was a soldier in the Royal Corps of Signals. It is difficult to know where to start with Scott. He took part in fieldwork at Chisenbury Midden and Perham Down and was also on other archaeological ventures such as the Waterloo Uncovered project. He discovered a real passion for this, inspiring others to join in, even it was just to keep him quiet. 'Scotty' died in August 2016 and the world is poorer for his passing.

Help for Heroes. Help for Heroes is a British Charity which was founded in 2007 to provide lifelong recovery support to service personnel and military veterans with injuries, illnesses and wounds sustained while serving in the British Armed Forces. We have had many dealings with them and their recovery centre of Tedworth House in Tidworth, Wiltshire, on **Salisbury Plain**. A number of the archaeologists on the Operation Nightingale project gained their crucial Mental Health First Aid (military) qualifications through Help for Heroes.

Paul Hemingway. Joined the Light Infantry before finishing his military career with 5th Battalion, the Rifles, serving on many operational tours, including in Iraq. 'Hem' is the lead of our metal detecting wing, and for good reason. Not only did he discover the parachute pull and a dog tag from Aldbourne, his work was crucial at Barrow Clump. On one of the projects here he located a sword and a shield boss when, even to the most experienced archaeological eyes, there was no discernible cut into the chalk or difference of fill; very unusual on this bedrock. Paul has been on many of the field excavations and pretty much always has the best 4 × 4 vehicle.

Historic England. Formerly part of **English Heritage**, Historic England is an executive non-departmental public body of the British Government sponsored by the Department for Digital, Culture, Media and Sport and is the government's statutory adviser on the historic environment, championing historic places and helping people to understand, value and care for them. They correlate the *Heritage At Risk Register* and if anyone wants to carry out any archaeology on a **Scheduled Monument**, they will need permission from Historic England: a consent called 'Scheduled Monument Clearance' within the Ministry of Defence.

Historic Environment Record. Most counties in Britain have what is called an 'Historic Environment Record' (HER) to aid Planning Departments with their development control. This is effectively a database of all known historic elements in the region – from protected buildings to archaeological finds and monuments, and important sites such as Historic Battlefields or areas of heritage conservation. This record is consulted by all applicants before building and infrastructure projects to gain permission for work.

Rowan Kendrick. 'Kenny' was an infantryman with 1st Battalion the Light Infantry and then 5th Battalion, the Rifles, doing two tours of Iraq. Kenny is one of our superstars. In 2022 he celebrated his tenth year as a professional archaeologist having left the armed forces. He has worked for several companies including **Wessex Archaeology** and, currently, West Yorkshire Archaeological Services. Kenny's celebrated find of a 6th-century drinking vessel can be seen in the Wiltshire Museum in Devizes and a picture of it is in the British Museum in London.

Phil Kimber. Having served in the Royal Air Force Regiment, Phil joined us on several projects, including at Chisenbury Midden and Bullecourt. His practical skills often came to the fore and hence it was no surprise that he showed great capabilities in driving the tracked excavator for us at Bullecourt, and also in helping to construct the roundhouse at **Butser**. Phil may well be one of the very few military veterans to have built two roundhouses; he had already helped build the **Help for Heroes** Iron Age example at their centre of Tedworth House in Wiltshire.

Jan Kirchner. As a former Non-Commissioned Officer in the German Luftwaffe, Jan's participation with us on our First World War excavation at Bullecourt in France was a formative moment for us all. He worked alongside British, French and Australian participants in a cathartic bonding of nationalities that had been on that site 100 years beforehand in more trying circumstances. Nobody who was there when Jan gave an address to the remains of the German soldier we recovered will forget that moment or his words.

Nick Márquez-Grant. Nick is Senior Lecturer in Forensic Anthropology at the Cranfield Forensic Institute, University of Cranfield, and has been a genial provider of expert knowledge on the Rat Island work.

Paul McCulloch. Paul is an incredibly experienced archaeologist, based in Winchester, Hampshire, as well as being a good friend! He is a Regional Manager of **Pre-Construct Archaeology** for the south of England and ran the Barton Farm excavation work, on to which Operation Nightingale was invited.

Jackie McKinley. Jackie is the Principal Osteoarchaeologist for **Wessex Archaeology**. I cannot imagine there is much she does not know about the human skeleton and thus, given her work with us at Avon Camp, Barrow Clump and Netheravon, we are able to draw upon a leading expert for our projects. She also gave the team calming advice on how best to recover the remains at Rat Island, when standard archaeological procedures were out of the question and/or unsafe, and this was a great comfort given Jackie has written many of

Gathering round to watch as the Hurricane propeller hub is uncovered at Saddlescombe Farm, West Sussex. © Harvey Mills

the guidelines for this sort of work in the UK. For the veterans, learning how to excavate burials or cremation deposits from Jackie means that their work on any site will be of the highest of standards.

Harvey Mills. Harvey is a professional photographer based in Winchester. Just look through this volume – the photographic skills of Harvey are often what make our projects accessible. We all see the same things that Harvey does but he truly composes them, and the results are phenomenal. Harvey has worked with us since our War Horse dig at Larkhill in 2014 and has covered all the southern-based projects since then. Our daughters were in the same year at school (and sometimes the same class) so were thus dragged onto field projects with us. We think this to have been 'character-building'.

Dave Murdie. Dave is one of the mainstays of the project – a professional archaeologist with **Wessex Archaeology** with an incredible eye and also a knack for finding things. His work really is phenomenal, and he also introduces team members to his specialised bespoke range of tools, such as adapted shovels that work better for those with back ailments. Dave has become a close friend to many on the Operation Nightingale project, not least for his wonderful story-telling. One example was so gripping that it caused **Phil Andrews** to miss his last bus home.

Ryan Parmenter. Ryan was an officer in the Royal Military Police and formulated the plans for the training programme for this unit based around the excavations at Rat Island and Bullecourt with us. This not only provided us with a team that were still serving in the military and who could support our veterans (and draw upon equipment) but also provide useful and cost-effective training for the MOD.

Portable Antiquities Scheme. The Portable Antiquity Scheme (PAS) is run by the British Museum and Amgueddfa Cymru – Museum Wales to encourage the recording of archaeological objects found by members of the public in England and Wales. Every year thousands of archaeological objects are discovered, many by metal-detector users, but also by people while out walking, gardening or going about their daily work. Finds recorded with the Scheme help advance knowledge of the history and archaeology of England and Wales.

Pre-Construct Archaeology. Pre-Construct Archaeology is a commercial archaeological company in England of some 30 years standing. We worked with them on the *Exercise Sleepy Hollow* dig in Winchester.

Alice Roberts. From her own website entry, Professor Alice Roberts is an 'Anatomist and biological anthropologist, author and broadcaster, and Professor of Public Engagement in Science at the University of Birmingham'. If that wasn't enough, she is also a wonderfully talented artist and a good friend. Among her television credits is the BBC series ***Digging for Britain***, which has provided an invaluable platform for our veterans to showcase their fieldwork over many years (and sometimes with several sites in a single series). This not only enables their work to be seen by as wide an audience as possible, but also enables them to spot and tease one another as the programme airs. Very human stuff.

Jack Robson. 'Big Jack' is one of those people who is wonderful for morale on site and a real 'grafter'. He only believes that archaeology of the 20th century (military) is relevant so it is fortunate that we have been able to provide several of these sites for him. He served with the 4th Battalion the Yorkshire Regiment and has been fascinated by the TV series *Band of Brothers* for many years, making him an obvious choice for this particular project, and enabling him to improve his collection of ephemera from the series by getting every actor that visits the dig to provide him with autographs. Interestingly, Jack's twin brother Harry is an archaeologist!

Salisbury Plain (Salisbury Plain Training Area). At 38,000 hectares (94,000 acres), Salisbury Plain is the largest military training area in the United Kingdom. It includes over 300 **Scheduled Monuments** (those protected by Government Statute) and a large part of the Stonehenge World Heritage Site. Additionally, there are many thousands of undesignated monuments that still need careful protection. Perhaps surprisingly, given artillery fire, tank manoeuvres and infantry digging, it is one of the best-preserved archaeological landscapes in Western Europe, as military purchases since 1897 have largely prevented deep ploughing, house building and road schemes. It is by turns bleak and achingly beautiful – often on the same day.

Guy Salkeld. Guy is based at Westdown Camp and is the archaeologist with the responsibility of looking after the Ministry of Defence southern holdings. He has helped me out on some of the Operation Nightingale excavations on **Salisbury Plain** as well as running his own excavation at Flowers Barrow in Dorset, an Iron Age hillfort with one of the most idyllic and dramatic settings in Britain situated on the Dorset coastline.

Scheduled Monument. A Scheduled Monument is one protected by Government Statute and it is a criminal offence to damage one. There are 772 on the Ministry of Defence Estate as things stand and it is the role of the team of archaeologists within MOD to ensure that these special sites are safeguarded. A Scheduled Monument may be many things: a single standing stone, a collection of many burial mounds, or a Roman village that covers vast tracts of land, for example.

Kieran Scotchford. 'Scotchy' served with the 8th/9th Battalion Royal Australian Regiment and followed in the footsteps of the Australian infantry a century ago with his participation in the excavations at Bullecourt. He also joined us at Aldbourne for the *Band of Brothers* dig where, bizarrely, he found that a close relative had once lived in this very village. Clearly fate brought us all together.

Subeg Singh. Subeg was an infantryman in 1st Battalion, the Rifles and was on the very first of the Operation Nightingale projects at Chisenbury Midden on **Salisbury Plain Training Area**. He found it a 'great experience following my return from Afghanistan. It's been brilliant to work on the project and find fascinating items such as fragments of pottery dating back some 2700 years'.

Darius Smith. 'Daz' served with the Royal Engineers and is especially interested in the projects with military heritage. Whilst he was still serving, he worked as a cartographer, producing our map of Burrow (Rat) Island for example. As the owner of a jeep, his presence is much in demand on the *Band of Brothers* dig and his sense of humour and positive attitude is always a highlight on sites.

Matt Smith. Matt joined us after recommendation from **Scott Hawkes** as they served together in the Royal Corps of Signals. He made the discovery of the Visigoth brooch at Barrow Clump and was one of the Welsh participants at Mametz Wood on the Somme dig in France, joining **Ant Cook** in the rugby session with Gareth Thomas. Not only has Matt dug on the project, he has also helped **Dickie Bennett** out with site administration and logistics over a number of years.

Alex Sotheran. Although Alex works for Ministry of Defence, alongside myself, Guy and Phil. I first met him on excavations of the First World War and he was one of the supervisors at Mametz Wood on the Somme in France. Since then he has helped me organise the work at Bullecourt and has run the Operation Nightingale excavations in the north of England with his colleague **Phil Abramson**.

Rob Steel. We first met Rob, an infantryman from the Princess of Wales's Royal Regiment, at the **Cranbourne Ancient Technology Centre** and this is perhaps what sowed the seeds of his ultimate ambition of establishing his own experimental site. Rob has worked on lots of our projects since, from Rat Island to Bullecourt and Perham Down to Barton Farm. He was another of the primary cohort of veterans attending Winchester University so he too now has a degree in archaeology and has since worked for the commercial archaeological company Museum of London Archaeology (MOLA).

Time Team. *Time Team* is a much-loved television programme that first aired on UK television in 1994 on Channel 4. The format saw a collection of archaeologists, historians, artists and surveyors investigate chosen sites over a three-day period. The Operation Nightingale project was featured in 2012 in an episode entitled *Warriors* and is currently filming a new episode for the online version of the programme at Aldbourne – our *Band of Brothers* dig. Many of the presenters – from **Phil Harding** to Professor Carenza Lewis – have been staunch advocates of our programme.

David Ulke. David is an extraordinary model maker as well as being a former officer in the Royal Air Force. He joined us for the excavations of an aircraft at Lulworth in Dorset and has taken part in many projects since then, in particular, helping make some of the more important discoveries at Aldbourne and the *Band of Brothers* dig. David has an archaeology degree too from the University of Leicester, where he is now an Honorary Visiting Fellow at the School of Archaeology and Ancient History and works as a key part of the Waterloo Uncovered project.

Diarmaid Walshe. Diarmaid was in the Royal Army Medical Corps attached to 1st Battalion, the Rifles when I met him, and we established the concept of Operation Nightingale together. He worked on the programme for a number of years.

Wessex Archaeology. Wessex Archaeology is a commercial archaeology company of over 44 years standing in the UK, with offices in Salisbury, Sheffield, Bristol, Edinburgh and Kent. Wessex has been key to many of the Operation Nightingale projects in the south of England.

Steve Winterton. We are all here because of 'Winno'. Following injury in Afghanistan, it was his desire to try some archaeology thanks to a love of the television programme ***Time Team*** that was the catalyst for the inception of Operation Nightingale. 'Winno' served in the infantry with the Devon and Dorset Regiment and then latterly with 1st Battalion, the Rifles. After medical discharge, Steve worked for **Wessex Archaeology** for a number of years and still visits some of our events.

Giles Woodhouse. Giles is probably the only one that can claim to have been a part of all sides of this programme – a former officer with the Staffordshire (and latterly the Mercian) Regiment who served in Afghanistan, Iraq and other theatres, as Head of Recovery South for the charity **Help for Heroes** and know working for **Wessex Archaeology**. Giles has a degree in archaeology as well as field experience and also focuses strongly on the wellbeing aspects of the discipline.

Łukasz Zub. Łukasz served with the 12th Mechanised Brigade of the Polish Army and his presence, alongside his colleagues, at the excavation of the Hurricane aircraft at Saddlescombe Farm in Sussex highlighted to me the importance of having participants of other nations working with us, just as they did in operational theatres.

Our three Polish veterans work on the site of a Battle of Britain Hurricane crash from 303 (Polish) Squadron

Gloucester
Abergavenny
Cotswolds AONB
Oxford
Stroud
Cirencester
Chiltern Hills AONB
Watford
M1
Cherington
Newport
M4
Swindon
A34
Cardiff
Bristol
Reading
Windsor
Chippenham
North Wessex Downs AONB
Bath
Weston-super-Mare
Trowbridge
Basingstoke
M25
M5
Andover
Surrey Hills AONB
M23
Bridgwater
M3
Salisbury
Barton Farm
Winchester
A3
Taunton
A303
Cranborne Chase AONB
South Downs National Park
Yeovil
Lurgashall Hurricane
Southampton
M27
Chichester
New Forest National Park
A27
A31
Portsmouth
Dorset AONB
Worthing
A30
A35
Rat Island
Dorchester
Poole
Bournemouth
Weymouth
Broad Hinton
Aldbourne
Lambourn Woodlands
Great Shefford
Ogbourne St George
A346
Berwick Bassett
Shefford Woodlands
Ogbourne St Andrew
Ramsbury
Hungerford Newtown
Avebury
Beckhampton
Marlborough
Stitchcombe
Elcot
Fyfield
Lockeridge
Froxfield
Little Bedwyn
Kintbury
Great Bedwyn
North Wessex Downs AONB
West Woodhay
Ball Hill
Shalbourne
Honey Street
Pewsey
Burbage
Combe
Woodborough
West Grafton
Manningford Abbots
Beechingstoke
Wexcombe
A338
Fosbury
Faccombe
Crux Easton
Upavon
Conholt
Collingbourne Ducis
Chisenbury Midden
Upavon Spitfire
Chute Standen
Hurstbourne Tarrant
Everleigh
Coombe
Ludgershall
Dunch Hill
Netheravon
Tidworth
Knights Enham
Avon Camp
Netheravon Barrow
Picket Piece
Barrow Clump
Perham Down
Weyhill
Fyfield
Shipton Bellinger
Thruxton
Andover
Milston
Larkhill
Durrington
Monxton
Anna Valley
Longparish
Bulford Camp
Stonehenge
Cholderton
Grateley

Above: Map of southern England showing sites investigated by Operation Nightingale and outline of Map 2. © Sarah Holloway

Inset: Map of Wiltshire and Operation Nightingale dig sites. © Sarah Holloway

INTRODUCTION

IT IS A HOT JULY DAY and a soldier lies prone in the dusty earth. He is a Royal Engineer and his duties include disarming explosive devices buried in the soil. He works slowly, carefully, ensuring that no mistakes are made; his face a picture of concentration. And yet, this isn't Afghanistan or Iraq. He is working on an archaeological excavation at Bullecourt, France, and the battlefield he is helping to excavate was last fought over in 1917. He is uncovering a twisted and frayed mass of leather components, with rusted metal fittings throughout – all that remains of what was once a boot. A careful examination of this object as the mud is slowly scraped away shows that, within this boot, a foot is still in place, the bones yellowed and dry. As is standard procedure for such sites in France, the work is stopped while the mayoress and police are contacted (making sure it is not evidence of a local murder) and then the Commonwealth War Graves Commission come to collect the remains. A representative from the latter informs our dig team that the bones will be buried in what is called a 'scant remains' grave. A headstone will proclaim the burial to be of remains of soldiers from the First World War rather than an 'unknown soldier' as, of course, the soldier 'might have survived the loss of his foot'.

This, however, we already know, as our archaeologist has only one foot himself. Oh, and one eye – the results of his military service; such are the unique circumstances of Operation Nightingale. This book tells the story of the genesis of our programme and the aims of using archaeology to aid the recovery of military personnel.

I have never been a part of the armed forces – it has always been archaeology for me; something I wanted to do from a very early age. And yet, I was still aware of the enormity of warfare in general as a young boy. Both of my grandfathers had fought as artillerymen in the First World War (one in the British and one in the Australian army) and their

Opposite: Two soldiers recover remains from the graves at Rat Island. © Harvey Mills

Below: Royal Engineer veteran John excavating the remains of an Allied boot at Bullecourt: empathy personified. © Harvey Mills

Signage at Chisenbury Midden making it clear to soldiers that 'no digging' is permitted. Badgers, however, cannot read. © Harvey Mills

experiences were harrowing. My Dad had been in the British Army in the Second World War (the 5th Royal Inniskilling Dragoon Guards) and took part in the campaigns through Normandy and the Low Countries in 1944. He was a gentle person, academic, and not somebody one would consider at all when conjuring up martial images. He wanted to be an actor but the events of 1939–1945 made this dream much tougher to achieve – though he did appear as a news reader in the last ever Laurel and Hardy movie.

As I grew up, my love of history was clear and I was, of course, fascinated by everything he might or might not have done in the war. Somewhat disappointingly, I was only ever given the funny stories of amusing mishaps or brief episodes of jollity facilitated by camaraderie. In the last week of his life, however, as he was dying of cancer, he would wake up from sleep in a panic, believing himself to be back in Normandy and, once again, suffering the horror of being on the radio to a friend in a neighbouring tank when it was hit, immolating the entire crew. Which he heard. I have no doubt that this was simply his body and mind releasing all those elements that he had suppresed, not wishing his family to know: that he, without doubt, had what we would call Post-Traumatic Stress Disorder (PTSD) today and which I just called 'depression'. You could always tell when Dad was in one of these moods and I had the happy knack, at least superficially, of being able to draw a smile from him even at those times – and what to do with him. He died in 1997 and I find it almost impossible to put myself into his boots, to imagine what my closest relative went through in his early twenties.

Fast forward to 2004 and I've landed a job as the archaeologist for the military training area of Salisbury Plain. It surprises some that the Ministry of Defence (MOD) in the United Kingdom employs archaeologists but, as owners of 1% of the UK mainland, parts of nine World Heritage Sites, over 700 Scheduled Monuments protected by law, and 800 plus Listed Buildings – the Ministry of Defence has a great deal of heritage that needs looking after, while still facilitating the military training requirements. I do this alongside wonderful colleagues and it is a genuine privilege.

At 38,000 hectares (around 94,000 acres), Salisbury Plain is the largest of the British Army training areas in the UK and, in geographic terms, the same size as the Isle of Wight in southern Britain. It might not seem that large for any readers from Canada or the United States but, believe me, for the UK this is BIG. A dream job therefore. With unspoilt monuments from the Neolithic to the 20th century – and with parts of the Stonehenge World Heritage Site all in glorious Wiltshire countryside in the west of England. I still feel this about my job and believe the area to be the most glorious archaeological landscape in western Europe (though my colleagues in the archaeology team within the MOD may well plead the case for their areas!). As I started, British armed forces were still engaged in visceral fighting in both Afghanistan and Iraq and there were, of course, casualties. As we worked to gain them the training facilities they needed, you could see the military units that were coming onto the Plain for pre-deployment exercises and were painfully aware that you would read about men and women from these groups being killed and wounded in action a few weeks later. It was an incredibly sobering experience and one that really did focus minds.

Some years on and I received a phone call from a medical sergeant attached to the 1st Battalion of the Rifles – an infantry unit based in Chepstow in south Wales. This regiment were on an operational tour of Afghanistan but had suffered quite a few casualties and thus had several men unable to deploy. In amongst soldiers of the 'Rear Operations Group' as this collection of 'Wounded, Injured and Sick' (or WIS) were called, was a corporal called Steve Winterton. 'Winno', as we knew him, had been wounded by a mortar blast and his career in the military was thus going to end. As he had been a soldier all of his life, this was a second family to him and the imminent loss (setting aside the physical pain) was palpable. Given he had been on national television in the UK stating this, I'm not breaking any confidences in saying that he was so low that he seriously considered ending his life. And this is where archaeology comes in, and Operation Nightingale began, because the thing that kept Steve going was watching the popular British television programme *Time Team* and enjoying the discoveries made by their archaeologists, their interpretations, and the characters themselves.

The sergeant, Diarmaid Walshe, asked me

Stonehenge, one of the most recognisable monuments in the world and a frequent reference point for military units on Salisbury Plain. © Harvey Mills

On site at Dunch Hill: the dig team watch an armoured vehicle trundle past. © Harvey Mills

whether I could set up some archaeology for Steve and the others in the group, given we were an in-house team and managed a very great deal of archaeology. The answer was 'yes' and Operation Nightingale was born; its name a nod to the most famous of all medics that dealt with the military, Florence Nightingale, a nurse in the Crimean War of 1853–1856. We have now been running for well over a decade with a huge range of field-work – from early prehistoric to archaeology of the conflicts of the 20th century – and it is high time that this tale was told. Almost all of the sites have been published academically or in what is known as 'grey literature', field reports that are given to the local Historic Environment Record. This, instead, is a story of the sites themselves, of the men and women that have made the project. Several have moved into professional archaeology or have higher level qualifications. It is a story of friendship, of discovery, of a fascination for the past and landscape, of the indomitability of the human spirit in spite of the challenges people face after conflict. The saga will take us from the fetid and ominous prison hulks of the 18th century to the smoky claustrophobia of First World War tanks. We shall attend Celtic feasts and marvel as the sun shines through amber jewels from 1500 years ago sending honeyed rays down onto the chalk. We will witness our veterans walking in the footsteps of the *Band of Brothers*, the hoofmarks of the 'Sleepy Hollow' horseman, and the shackled feet of Abel Magwitch. There are so many stories within the stories.

Archaeology may seem the strangest place to

contemplate recovery, to gain catharsis – especially given the truism that we are, for the most part, dealing with the lives of those long-dead. I mean, how much more incongruous could it be than to take modern veterans to the tortured fields of the First World War, among the Iron Harvest of explosives, the sherds of bone, uncovering destroyed lives for which there had often never been any resolution back home? And yet we did, and it worked.

Perhaps ours is not an original idea however. In his beautiful novel *A Month in the Country*, J.L. Carr wrote about the lives of two men brutalised by the First World War – the book later adapted into a film starring, among others, the Oscar-winners Sir Kenneth Branagh and Colin Firth. These two played former soldiers excavating an Anglo-Saxon cemetery and restoring a medieval church wall painting respectively in a beautifully linked narrative. I won't give any plot-spoilers but heartily recommend this work, which has been to the forefront of my mind throughout our project.

In designing the project a motto we all worked towards was 'do no harm'. If we tried to improve the lot of the participant but they left the programme with no change in their wellbeing, well at least we had not made things worse. The same was to be applied to the archaeology – it is important that any work was done well, that we wrote it up and that our interventions not only did not

The opening of the Bronze Age roundhouse at Butser Ancient Farm. © Harvey Mills

contravene professional standards and ethics but would perhaps enhance them and, certainly, contribute to the narrative surrounding the worth of archaeology for society. In retrospect, and at the risk of hubris, I really hope that we have, in fact, contributed something positive and empirical to the time-honoured undergraduate essay topic of 'What is the point of archaeology?'.

We began all this work with a belief that sites would need to be carefully selected. Initially these were on the Estate of the Ministry of Defence – at 1% of the British mainland there is enough archaeology to be worked on – but we have since moved further afield too. Sites chosen had to have a legitimate need for our endeavours, a genuine research design. This could include the fact that the sites were under threat, or that we aimed to set new standards in the examination of site types. It could be to draw together military agencies and utilise our archaeology in the training for their specific roles; this could be surveyors in the Royal Engineers through to human remains recovery teams within the Royal Military Police. My experience, both as an archaeologist and also in working for MOD, suggested that we also needed to select sites that would engage – thinking of ones that would yield finds or discoveries and perhaps even link to their military forebears. Late Bronze Age linear ditches cut into chalk are things of structural beauty, incredible testaments of the ingenuity or societies some 3000 years ago but would they hold the attention of wounded veterans? I had my doubts. And I have learned that a bored soldier can be both a mischievous and inventive entity!

Another element we looked at was having ancillary components that would further expose the participants to heritage; making pottery, visiting museums, witnessing the alchemy of bronze smelting and casting. We joined with local museums so the veterans could see the sorts of items they might find on excavations and with experimental archaeological sites to see how the places excavated might once have looked. It was also important to highlight that excavation is only a very small part of the archaeological process, so trips to County Historic Environment Records and to the Historic England Air Photography archives in Swindon were made. Team members went to Cardiff University to assist with isotope assessment of animal bones from an Iron Age site, and to Cranfield University pathology labs to examine 200-year-old human remains. We invested in some cutting-edge facial reconstruction work from Facelab at Liverpool John Moores University to highlight our human story in the fieldwork, we even persuaded owners of a Hurricane and Dakota aircraft to fly over a relevant excavation. Such is the generosity of people we have worked with.

Social media has revolutionised how such 'community' projects can work – inevitably we have our Facebook page where we share stories of the digs, photographs, results and reports. We can put out team information here too and enable our expanding archaeology 'family' to keep in touch with one another – often to share jokes and to organise their own social events beyond the project with their new friends. Much of the fieldwork has been filmed and appeared on television from *Time Team* through to the brilliant *Digging for Britain* – a testament to the quality of the work of the personnel and also, I think, the fact that there is a general belief that such projects really do need to happen and genuinely make a difference. Of course, you can share links to these programmes online and hence reach a wide and global audience. This book also only details some of the projects that I have run; there have been so many others led by the other archaeologists in the team – Phil Abramson, Alex Sotheran, Guy Salkeld and Martin Brown.

We will see what seems to work for our participants, how archaeology may be uniquely placed to aid their restoration – perhaps the open air, the teamwork, the physical exercise, the frequent idyllic settings of the sites and their proximity to nature, the fact that there really is a job for everyone. Ours is the story of people – both in the past and today.

Although our subject is historical, I wanted to avoid a linear narrative; not to work through our sites in chronological order of their excavation or their formation; instead this work is arranged to consider the themes that have built the bonds of the project. We continue to learn as the years move on and to increase our ambition and scale of operations – we have seen many people pass through the programme to achieve great things, but all will still remain part of our 'family'. This project is just their latest battle honour and one for which they should all be saluted.

The trowel of Asclepius. Professor Simon James designed our logo combining medical and archaeological elements. © Crown Copyright

1 ORIGINS AT THE MIDDEN

The beginnings of Operation Nightingale at an Iron Age feasting site

AS THE TENTH TRAY of Iron Age pottery is brought to the finds tent, the soldiers begin to become suspicious: 'you've laced this site, haven't you? Just so we find stuff'. They are, in part, right. We are determined that participants on our new project will make discoveries – however, none of the finds have been placed in the ground by archaeologists. Instead, these are relics of feasting some 2700 years or so ago. The site is the East Chisenbury Midden, and this is the birthplace of Operation Nightingale.

The monument is one of the most curious and enigmatic on Salisbury Plain, yet surprisingly it is not protected as a Scheduled Monument – the rumour being that there is no designation category for such a dump of material. It is, however, shaded in blue on all military training maps as what is called an 'Important and Fragile Site' and therefore one to be avoided where possible by the army. Discovered initially by a couple of members of the Royal Air Force in the Second World War, this site is one which has had a great deal of work to try to protect it. Initially a series of white-topped palisades, with accompanying signage to make it very clear that 'no vehicles' or 'no digging' was to be permitted, were placed around it. Subsequently, Dave Norcott of Wessex Archaeology took a number of cores with an augur (something that resembles a large corkscrew) to establish the sheer extent of the midden and we enclosed this area within a pen. This fence not only demarcated the midden site, it also held in a number of badgers.

Above: Decorated Iron Age bowl sherd, Chisenbury Midden. © Alice Roberts

Opposite: Perhaps the first feast at Chisenbury Midden in 2700 years. Sampling the Iron Age cooking of Pario Gallico. © Crown Copyright

These industrious creatures appreciated the soft soils of this Iron Age site and this soon became a chosen place for some of their many setts.

This is a mixed blessing of course. The archaeology is being damaged, but there is a lot of it here and I can't help finding it exciting to walk over this artificial hill (up to 3 m high in places) and see material brought up to the surface by the animals: burnt flint, bones and lots and lots of exquisitely decorated pottery. I have been on official organised excavations over several months that have not yielded as much material as this site from a couple of minutes of walking over freshly burrowed soil. So, what to do? This material was in many cases lying on the surface, in other places covered with badger sett soil, and I needed to recover as much of it as possible, to try to learn more about the site and to improve its conservation. It was perfect for Operation Nightingale.

Our first 'deployment' therefore came in the early autumn of 2011 with what was called the 'Rear Operations Group' from the 1st Battalion, the Rifles, based in Chepstow, south Wales. This included Steve Winterton: his first experience of an archaeological site apart from watching the TV programme *Time Team*. The army does logistics well – we had trucks, land rovers, catering, tents and camping beds – items that most archaeological site directors can only dream about acquiring. Over twenty of these wounded men (and it was all men in the first iteration, an infantry unit) were on site, with archaeological supervision from several people, including Phil Abramson and Martin Brown in my team.

Each morning, to the hum of the generators

Clouds scurry over the rolling fie ds of Salisbury Plain at East Chisenbury. © Harvey Mills

Left: Riflemen uncovering their training area. The first days of Operation Nightingale. © Crown Copyright

Below left: A few minutes work at the Midden: one of many finds trays. © Harvey Mills

Below right: Completing a section drawing at the midden before the storm arrives. The author Herman Melville believed the Plain to be one of the bleakest places on the planet and I wasn't hanging around to investigate this. © Harvey Mills

Surveying the future perhaps? One of the many skills archaeology can provide, in this case taking levels at the Midden. © Crown Copyright

that did an audible battle with the sound of snoring from the barn next to site, which we used as our headquarters, the chefs made breakfasts for the soldiers who gradually woke and moved to the excavation through the mists of the September dawn. If you've read *Moby Dick* by Herman Melville, he refers to the Plain as being one of the two bleakest places on the planet – the other being the Pine Barrens of New York State (the name being the giveaway). But I think it's magical, this mist would soon burn off and you can gaze for miles and miles under huge skies, over to Sidbury Hillfort in one direction, to a white horse and the Vale of Pewsey in another, and a colossal barrow and field systems in a third vista. Today, however, we were firmly in the Iron Age.

The badgers were unearthing vast quantities of finds and this was going to play havoc with our initial thoughts on how to record the material. Cutting a section through the spoilheap and drawing as section – easy; trowelling different surfaces – a delight; taking levels – rudimentary. Opting to three-dimensionally spot-record every sherd with differential GPS (Global Positioning System)? – foolhardy, if a noble aspiration.

We soon decided that, as the material was out of context (i.e., not where it was originally deposited), learning about layers and the context sheets used to record descriptions of them was probably more beneficial to the participants. What was also intriguing was the way that some people gravitated to specific tasks. Some of the riflemen really enjoyed the surveying aspects (indeed one promptly joined the Royal Engineers to do more of it afterwards), others liked the site drawing. Some were more interested in the digging itself, possibly to their own surprise given the usual reticence of infantry when asked to perform this as a training task on the Plain. I don't think it was because it was warm and near to the tea and coffee that others wished to be working on the finds processing and cataloguing but this probably helped. Without exception they all appeared to relish being part of a functioning team again, working towards specific goals. One of the beauties, I think, of archaeology is that there are so many disparate tasks – both physical *and* intellectual – which come together to produce an overall outcome and result.

A shared excitement in all of this was one of discovery. One moment that will always live with me was the sense of wonder when one of the team, Rifleman Singh, noticed that there were decorations made in the pot sherd he had found, created by the fingertips and fingernails of the potter some 2700 years ago. He felt a direct connection to this person – being almost certainly the first person to touch these human traces since that time. He told me of his thrill in connecting here to his ancestors. For him, use of this land, of place, was such a personal connection. This is the thrill I still get in archaeology – of seeing the past directly, of time-travelling, of reaching out to touch those that knew this land millennia ago. Our time on the planet is so brief and fleeting and I would love anything I have made to inspire such reverence in 2000 years. The fact that this man, a soldier, felt exactly the same as me in spite of his having no background in the subject whatsoever was illuminating to me as an archaeologist that this project really could be inspiring to the participants. And I could see this being replicated across the site – with the find of a bone awl, a clay spindle whorl, part of a quernstone. From day one on this project, therefore, it was evident that there was something at work, an alchemy as people relaxed, smiled, enjoyed themselves.

Throughout the dig, the team was monitored by medical professionals to ensure that the positive aspects we intended all participants to experience were genuinely possible. This resulted in the very first medical assessment, by Dr Nimenko, in a military medical journal. The sample size and duration were, however, small, so perhaps it was almost a good thing that the team asked if they could do another week on the same site shortly afterwards. There was certainly enough archaeological work to facilitate this.

Another week thus ensued and after this we looked back on all that we had found – bone pins and combs, possible bobbins and quernstones and rubbing stones, spindle whorls, shale bracelet frag-

Dark soil clear against the chalk showing the holes left by hut posts.
© Crown Copyright

The thin green line: soldiers from the Rifles trowel away topsoil to make their discoveries. © Crown Copyright

ments, worked bone awls and combs, butchered animal bones and SO much pottery! We had also, rather delightfully found ancient mineralised poo known as a 'coprolite', largely dog in origin, of course causing much amusement. Some years later we even caught one of the veterans, who is a double amputee, washing one of these in the finds tent – almost literally 'polishing a turd'. I said to him that it was a great relief to me that he didn't have a compromised immune system (suspecting of course the reverse to be the case). Humour always seems important on these projects – it can be pretty dark at times and can take some getting used to.

Not only does one find copious amounts of bone and pottery on this site, there is also a vast quantity of burnt flint. To what end? There are several theories. You can arrange them in a circle surrounding your fire, preventing it spreading into areas that you don't wish it to affect; you can heat stones to place in and subsequently assist to boil liquids – so called 'pot boilers' – although heating flints can cause them to explode so this is perhaps not an ideal material. There is another possibility, and one I suggested to a former Commander of Salisbury Plain which led to him forever calling it the 'Rave Site'. Perhaps it was an error in hindsight. In Book Four of his *Histories*, the Greek historian Herodotus, who lived 2500 years ago, talks about the Scythians, a nomadic tribe of the Iron Age who migrated from central Asia over towards Ukraine and southern Russia. He mentions how these people threw hemp seeds onto heated stones and would howl for joy from the vapour it produced. He seemed to be of the belief that these simple folk were gaining astonishing amounts of joy from what amounted more or less to a rudimentary sauna. Clearly, however, these people were deriving all manner of narcotic pleasure from the hemp seeds and getting utterly stoned. There has been no evidence for hemp in the archaeobotanical record from the midden site but its reputation had been sealed for a few years. And I do like to think that the parties there must have been pretty spectacular affairs anyway.

The midden is incredible, and this work seemed innovative, so it seemed to catch the eye of the press. We always produce academic site reports, but we want to make the results of the work as available as possible; having news of the work on British Forces Broadcasting... or on local television really does share the excitement of discovery. On this first venture we were lucky enough to welcome *British Archaeology* (the magazine of the Council for British Archaeology) to site and this ensured that several of the soldiers were able to see themselves in print, much to their chagrin/delight. Further to media involvement, another requirement on the bigger projects is the chance for participants to branch out; to see wider heritage opportunities and to fire their historic imagination. So, trips to the middle of Stonehenge (thanks to English Heritage) and to the Butser Ancient Farm in Hampshire were organised.

On completion of the excavation, our first cohort of military 'students' went back to barracks; their regimental haberdasher (such a thing really *does* exist at their regimental headquarters in Winchester) approved an official 'Rifles –

Archaeology' patch, which could be worn on their uniforms, and we had even had the visit of a general to site, digging, as he put it 'through badger shit' with good humour and even engaging in an astonishingly detailed discussion of the long-running British television 'soap opera' *Coronation Street* with the rifleman he worked alongside. The general was hugely supportive of our efforts and most empathetic with the soldiers – his own son, himself in the Rifles, having lost both legs in an explosion in Afghanistan.

The soldiers' parting gesture even showed how good the two weeks of training had been as it demonstrated that they were thinking like archaeologists. From the very beginning of the discipline, those that have taken part have enjoyed illustrating their presence. Antiquaries and early archaeologists like Sir Richard Colt Hoare and Lieutenant General Pitt Rivers left tokens at the bottoms of the features they had dug, with their initials on, or elaborated skulls and picks depicted on them. I have seen wheelbarrows left in Iron Age pits or old worn-out boots in larger postholes. The soldiers, however, left a 'Rifles' mug (perhaps their own form of 'Beaker' burial (one that includes a very specific type of pot alongside a burial and which belongs to a relatively short time period at the start of the Bronze Age) with a coin and a cap badge at the bottom of one of the very deep sample cores we took. If ever this is excavated by future archaeologists, I hope it will cause amusement. It was not the last special deposit we left here.

As this site is guaranteed to produce results and the badgers are never-ending in their efforts to reveal material, the midden has been a very useful training ground for Operation Nightingale. We have also been able to invite other groups over to share in its bounty. This included a group from the United States. One of the privileges of my job is working with my opposite numbers from other countries and one of my absolute heroes is Dr Laurie Rush, based at Fort Drum in New York State. Laurie is one of the pioneers of Cultural Property Protection and has worked with NATO and even been deployed into zones of conflict like Iraq to advise the American military on protecting heritage. She and I chatted about the potential for American partnership with us and it wasn't long before a group of veterans, led in 2015 by Dr Duane Quates, from the State University of New York, Oswego, were joining us. I say it wasn't long, but their arrival was later than planned as they were delayed at the airport by the presence of Air Force One and President Obama – cue all sorts of jokes from the Brits involved in the programme – late in 1914, late in 1939, late now ... This was all good-natured as we found that several of the service personnel had been in the same theatre, at the same time, in different armies. Indeed, for Kenneth Cisson, an infantryman with the 10th Mountain Division and veteran of the conflict in Iraq, some of the more memorable aspects of the dig were 'the jokes, attempts at accents, what military branches were the best, and what seemed to be non-stop banter. I came with a camouflage hat that had a velcroed American Flag on it and one of the UK Veterans had one with the velcroed Union Flag. Before the end of the day we traded those flags'.

Our American friends teamed up with their British counterparts and, again, made dramatic finds of Iron Age material. Social aspects were to the fore once more with a barn quiz, which involved teams having to give answers requiring both a US and British knowledge-base. Ken Cisson recalls:

> For many Veterans with PTSD, taking part in a project with new faces in an unfamiliar territory can be an incredibly daunting task. During combat our brains rewire themselves for survival. We carry a hypervigilance for any potential dangers in our environment. For me, it's something that is hard to shut off. However, when speaking with other Veterans about my experiences and discomforts along with them expressing theirs, we are unconsciously rewiring our brains and rebuilding our frontal lobes to better connect with our current environment. Slowly realizing that there isn't a need for constant vigilance – allowing ourselves to let our guard down. Culture plays a remarkable role in recovery and for members

of the military, we are a culture within cultures. A Warrior Culture. The very reason we subconsciously seek each other out in whatever environment we find ourselves in. On this trip, it didn't matter that we served in different branches and for different countries. To us it was a new mission with a shared purpose. It was an extraordinary experience!

Another boon of this site was the opportunity to try to make versions of these Iron Age pots on site with Briony Clifton, our experimental potter and archaeologist with the National Trust. One of the experiments was to try to make a vessel that could hold the white inlaid decoration that we were discovering. Was it chalk, or bone – perhaps even human bone? Analysis by Manchester University seems to demonstrate that it was the former – but this is certainly very difficult to adhere in firing the pots. These pots worked really well and were very different in form to those we made collectively on our first foray to Butser Ancient Farm in 2011, where the pottery the veterans attempted to make resulted in almost thirty ash trays. As we had been looking at a site pre-dating the arrival of tobacco in the UK by over 2000 years perhaps this 'experimental work' was not entirely accurate

Further flames assisted in a ceremony run for us on-site by our visitors from the States. A ceremonial cleanse or 'smudge' smoked local herbal material over this fire as an act of healing for the military participants from both sides of 'the Pond', of remembrance. We were led in this very moving ceremony by one of the veterans, Rebekah, who was of Wendat (Huron) descent: a confederacy of peoples who have now resettled around Ohio and southern Michigan. Rebekah's father was a member of the US Navy during the Second World War, a witness to the trauma of Leyte Gulf and was present in Tokyo Bay at the signing of the 'End of War' declaration. Family stories are certainly important for many of those of the project, in addition to the ones they created for themselves.

Phil Andrews recording the excavation. A truly wonderful archaeologist in his natural setting. © Harvey Mills

Contemplating discoveries at the Midden: veterans and volunteers together. © Harvey Mills

I am always in awe of those that participate. On this project, for example, we had one of the first female Black Hawk helicopter pilots from America working with a female British bomb disposal officer. We had people that could work the most complicated signalling equipment alongside those able to drive incredibly heavy tracked vehicles with minute precision. All had ailments, none of them complained about them. One of this group, Scott Hawkes, was in almost continuous pain but archaeology very definitely appealed to him. One of his colleagues, Matt Smith, joined us too as Scott wouldn't shut up about how good it was! Matt was not initially convinced, as he told us that, as a soldier, he couldn't think of anything worse than being asked to dig holes on Salisbury Plain. Scott worked with our Anglo-American team at the midden and then joined in other archaeology programmes such as Waterloo Uncovered afterwards. Not long after this we received the dreadful news that Scott had been found dead at home. He was 38. The nature of our programme has meant that there have been a number of participants who have died and to whom we have had to say goodbye.

After our partnership with the Americans, we returned to the midden with Phil Andrews and Wessex Archaeology for formal excavations and, as a part of this, we were able to invite Scott's parents to the site he had loved and which had really sparked his interest in archaeology, something he showed a real aptitude for and which was offering him a potential direction after the armed forces. We gathered around our excavation trench towards the end of the dig and all shared a few words about Scott. To close, we placed the experimental pot he had made in a now excavated and recorded posthole complete with items that reminded us of him, and a plaque inscribed with his name in white chalk inlay as per the Iron Age. This was a special deposit in the truest meaning of the word. I like to think that Scott would have

A bird's eye view of the excavation of the settlement associated with the midden. © Harvey Mills

approved, as would the ghosts of all those early archaeologists. *'Scotty' – Scott Hawkes 19th Oct 1977–10th Aug 2016.*

As this midden has been our most visited site, even though the monument is vast and our attention relatively small-scale, we have indeed been able to fulfil this aspiration writ large. Our projects have, through both excavation and geo-physical surveys, such as the magnetometer work by Wessex Archaeology, illustrated that this midden was around 150 m in diameter and up to around 3 m in depth in some areas – astonishing! The radiocarbon assessments of some of the bones recovered highlight that the area was in use for hundreds of years, from around 1000 BC through to 500 or even 400 BC. There has been

some debate as to whether the midden lay within an enclosure or, indeed, if it was established at a meeting place of several other later prehistoric entities, such as pit alignments on linear ditches familiar to students of the Late Bronze Age. Debate no longer! Geophysics picked up all these elements beautifully and, in our more formal excavations in 2015–2017, were even able to dig some of this surrounding ditch – and a whopper it was! Up to about 10 m wide and 2 m deep in places, it was of a scale almost consistent with an early hillfort and was clearly a colossal endeavour to construct – a fact not lost on our veterans.

Just inside the ditch to the eastern side, we had found over 150 postholes in a relatively small excavation, features representing roundhouses of the Early Iron Age population. So, in addition to this being a place of feasting, of bond building, meeting and trading, this was also a place where people lived and farmed. Not necessarily surprising, but our empirical evidence showed, for certain, that this was not just simply a gathering marketplace.

Although we had found evidence for housing, the people themselves remained elusive. On many of the Operation Nightingale projects we have found human remains. This had always concerned me and, perhaps naively, I thought that this could prove to be an obvious trigger for episodes of Post-Traumatic Stress Disorder (PTSD). In fact, this has very rarely proved problematic and we have spent a lot of time excavating ancient cemetery sites. Here at the midden, only a small number of human bones were found. This biggest collection was jumbled – in archaeological parlance 'disarticulated' – and lay on the ground surface alongside animal bones within the areas of postholes. Two of these bones displayed some evidence of trauma, exhibiting traces of possible violence. Incredibly the radiocarbon dates for these bones came back as 1043–907 BC and 1044–910 BC; around 300 years before the main settlement we excavated! Was this therefore evidence of curated human remains, for ancient relatives being brought to special events or at least kept within family housing?

It has always been important on our programme to offer the team the opportunity to engage in archaeological elements that go beyond excavation. This could be documentary research in an archive, an examination of aerial photographs or, in the case of the midden, cutting-edge science with Dr Rich

Bone, stone and pot. Enigmatic traces of Iron Age life recovered by the team. © Harvey Mills

Madgwick of Cardiff University. The project, called FEASTNET, enabled them to process samples in a laboratory taken from the bones of animals we had all excavated at the midden, in particular, to examine the presence of certain stable isotopes – Strontium, Nitrogen, Oxygen, Carbon – to discern the geological component of the water drunk by the animal when young, or the plants and food they had eaten, and whose chemical signature was retained in bones and teeth.

The veterans' work with Cardiff looked at the signatures of stable isotopes within animal bones and could discern that the sheep, pigs and cattle represented by the feasting remains had been raised and slaughtered locally, though the cows had perhaps moved in from slightly further afield – probably still within the area of the modern county of Wiltshire. The sheer quantity of butchered animal bones and pottery, along with ancient charred plant remains including wheats and barley and foraged materials, showed that these were some parties – even if it had taken several hundred years to make a deposit of this depth. I wonder whether specific mounds reminded the participants of particularly special and important events, and that, by the end, the dark soils they engendered had magical and important properties in their own right.

We could see also that there even seemed to be certain patterning in the types of finds revealed by the badgers. There were far more spindle whorls and bone items perhaps associated with weaving, like pins and combs, at the southern end of the dark soils deposited. Even when you make finds that are 'out of context' it is therefore worth considering their localised differentiation.

Mysteries still remain and you could spend a fortune on looking at this site, keeping me (and Operation Nightingale) going for decades to come: after all, where is the southern end of the enclosure ditch? What on earth is the little human-shaped bronze figure we found? What were the specific links between our midden site and others that have been discovered close by at All Cannings or Potterne? We might be able to assess the latter with the team looking for Iron Age fingerprints on pot sherds from all three sites – thereby enabling our inclusion of military police techniques too!

The site of Chisenbury Midden with its wonderful views and memories of celebrations and festivals went out of use in the Middle Iron Age (around 300 BC and we believe that the huge enclosure ditch had largely been levelled by the late Roman period (3rd/4th century AD), Roman pottery being found in the fill of these upper layers. Prehistorians (and other archaeologists to be honest) sometimes like to tease their colleagues who study the Romans and this was certainly the case when we noticed that one of our veterans seemed to be really keen on finding Roman material; this was the era he was most interested in, he said. As if to prove the case, Rob Steel then showed us his latest tattoo – a ghostly face of a Roman soldier. This has ended up being something of a recurring theme on the Operation Nightingale excavations, with participants having pre-existing tattoos associated with the topic we are addressing, be it First World War Tank through to the burials of Barrow Clump we shall see later.

If the midden was a place of building bonds some 2700 years ago through feasting and fire, then how much more appropriate could it be for our project? It was here that we began forging friendships that have lasted for over a decade and counting. Many evenings here have been spent around a campfire, where the veterans can relax, 'decompress', share their stories, make puppets (I kid you not), and marvel at the fire itself. Something utterly elemental. Some of the soldiers have told me that on exercise or in theatre they can often be found staring at the remains of their hexamine burners having cooked their food or made a 'brew' or a 'wet' – 'Hexi TV' as they call it. A relationship between humans and fire is fundamental, watching the dancing sparks flicker skywards as we think, and is something we see time and time again on our digs. Coming together to eat food on this site was important some 2700 years ago and so we decided to resurrect the tradition. An experimental archaeologist called Caroline Nicolay put together a mouth-watering banquet of items that might please the Iron Age palate and which would not have been impossible for our East Chisenbury residents to have foraged or made some 2700 years ago. In 1954, for a BBC television documentary called *Buried Treasure*, the famous British Archaeologist Sir Mortimer Wheeler was given a meal based on the ingredients found in the stomach of the Danish Iron Age bog body Tollund Man. Famously, Wheeler felt that the food served to this man was so bad that his cause of death was probably suicide. It was therefore with a degree of trepidation that we awaited our equivalent. We needn't have worried as Caroline worked wonders cooking over a fire and there was certainly nothing left afterwards. Such cameos as trying to add as much archaeology in as many different forms of experience has been a crucial element of Operation Nightingale. Engagement in many different forms is key as not everyone is inspired simply by digging holes and there are many educational ways to inspire.

U.S ARMY
24879511
TP 25
NVS 464
101

2 THE PHOENIX AND THE EAGLE

Searching for Hessians and the *Band of Brothers*

THE SYMBOL OF THE PHOENIX is one we encounter frequently in this project – a mythical bird that obtains new life through regeneration from the ashes of its former self. Rising from the flames of one's past life makes for good symbology – it appears on T-shirts for the charity Help for Heroes in the UK as well as being the name for their recovery centre in one of the major garrison towns, Catterick in North Yorkshire. So many of our participants have been through fire and flame and are rebuilding lives – it surprises me how frequently fire and smoke features in the excavations in some shape or form and that its very presence is cathartic and plays a role in recovery.

It is winter 1756 and a bitter wind whips across a large open field near Winchester, in Hampshire, southern England, sending smoke wisps dancing like ghosts to escape its path. Thousands of men try to keep warm here, foraging wood from nearby copses to feed their campfires, for this is the site of an encamped army – a German one at that. These troops all come from the state of Hesse in what is now Germany and would go on to fight for the British in the American War of Independence in the 1770s. For now, their role is more one of policing and helping to guard Britain from possible French invasion during what became known as the Seven Years War. So here, in Winchester, they create shelters in which to

Above: A little boy's memory of the Americans; Switzy the Monkey. © Alice Roberts

Opposite: Driving around in Daz's jeep is one of the perks of this excavation, and always popular with the dig team and site visitors alike. © Harvey Mills

huddle, dig latrine pits, and build kitchens for the vital task of feeding so many soldiers. If an army marches on its stomach, then a hungry one is to be avoided at all costs.

Over 250 years later and a small team of veterans from Operation Nightingale joined an excavation of this site, Barton Farm, being run by a commercial archaeology unit, Pre-Construct Archaeology, under the direction of a good friend, Paul McCulloch. The modern housing that was going to be built on this land would replace those created by the Hessians (and some Hampshire militia forces) all those years before but not before the old features were excavated and recorded. This project took place in 2018, years after our first forays at Chisenbury Midden and we thus worked to a well-tested planning methodology, with risk assessments, administration instructions and, vitally, a snappy project name (we have now added dig T-shirts to this extensive list too, a popular move). We called our week on this site *Exercise Sleepy Hollow* in due deference to perhaps the most famous Hessian soldier of them all; the 'Headless Horseman' from the American Gothic novel *The Legend of Sleepy Hollow* by Washington Irving. Although some burials were indeed excavated, they were Early Bronze Age and Roman, and all still had their skulls so we could obviate the need to include potential attacks from phantom riders from the risk assessment.

Chalk is the most marvellous bedrock on which to excavate: mud-filled archaeological features show up brown against the hard, white geology. Dig the brown, leave the white and you rarely go wrong. Fortunately Barton Farm is on chalk, as are almost all our sites on Salisbury Plain. Not only is the archaeology relatively clear, it also shows up extraordinarily well in site photographs.

Forging memories in the flames. Many of the stories revolve around fire: here with a ship burning at Butser Ancient Farm. © Harvey Mills

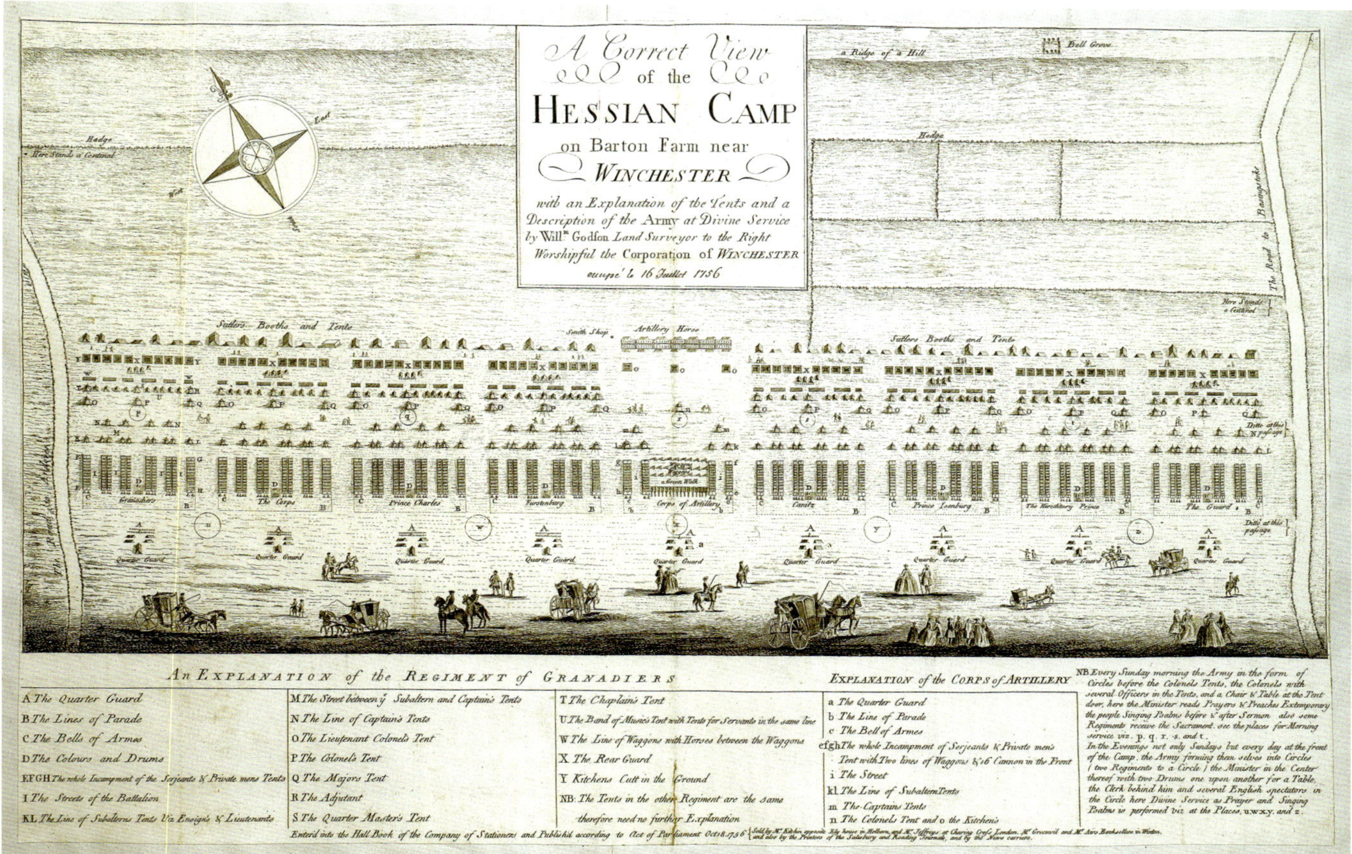

1756: a correct view of the Hessian camp on Barton Farm near Winchester (Hesse archives)

The Hessian camp itself was, in fact, really well mapped by a surveyor called William Godson in 1756 and his map was a marvellous resource for the team, not least as it proved to be pretty accurate in its depicted configurations of structures and dispositions of particular elements of the army. Our team was allocated a number of features: a (square) kitchen used by the Hampshire militia, a circular version of Hessian origin, and a couple of dugouts. From an ethos perspective this was perfect as three of our veterans were former infantrymen; a Scots Guardsman (Rob Cummings), along with Kris Conlin and Rob Steel who had both been in the Princess of Wales's Royal Regiment, a unit that succeeded the old Hampshire regiment. In fact, the Hessian soldiers had, in 1759, fought alongside the Hampshires at the Battle of Minden in Prussia – 'Minden Roses' are worn in the regimental head-dresses of soldiers belonging to the regiments that fought in this engagement.

The field kitchens that Godson said were 'cutt into the ground' tended not to produce many finds – perhaps testament to the fastidious nature of the Hessian troops or, more probably, to the excellent site clearance of the contractor later detailed to tidy up the site. 'Hampshire' Rob did find a small cache of 18th-century pottery in one of the ovens, perhaps pushed into the redundant structure on its closure – a worthwhile discovery.

The areas that really excited us were, however, the dugouts and these were surprisingly elaborate, at least for the officers. Rectangles cut down up to 2 m into the chalk, each had a staircase carved at one corner and on one occasion even curving,

Above: On the trail of the Hessian army: the site of Barton Farm. © Harvey Mills

Left: Some of the Operation Nightingale volunteers in a dugout 250 years after it was used by their Regimental predecessors. © Harvey Mills

perhaps to help exclude drafts. There were recesses and ledges chipped into the rock to act as shelves to hold items, or to house candles and lanterns if the sooty smoke marks were anything to go by. A series of postholes around the edges of floor of the dwelling perhaps were revetments to retain wicker wall lining or panelling or might have been structural to hold a tent-like roof structure in place. The floors too, although largely clean, still had the marks of burnt material where embers and ashes had been swept away as part of cleaning up the fireplace. And *what* fireplaces! Unlike those we would see on construction work for roundhouses of the Late Bronze Age, these were brick-built structures of genuine durability. They had, after all, survived intact in spite of being buried in the ground for hundreds of years. Driving past the new housing estate on this site today, I really wonder whether the chimneys that now pierce the skyline on the regimental lines of new buildings will enjoy half the duration spell of their predecessors.

There were also circular dugouts possibly for ordinary soldiers with concentric ledges inside, far more spartan and rudimentary and probably quite cramped even though they were larger than the rectangular versions. Many had pieces of broken pottery, of clay pipes, bottles, in fact any item you might expect to find on an army encampment. One particularly pleasing items was a fragment of a brightly painted Schnapps bottle from Germany – a direct link to our Hessians perhaps. In terms of artefacts you always seem to find associated with the presence of the military, there are very definite recurring themes. Tobacco and alcohol are two of the groupings and Barton Farm had thus not disappointed.

If food is important to the soldier, shelter is its equal – for the veterans on the programme, even a tent is a luxury on occasions. Nights spent in the open are not uncommon on exercise or in theatre, although there is the inevitable teasing amongst the various branches of the forces relating to this – and relating to stars – the joke being that the Army sleep under the stars, the Navy navigates by the stars, and the Air Force judges the quality of its hotel by the number of stars. Anyone can be uncomfortable, so I am firmly in support of good accommodation. These Hessian dugouts were certainly substantial – having had many a wet winter in nearby Winchester myself, this was a sound design decision. Our soldiers certainly reminisced both on the quality of the dining facilities and also the sleeping arrangements in comparison with their time in the Army.

Kris felt that these shelters are crucial in the bonding experience that soldiers undergo and he told me that:

> Transit accommodation, and any situation where soldiers are grouped together for extended periods of time in less than comfortable surroundings, is where the real bonds of brotherhood and friendship are made. They provide an area for soldiers to gather and release frustrations, whether this is complaining about a rubbish task, poor exercise conditions, the cook house (always a favourite), and especially the command elements within the company or battalion.

Warmth in a cold shelter: the remains of a brick chimney in a Hessian dugout. © Harvey Mills

A row of circular field kitchens stretch across the field at Barton Farm.
© Harvey Mills

Kris told me that this complaining is sometime called 'Monking' and creates bonds that last a lifetime:

> it is not on the march: marching is silent. It isn't on the battlefield: there is too much going on. It's in these gathering places where the military micro-societies form, where the new guys learn their place, but also where they find their way into a close-knit group.

So how then did Kris feel that our structures at Barton Farm were important? He told the popular magazine *Current Archaeology* that:

> In essence, although these closely-confined, poor-looking accommodations dug from the chalk may look like a cruel way to house our heroes during a critical period (and they are), they also provide the backbone for the brotherhood that remains today in our modern military. While digging this site, in my mind's eye I could almost see the group of men gathered around, sharing a smoke, a drink, a story, and a nugget of wisdom on any given situation. Every man has his say.

These links of bonding through shared experience and shared hardship are interesting. Perhaps digs do have this themselves on a smaller scale – think about sheltering behind wet site huts as storms come in and you are digging linear features with nothing in them!

We will meet both Robs and Kris again in this story – they are great exemplars of what can be achieved. All three went to the University of Winchester to study archaeology (a wonderful scheme of partnership between the University and Help for Heroes) and were thus 'locals' for the duration of this dig. They all graduated with an Honours Degree and all, at the time of writing, work in professional archaeology.

Flames and smoke – elemental reminders of the past that are central to the present and thoughts of the future. Creating bonds of friendship over shared experiences just as those at East Chisenbury did around 3000 years ago. We have had stories told to us in the smoke of a roundhouse at Butser

*T*wo Hampshire veterans at Barton Farm; Kris (left), Rob (right). © Harvey Mills

Ancient Farm, following this up with our own chats in the Saxon longhouse as we shared mead and spent a night in this hall with the orange glow slowly dissipating to glowing embers as we all fell asleep. We witnessed the burning of a 'Viking ship' at this site too (and indeed a wicker man!) all to the rhythmic chants and beats of drummers (and the nervous glances to see that sparks did not flicker onto the thatched roof of our nearby Bronze Age roundhouse). We have seen the firework sparks of the forge as Ian, our experimental blacksmith, made copies of the iron knives we had just excavated. We have gazed in awe at the green flames emanating from the crucible as alchemy occurred when stones of an emerald hue are forced to yield shiny metal in the copper smelting process – and in bewilderment as an urban myth that a particular brand of crisp (potato chips to our American cousins) that comes in a tube would burn with a similarly colour flame, failed to deliver in spite of a complete packet of these snacks being offered to the fire deities. Our choreography and events do seem to place fire as a focal point.

On almost all our digs, the campfire becomes a central place – to stare into the light, to feel warmth, to share tales. Around a brazier on a bone-jarring cold night at Barrow Clump, the bonfire at the Midden as we fire our experimental pots, or the fire on the old camp site of the 'Screamin' Eagles' of the 101st Airborne at Aldbourne.

Easy Company of the 506th Parachute Infantry Regiment, 101st Airborne, are perhaps the most famous Allied military unit of the Second World War. Immortalised by the book written by Stephen Ambrose, and world-renowned television series of the same name: *Band of Brothers*. If what we have discussed on shared experience, privation and

Smith Ian Thackray and veteran Chris working the forge on an Operation Nightingale project. © Harvey Mills

Kris Conlin (British 2nd Battalion, the Princess of Wales's Royal Regiment, age 42)

Kris told me his extraordinary story as we sat in one of the chalky dugouts at Barton Farm – a triumph over adversity, from severely wounded infantryman to established professional archaeologist. It is worth him telling his story in full as I could almost feel the ghosts of the Hessian soldiers crowding round us to listen in too.

The following is an account of events both preceding and following an incident that took place early 2009. This incident is recollected by myself from my own experience and observations with the gaps filled in by others that were there with me.

I was serving with the 2nd Battalion, the Princess of Wales's Royal Regiment (2PWRR) and had been since 2006. It was my company's second tour of Afghanistan. We headed out with experience in the field and full understanding of what we were getting into. We were based in a small patrol base called Patrol Base Tanda, which I believe translates to thunder. Our little slice of purgatory certainly lived up to its name. After a month or so of constant attacks with fire fights happening twice daily including whilst we were out on patrol, we developed a communications issue that would cripple our ground controlling patrols. An issue with communications would mean that we couldn't safely conduct patrols as we would lack the ability to call for support if things went wrong. The upside of this is no patrols in 50°C heat with 40 lb of kit on our backs into enemy held territory that could expose us to Improvised Explosive Devices, Rocket Propelled Grenade attacks, exposed small arms fire fights and the like. The downside is we couldn't control enemy movement, which led to them getting braver and closer.

One morning I was coming off guard duty. This is a four-hour rotation in the middle of the night staring out into the province and employing various night-vision equipment in an attempt to locate enemy movement whilst protecting the camp and my sleeping brothers. This is conducted from a sangar or watch tower built from pieces of wood and Hesco. It is a roofed elevated platform that sits a few metres off the ground and stares out to guard against potential threats. Equipped with night vision, binoculars, two General Purpose Machine Guns (GPMG), claymore triggers and illumination flares. It provides protection for the two fed up, tired, bored and stinking soldiers who have spent most of the night discussing what food they were going to eat when they got home. But my shift was done, my relief came and I went off to carry out my morning duties, such as burning the shit tins from under the long-drop toilets. With my duties done I was heading off to the mess tent to get a drink and some breakfast. But first I was going to remove all the kit I had been lugging around all night: body armour, day sack, helmet, rifle, pistol. I had dumped it in a pile outside the accommodation and was stood rolling my shoulders to get rid of the night's stiffness and aches when the first round came in. A low crack sounded and a bullet flew in over the patrol base wall and slammed into the Hesco I had just propped my kit against. Now, I had just stood for four hours in the cold of night staring out into the nothingness and the moment I leave the sangar the enemy attacks? Was I about to let my replacement get all the action after I had been there waiting for something to happen all night? Was I fuck.

I threw my kit back on and stopped up into the sangar and briefly told my relief (a lad by the name of Jack) that I am taking over and he was to go grab us some more ammunition for the GPMG. The lad beside me in the sangar was Jamie. Jamie and I had been through everything in our military careers together, from training to joining the same battalion, same company and same platoon. I was confident in his abilities, confident in my own abilities and I was angry at the timing of the situation. With this frame of mind we set about returning fire and attempting to locate the firing point. One thing to note here: it's not like the movies. You can rarely see the enemy; they are not charging in, guns blazing. They know that we are capable of unleashing hell on them. So, they hide. Sometimes they will poke a hole through a compound wall just big enough for their rifle barrel. So, in order to find them we fire at the direction of the noise or previously used firing positions. In this case we were able to follow the line of fire as the rounds skittered along the ground up the sangar wall and past us. Jamie and I continued to fire a deliberate rate of controlled fire at the compound that was suggested by both noise and line of fire as the location of our aggressor. By this point our section commander Corporal Bell (Dinger) had joined us and was crouched behind the Hesco wall that we were using to provide cover. He was to my left, as was Jamie. This is why no one noticed the steady stream of blood that was pouring down my right side. I had not noticed it either and continued the fire fight. I remember thinking 'did I hit my head on the sangar as I climbed up?' but it was a passing thought. I suddenly started feeling a bit dizzy but the adrenalin was pumping and, as I said earlier, I was confident and angry. After a few more minutes of back and forth firing I started to lose feeling in my right hand and at one point I had to physically make sure my finger was on the trigger. Then I started receiving waves of dizziness and nausea.

This is where my recollection and the testimony of my comrades mix to complete the story. My recollection would suggest that I turned to Jamie and Dinger and said 'I'm feeling dizzy, I'm going to go lay down and I'll get Jack back up here'. What actually happened is that I turned to Jamie and collapsed. 'MAN DOWN!! MAN DOWN!!' came the shout from sangar one. The stretcher was grabbed, a team assembled, the medic informed (we had practised this). At this point I could have been dead. I was believed to be dead by Jamie and Dinger. In any case I was out. With the full horror of the amount of blood that was caking the side of my face and body armour and running in rivulets down my leg I was unceremoniously thrown from the sangar. Bang! I hit the ground. I come back, I'm awake, I have a mouth full of stinking Afghan dust and several brothers are trying to lift me, body armour and all, onto the stretcher. I lost consciousness again. The guys are carrying me to the medical tent, the front man slips down a mortar pit and again I'm dumped onto the ground, crashing through Jamie's tent that he deployed in the mortar pit. Again, mouth full of Afghan dust, bleary images fading in and out, 'what the hell is happening?'. I'm lifted back onto the stretcher and again I lose consciousness. Next memory for me is a sharp pain in my head. I open my eyes, I'm groggy, Jamie is sat behind me trying to apply pressure to my head, there's a bandage wrapped around my skull. 'What is going on?'. Jamie fills me in. 'You're a fucking legend mate, you've been shot in the head!'. Jamie was told to keep me conscious. I have to stay awake. All I want to do is sleep. I'm telling him I'm fine, I'll be alright, it's just a scratch. The medical Chinook helicopter (mert) is inbound. Later I was told that as soon as I found out I was going home I started ordering people to go get my stuff, get my iPod,

The face of battle, Kris in Afghanistan. © Kristoffer Conlin

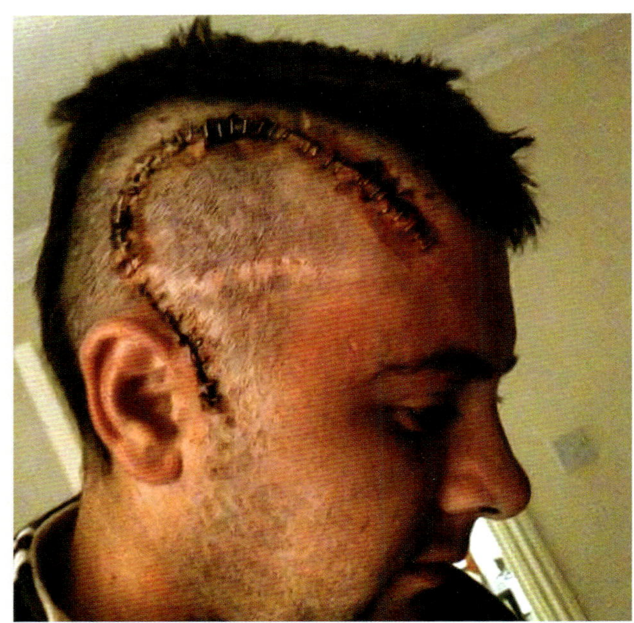

The face of battle, Kris in Afghanistan. © Kristoffer Conlin

etc. I'm arguing with Jamie telling him to stop squeezing my head, go get my stuff, let me sleep. He saved my life by being stubborn. The mert arrives and I'm stretchered out. My brothers are watching. I can't let them worry so I do the Help for Heroes thumbs up as I'm lifted onto the Chinook. Next thing I remember is glimpses of inside the mert, there are people around me, they are cutting off my body armour and uniform. This I remember because I thought, 'damn, I'm gonna get charged for these trousers'. I lost and gained consciousness several more times on the journey to Bastion. I remember the three minutes to Bastion, two minutes to Bastion then I wake up in Queen Elizabeth Hospital in Birmingham. The strain of coming back and so many times had taken a toll on my body and the decision had been made to induce a coma.

My recovery was long and never really completed. I had fifty staples in the side of my head – the whole right-hand side of my skull had been shattered and the frontal lobe of my brain had been smashed up. Since then I have had multiple brain scans and have seen the damage for myself. The front of my brain to this day remains a dark mass of damage on the CT scans. It took a year for the doctors to replicate my skull in titanium and replace the damaged side and although I eventually rejoined my unit in London, I was never going to recover to the same capacity. In 2015, whilst on guard in Cyprus, I had a seizure that ended my military career for good.

With the sheer amount of time I had on my hands I developed an interest in history. I was soaking up information on past cultures, why the world is the way it is now. Who were the Romans, Saxons, the Normans and who were the original inhabitants of Britain. It was all fascinating to me, and I read articles and watched documentaries to sate my thirst for knowledge. This inevitably led me to discover archaeology. And wow archaeology is so exciting. Imagine finding the evidence and artefacts from the cultures I had been learning about? I never thought that this could be approached from any other angle than a hobby or interest. With no idea that this was a genuine achievable profession, I blurted out when asked what my interests were by a career guidance counsellor that I'm really interested in archaeology. I was informed that I could use my enhanced learning credits from the military to achieve a degree in archaeology, which is the first step in making my passion a career. During this process of filling out a million forms for UCAS and ELCAS I was approached by Giles Woodhouse from Help for Heroes. He informed me that not only would they fund the degree but that there were four other veterans in the same situation. It was a very unstable time in my life. I had no home, I was living with my girlfriend and chasing various veteran aid housing schemes to help me out. My girlfriend (Katie Seymour), who remains my partner to this day, was so supportive and gave me the belief that this was an achievable dream. With her support I could do a four-year degree with the University of Winchester and the rest of life's barriers we would scale together. We gained a house through Hampshire County Council, my girlfriend was pregnant with my now five-year-old son and I was following my dream.

The other guys I was doing my degree with (both called Rob) informed me that there was a series of veteran-led archaeological experiences that I could partake in to gain that much-wanted practical experience that I felt was essential if I then wanted a career in archaeology. They informed me that there was a whole host of activities including excavations that I could get involved in to gain experience. I signed up to take part in the Barrow Clump excavations and was rewarded when Dickie Bennett and Richard Osgood granted my request to take part. This was another world entirely full of hard-working, like-minded veterans with all the banter and fun that accompanies them. Amazing archaeology, a relaxed atmosphere, and like-minded participants and a real sense that you are contributing to the archaeological narrative. During this excavation I was invited to take part in the Barton Farm excavation of a Hessian camp. Given our military experience we were also chosen due to one of our regiment's battle honours (Battle of Minden) where the Hessians fought alongside one of the forebears of our regiment, the Hampshires. Our insight and connection with the site along with our military background provided us with a unique experience when excavating. We could picture the conditions, the mood, the atmosphere of the site and were rewarded with the sense that our opinions and views were an essential part of the narrative. This sense of value overshadowed our inexperience and created an enjoyable and informative experience that served to germinate the archaeological seed of passion that had developed within us.

I can't emphasise enough the number of people I counted on for help during this period. Dr Paul Everill made it his personal mission to support myself and the other veterans throughout our university journey and helped massively with our shared worries that we would just not fit in within an academic environment. He organised a placement with Wessex Archaeology, where I would find that I really do fit in and have a valid skill set created in the military that meshes so well with archaeological excavations. During my time at Wessex I was mentored by the legendary Dr Phil Harding, which was an amazing opportunity and experience within itself. We even had the opportunity to travel to Georgia in Eastern Europe in 2017 and take part in his own project. Giles from Help for Heroes joined us on this excavation to monitor our progress and provide support and, just as likely, to rekindle his own passion for archaeology. He now works for Wessex. Following this, which was my first experience in the field, I wanted to soak up as much information and learn as much as I could about the practical side of archaeology. People like Paul and Giles, Phil, Richard and Dickie have been there providing me with the opportunities that were essential to promoting the idea that this was an achievable career path. Adding that to the support I receive from my partner it is safe to say that many have held my hand and encouraged the evolution within me that has seen me progress in the little-known archaeological sector.

Since leaving university I have been employed as an archaeologist in a number of commercial companies. I found my home in a company called L - P : Archaeology where I grew from field archaeologist to team leader on one of the biggest HS2 [High Speed 2 rail link project] excavations at St Mary's church in Stoke Mandeville, Buckinghamshire. From there I was promoted to supervisor and then quickly elevated to project officer. I now run sites but the passion to get out there with trowel, mattock, shovel and wheelbarrow will never leave. You will often find me on site hiding under a white hard hat happily digging away at the most complex feature I can find, content, happy and at home unravelling the past.

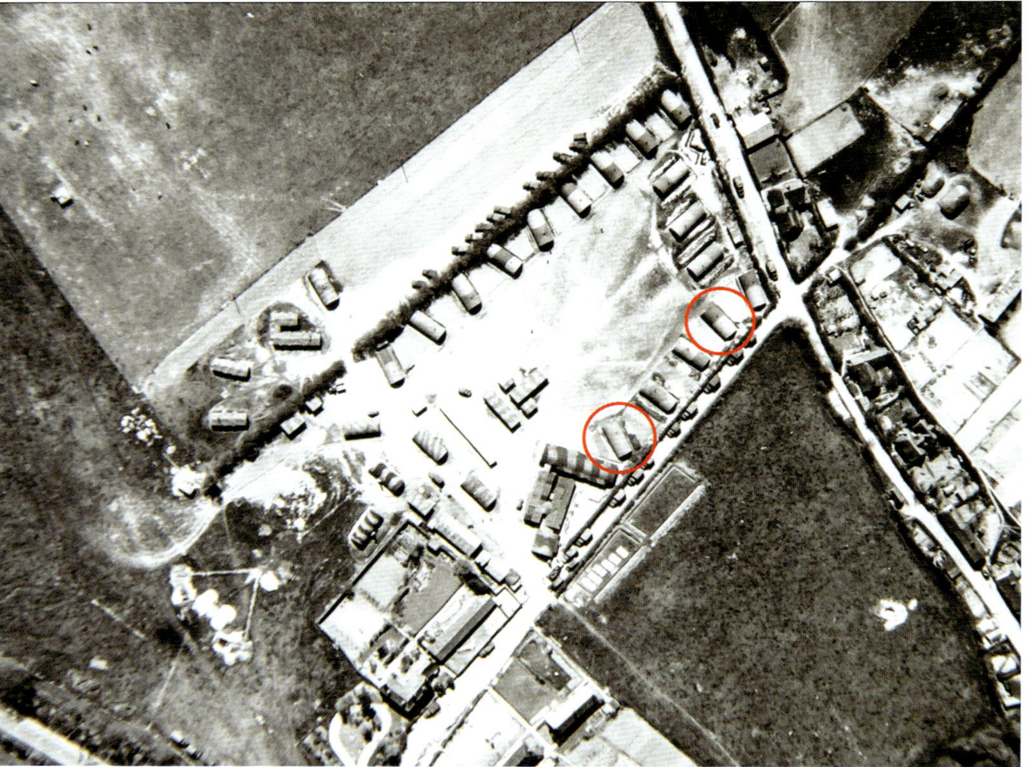

Photographed by the Royal Air Force in 1946, this image shows the camp used by Easy Company and the focus of our excavations at Aldbourne. 4315/106G/ UK1415/14 Apr 1946/ F20/540 Sqdn. © Historic England

bonding – in accommodation – is true, then much of what made this unit occurred in a small field in Wiltshire, in south-west England, for this is where Easy Company spent the longest single period of time in one place: in Aldbourne. From this village they moved to an airfield to drop into Normandy on the morning of D-Day, 6 June 1944, as some of the earliest liberators of northern France. Some would return before later deployments, many never did.

The soldiers of this unit discussed how welcome the villagers had made them feel in the 1940s recalling the youngsters pestering them for chewing gum or local women doing their washing. Indeed their famous leader, Dick Winters, had practically been adopted by a Mr and Mrs Barnes who lived in the general stores and shared their house with Winters and Harry Welsh. The Barnes' were living with their own war traumas as their son had been killed in the Royal Air Force; he is buried in Aldbourne. The paratroopers' campaign for 'hearts and minds' certainly seems to have been effective, with a number of wartime marriages and children – and the fact that the local village hall dancefloor was worn out by the end of their time here (the Americans paid for a replacement!).

The American troops arrived in Aldbourne on 16 September 1943 and, whilst some soldiers were based with local families or in stable blocks around the village green, others took on a camp site that had been created for British units on the village sports pitches. This included the sergeants of Easy Company, stalwarts of the unit and fundamental to how it would perform in battle. As always, winter brought its privations. In his 2010 publication 'In the Footsteps of the Band of Brothers', Larry Alexander highlighted the views of these huts held by a soldier from headquarters company called Williams:

> A gloomy light was shining through an open door of a Quonset hut. We entered and found wooden double-deck bunks lined down both sides. The hut was of corrugated iron construction and not insulated ... I got into bed, dog-tired, and could not stop shivering. The cold air came through the mattress and it was impossible to sleep. I found some old newspapers and put them under the mattress, which made things marginally better.

The sergeants included such luminaries as Carwood Lipton and Don Malarkey: familiar to anyone who has watched the television series. The latter wrote that each of these huts had a 'potbelly stove' within them; echoing our Hessians from Barton Farm in a different war.

A local historian, Neil Stevens, has made a lifetime study of the 101st Airborne in Aldbourne, even before the book on the unit by Stephen Ambrose came out. He knew many of the soldiers, stayed with them, discussed their stories with them. As such, his knowledge is incredible. He was given a photograph of the hut camp by none other than Carwood Lipton who is himself pictured standing with several other paratroopers in front of some of the huts on the sports pitches, behind them the rolling hills around Aldbourne with trees cresting the ridge like bristles on a boar's back. Our team of veterans, our band of brothers and sisters, thus made this their target; to excavate the hut in the photograph behind the soldiers. A sketch map given to Neil by one of the Easy Company men told us that this was the sergeants' hut itself and, just as importantly, the trees were still on the hillside and we could locate the position that the hut had stood on. Early stories from the villagers were not, however, promising; the area had been graded and levelled quite extensively when the sports pitches were upgraded. Only one

Carwood Lipton stands in front of his soldiers (second right in the image). The trees on the skyline still remain and the hut we searched for is in the centre of the photograph. Note the glider crate on the left. Courtesy of Neil Stevens

Veterans and volunteers search the layers beneath the hut used by the Sergeants of Easy Company.
© Harvey Mills

of the original camp buildings survived on site (a brick-built cookhouse) with the last remaining 'Quonset' hut having been moved to the edges of the sports area where it now functioned as a workshop.

Did anything survive? Were there any traces of Easy Company hidden under the turf? I really wanted this to be the case; our military 'archaeologists' could really empathise with the experiences of those young Americans over 75 years ago and form direct links. They would probably be able to recognise many of the finds and features immediately and, by now, I had come to see that the archaeological projects that worked on military sites were extremely effective and engaging. Given we had planned to watch some of the TV series with one of the cast in the very dance hall used by the Americans, to have a pint in the old haunts of Easy Company (the *Blue Boar* for officers, the *Crown* for other ranks), to host an open day, and to encourage a Skytrain (or Dakota) aircraft of the type from which the Screamin' Eagles jumped into battle to fly over us – much depended on the early stages of work. To this end, we had to thank a chap called David Sabin for his geophysical surveys tracing the magnetic signals left below the turf of the pitch. I had been to the Historic England archives with my friend, the wonderful photographer Harvey Mills, beforehand to look at all the holdings of historic aerial photographs. We were well supplied for Aldbourne, not least because the United States Army Air Force (USAAF) had used it as a regular training run for photography. We had photos of the huts, the paths, ablutions blocks, camouflage techniques and even parking areas with military trucks present. We thus knew the layout of the camp and could relate it to our sketch map with the sergeants' hut and with the photo with Sergeant Lipton. So, it was with some trepidation that we awaited the first viewing of David's scan on the computer screens.

From an early stage, we decided that all of the work was going to be done by hand (though ultimately we were thankful to a local farmer who helped us backfill the site with his tractor, saving both our backs and a modicum of sanity). Thus, on Day 1, the team cut the turves from one corner flag of the pitch before trowelling the surface neatly to expose any archaeology. How fortunate we were in that the grading of the pitch had, in fact, covered the remains of the camp with a protective mattress of topsoil. We soon made finds and, of course, the uppermost were the most recent. Crisp packets (pre- the 1971 decimalisation of the currency in the UK on occasion) were found, with many no-longer existing but nostalgia-inducing brands being present. Perhaps not a find to set the pulses racing but an utter godsend for the school visits that would come for an open day and which would beautifully illustrate the need for recycling and limitation of plastic consumption. Below that we found children's toys – marbles, cars, a tiny lead pig, and suchlike. This poignant discovery evoked the post-war years where the old huts had been given temporarily to 'squatters'; people whose houses had been bombed and who were now awaiting the new arrival of council housing to accommodate them. Interestingly enough, within this layer we also discovered stove components and a cooking pan, not from a pot-bellied stove but from the lives of the displaced civilians. Some of our visitors could remember those days, indeed Cecil Newton had been there on D-Day in one of the British 'swimming tanks', really highlighting the close proximity of history for us. Archaeology need not be ancient to be relevant, powerful or important.

What then of Easy Company? Well, the first stage was to locate the traces of the sergeants' building that David appeared to have located on his survey. Some dark lines on the printout were soon seen to be the lines of tarpaper remnants, waterproofing the building. A hardened stone path led to the threshold of the hut and its foundation stones also remained; these were the small punctuating dots we could see in the survey – clear ferrous signals; the concrete of each post pad having a solid iron spike in its centre to enable the hut to be held in place. Reinforced glass and bolts

Silk and stockings, 'hearts and minds'. The finds at Aldbourne related both to the military occupation and also to the recreational time of the soldiers. From left to right: part of a parachute, Brylcream bottle, nylon stocking. One is tempted to think of the liberal application of Brylcream before the user went to the local dance hall. The Americans paid for a new floor in the dance hall post-war. © Harvey Mills

and screws were liberally strewn across the area and were identical to the hut now used by one of the villagers, Stephen Sowerby, for the restoration of historic cars as a useful comparator. We could definitely rebuild this structure and almost feel the presence of Carwood Lipton.

In each excavation, I reach a point when I feel I can relax; when the team dynamic is working; when the weather is being kind; when I feel that we have answered key research questions; when I see smiling faces. The discovery of those post pads was that point for me as we had found our structure. But the team, not for the first time, surpassed all expectations. Soon the links to the soldiers themselves were being made – clips from a Garand rifle, spam tin keys, a Pepsi-Cola bottle fragment, a basketball supporter's badge, bullets. Gloriously, there were hints to the attempts at local liaison: a bottle of Brylcream and – perhaps even the success of such a 'hearts and minds' campaign – a nylon stocking, all redolent of the tales of the village dance hall we were by now familiar with.

They do say that war is a small amount of terror in amongst a vast sea of boredom and I have hinted at the imaginative nature of the bored soldier – well we found a British wartime-period coin (a thrupenny bit) with a perfect bullet hole through its centre. Right through the King's head no less. Hoping that no British soldier was guilty of such a treasonous act, one likes to point the finger at an American soldier for this.

Of course, we wanted to be sure we were looking at paratroopers now we had good evidence for our Americans. We were, by now, greedy. One of our veterans, Paul Hemingway, was our lead on metal detecting on this site working with friends David Ulke (Royal Air Force) and James Galvin (Royal Anglian Regiment). Paul made the find of the dig right next to Carwood Lipton's hut using a metal detector.

Archaeologists and metal detectorists have been documented as having a frosty relationship at times – there can be rogues that claim to be both. I find the ordered use of metal detectors to

The next generation of archaeologists? School children watch Daz at work. The children are taught about the Band of Brothers in school at Aldbourne.
© Harvey Mills

George (Rifles veteran) and Jo Hutchings (Aldourne resident) model the excavation T-shirt and monitor dig progress.
© Harvey Mills

be invaluable, however, and Paul and colleagues have definitely located items we would not have seen, often in tricky geology (I know of at least one 6th-century shield boss in this category). Metal detecting is prohibited on Ministry of Defence land, for the, perhaps obvious, reason that there is still a large quantity of unexploded ordnance around and you really don't want to excavate that. Ironically, of course, the origin of the metal detector itself comes from the military and in mine detection and the lives of many of the Operation Nightingale team were saved in operational theatres through use of this tool. Not surprisingly, they are very good with these pieces of equipment on our sites, and we really benefit from their skills as we plot the results.

Paul came over to us, initially quizzically, with a strange T-shaped handle he had discovered and flagged. Fortunately, there were enough experts on site, armed with illustrated books, to demonstrate that this was, rather incredibly, the handle of a reserve parachute; some of the red paint still adhering. Of course, this set the mind racing – why was it in the hut? Had it been lost in training? Had it been brought back as a souvenir of life-saving action when the paratroopers returned from D-Day and before they dropped onto Arnhem later in the war? We will never know, but it certainly enables us to write some tremendous narratives, to daydream and to reconstruct a tale of heroism (p. 40). Archaeology enables you to do this; it is so important to weave a reasonable evidence-based tale and theory around your discoveries (backing with science where you can of course!). Not far from this find was a small, ragged fragment of fabric – also from a reserve parachute. Our cup runneth over.

When I wrote this, I was also considering what makes a project good for wellbeing. Certainly, a beautiful location fits the bill, with kind locals, good food, fabulous weather, incredible finds and engaging participants also perfect additions. This excavation enabled the team to explore the wider landscape too: to visit carvings left behind on trees

Paul Hemingway holds the star find from 2019, which he has just made; the handle of a reserve parachute. © Harvey Mills

The reserve parachute handle found at Aldbourne still had some original red paint adhering and had all the team wondering how it ended up on site. We couldn't imagine any find coming close to equalling this discovery here. © Harvey Mills

by American soldiers, which had, in some cases, already probably outlived the carver by almost eighty years; to see practice infantry positions and shelters dug in training before Normandy and yet familiar to our dig team from their military days. We could enjoy the same pubs as the Band of Brothers and participate in the weekly pub quiz.

As we packed our tents away, we could even find the culprit of nocturnal discomfort to one of our number. Paul Barnsley (a former artilleryman) had had his sleep disrupted by evening scurrying and the mouse runs were clear for all to see as the groundsheet was lifted, the rodent itself scurried into the undergrowth nearby. In fact, Paul seems to have been a veritable magnet for the local wildlife as he had, foolishly, pitched his tent directly below telegraph wires, which hosted the 5 am meetings of most of the crows of Wiltshire. Very noisy indeed. I still chuckle at Paul shouting at them to 'SHUT UP'. He may have been a non-commissioned officer in the British Army but this impresses no corvid.

The finds were recorded, bagged and then curated at the village Heritage Centre where any pilgrim of the deeds of Easy Company can visit them today alongside other items associated with the American presence in Aldbourne.

With all the work our projects embark upon, getting the results out is crucial. If you don't publish your findings you might as well simply take to a site with a bulldozer. Heritage belongs to us all, not just the excavator. In addition to the more formal outputs of monographs, or articles in County Archaeological Journals, each site is written up for the local County Historic Environment Record, most of which are online and thus accessible to anyone. But you can't beat a site featuring in a glossy magazine or (best of all in my opinion) on television. *Digging for Britain* on the BBC with Professor Alice Roberts leads the pack I think in the way it makes archaeology accessible to a wide audience. This *Band of Brothers* excavation was covered in the 2019 season and so we filmed all the discoveries on site before the follow-up session looking in details at some of the artefacts we excavated. I felt a very small amount of guilt covering the finds table in her studio with my various elements of rust, glass and nylon, given they had been preceded in filming by the sumptuous sparkling priceless treasures of the recently discovered Staffordshire Hoard (the largest hoard of Anglo-Saxon gold and silver metalwork yet found in England). But this moment was only fleeting; these objects are still an important part of our island story. Linking to people who have now died but whose actions left a legacy in history. For sword hilt pieces and helmet fragments we had bullet clips and parachute handles – all parts of a 'warrior' panoply nonetheless.

The power of the broadcast media was highlighted just a day or so after the programme aired, and Alice emailed me to inform me that a man had written into the show prompted by what he had seen. He had been a young boy when Easy Company came to his village and he had many memories of their presence; ones he wanted to share with me. Such reminiscences are priceless and might well have been lost had it not been for the television. This was a local history that we could now capture and add to our records and I know that the team was delighted by the story offered by David Shaw-Stewart.

Whilst the tales of discarded ammunition were a little frightening, the picture of two small boys walking around a ghostly camp with its former occupants now heavily engaged in the morning of D-Day (or already wounded or indeed dead) set the hairs on the back of my neck on end. David's tale corroborated those of the veterans that the local youngsters and the paratroopers got on famously. Switzy (and Colin) visited us in our second field season at Aldbourne in 2022 and they were the stars of our open day. In addition to the badges on Switzy's little jumper, it also had a couple of pockets. One used to hold a tiny ration book, the other now holds a small folded obituary from the *Daily Telegraph* newspaper, of Dick Winters – erstwhile commander of Easy Company and that Band of Brothers.

An aerial view during our excavations of what we think was the Sergeant's hut at Aldbourne. © Harvey Mills

David Shaw-Stewart (resident of Aldbourne)

I used to watch the soldiers marching up Southward Lane every day to go on their training exercises up over the downs and also on to Pentico Wood. They would throw sticks of chewing gum to me. They also would go along the valley, opposite from the drive up to the house, to fire live ammunition into the hillside. They discarded belts of empty machine-gun bullets which we picked up and used as bandoliers. We also collected belts, water bottles, mess tins, helmets and bits of ammunition such as rocket grenades.

My Aunt Peggy and mother were very involved in helping the war effort in the village and were friends with many of the military personnel in Easy Company and also with the large Air Force base at Membury nearby. They would have drinks parties for officers of Easy Company. I remember the well-dressed soldiers coming to the house.

My mother was friends with one of the officers called George. I never knew his surname. He gave her two badges, which my mother sewed on to my brother Colin's chimpanzee teddy called Switzy. The two badges were the 101st Airborne and the eagle's head. I am not sure where the badge for the Anti-Aircraft Company came from. Switzy is still a companion today. On D-Day the camp was deserted. My cousin Peter and I went down to the camp. All the doors were left open and there were open boxes of live ammunition on the tables.

Switzy the monkey visits the American camp at Aldbourne, having been a regular in the 1940s. Switzy still has an 'airborne' and 'Screamin' Eagle' patch given to his owner by the Americans. © Harvey Mills

Our team shared so many links and experiences with the young men of Easy Company. The respect on the excavation for those that had lived here before was really tangible. In one final link, I remembered that Paul Hemingway had been a serjeant in the Light Infantry, which then became the Rifles – a British Infantry Regiment. One of the great characters of the *Band of Brothers* was Lieutenant Ronald Speirs. Speirs married an Aldbourne girl and they had a son; this son eventually becoming an officer in the Royal Green Jackets which also eventually became ... the Rifles, amalgamating with Paul's unit amongst others. The soldiers of Easy Company were deeply affected by their wartime experiences with the memories of what they had faced resurfacing frequently:

> And coming home, you can't just check in at the door like a hat or a coat. I'd see or hear things that would suddenly bring it all back: a combat movie at the McDonald. The eyes of some freshman who reminded me of that sixteen-year-old German kid I'd shot in Foy. The backfire of a truck; once, on Thirteenth Street, that happened and I literally dove for cover because it was still so ingrained in me. Every now and then, I'd wake up tangled in my blankets and sweating like a pig, sure some German soldier had just popped out from behind those skinny firs in Jack's Woods and jammed a bayonet in my gut. Or those bloody legs of Toye's and Guarnere's in the snow. But would you tell anyone about this stuff back then? Hell, no ... (Malarkey 2008, 230)[1]

The Operation Nightingale team could empathise with all these words of Don Malarkey and they created their own bonds around the memories of these young Americans. Perhaps it seems incongruous but gaining a degree of solace and alleviation from those challenges faced by the Easy Company soldiers as a result – I think those lads from the 1940s would have smiled at this.

The perils of writing this book whilst Operation Nightingale continues were made very clear to me in May 2022 when I thought I had already finished this chapter. The dig team had returned to Aldbourne after the enforced gap of the COVID-19 pandemic and we were able to investigate another hut in the row used by Easy Company as well as surveying more of the lines of their comrades in 'Fox' Company – if the sketch maps we had were correct. I was fairly comfortable that nothing would surpass the result of the previous fieldwork and hence I could write up this project without need for subsequent augmentation or alteration. How wrong I was. Even before we began digging we found out, quite by chance, that the relatives of one of our Australian veterans, Kieran Scotchford ('Scotchy' as we call him) had lived in the house closest to the church on the village green – he had had no idea when he signed up for the project. Scotchy said of this:

> The Band of Brothers dig was a memorable one for my family as I discovered my Nana had stayed in Aldbourne in the late 1950s whilst my Grandad was serving on one of the airbases with the RAF. We found the house and the locals helped research some of the history about that era. My mum was ecstatic, it was an overwhelming feeling to be added to an already amazing time in Aldbourne.

On excavation of the sports pitch, we could see that the camp buildings themselves were interesting, concrete footings of floor pads for the Quonset huts on the 'Easy' side, and more elaborate brick foundations on the opposite side of the quadrangle in the 'Fox' lines. We found more American ammunition and building furniture (along with parts of a German grenade, identified by our ammunition expert, Mark Khan, which must have been used for familiarisation in enemy weaponry training) and were able to match the location of our building with a wartime photograph of a very famous Easy Company man, Forrest Guth, sitting on a bicycle outside it (p. 44).

It was, however, the surveying that really surpassed even the most optimistic of pre-excavation aspirations. Magnetometry, ground-penetrating

One of the most incredible coincidences: Australian veteran Scotchy found that a relative of his used to live in this house in Aldbourne. © Harvey Mills

Above left: An aerial view of the excavation of the hut we looked at in 2022 with the square post pads clearly visible. © Harvey Mills

Above right: Excavating one of the Easy Company huts in 2022. © Harvey Mills

radar and resistivity showed that there were further brick structures and, once more, our detectorists found historic 'treasure' every bit as exciting as Sutton Hoo. David Ulke located a bus fare token (valid for one journey in Atlanta, Georgia). This was the same state as the jump school in Toccoa and conjures up images of a paratrooper making the most of a leave pass and the opportunities afforded by the city's public transport. Veteran Adrian Ledbury then brought us over to look at, on the face of it, a rather undistinguished small rectangular metal box – fortunately this was recognised instantly by Jack Robson, one of the veterans from the Yorkshire Regiment, as a 'cricket' or clicker, a child's toy used on D-Day by the paratroopers to identify one another in the dark, as portrayed in one of the most famous scenes in the film *The Longest Day* and featured in *Band of Brothers*. Archaeology is all about telling a story around the sites and objects found. This one small object screams about one single day in history: 6 June 1944, certainly, one of the most momentous in recent centuries and, as such, is a small item holding incredible power. The team was, understandably utterly thrilled.

Such items are also really useful for showing to the many tour groups, villagers and school children that came to see us, along with Tim Matthews, Rick Warden and Shane Taylor – some of the actors from the original television series – that rendered a number of our dig team rather star-struck (this means you Jack Robson).

And just at the point, when we felt that nothing could improve, it suddenly did. Twice. Paul Hemingway (once again) started it all off. We heard whoops of delight from the far side of the

Below left: When we thought no find could equal a parachute pull or our first dog tag – this was discovered; the identity tag of Carl Fenstermaker, one of the two pathfinders of Easy Company. © Harvey Mills

Below right: Evidence of an American presence at D-Day. A bus token from Atlanta, a clicker or 'cricket', and an American button. © Harvey Mills

The Royal Air Force fly over the excavation in 2022 as the team look on. © Harvey Mills

field and rushed over to see what he had found. It was an identity disc known as a 'dog tag': it was shiny and pristine-looking and almost appeared too good to be true, but it was undoubtedly genuine. The tag was for Richard Blake, an 'Able' Company soldier in the 506th from New York State who parachuted into Normandy on D-Day itself and was wounded badly enough on a subsequent jump, as part of the 'Operation Market Garden' campaign for Arnhem, that he never fought again. Paul had found an item that matched the 'clicker' in being a direct link to D-Day for the paratroopers but this time we had a name and, moments later thanks to an internet search, we had a face to go with it – a photograph of Richard. He was twenty years old when he first jumped into battle and for several months he called Aldbourne home. How did his tag get there? Did 'Able' Company live in this field? Had he dropped it visiting a friend? Had someone else placed it here? We'll never know but it still makes the hair on the back of my neck rise to think of such a tangible link to the events of 1944 (p. 45).

David Ulke led a Royal Air Force mental health team on operational tours: his experience required him to hear all the worst elements that people

the camaraderie on site continues 'long after we go home' is also important. David has been a key member of the metal-detecting element of the fieldwork programme and, for this reason perhaps, Aldbourne has been a memorable project for him; 'Recovering some really interesting artefacts, and then being present the days the two dog tags surfaced … priceless memories made right there and then'.

Tags plural? Well yes because, astonishingly, on the very next day after the first discovery, a second tag was found by Cassie, one of the local stalwarts that helped us. This tag was bent and slightly less shiny but the data it held was equally priceless. This time it was for an Easy Company man. One of the Band of Brothers, Carl Fenstermaker, a 21-year-old from Seipstown, Pennsylvania, took part in D-Day (in fact he was a pathfinder whose job was to mark the landing zones for his colleagues that came after him) and though his Dakota crashed into the sea, he also took part in Operation Market Garden and at Bastogne. There were lots of photographs of him, indeed several with Forrest Guth – the man perched on the bicycle outside the hut we excavated, as Carl was his friend. Forrest and Carl enlisted together in Philadelphia in 1942 along with Rod Strohl. All managed to get through the

Former Royal Engineer Adrian holds his discovery of an American button. © Harvey Mills

had gone through, leading to him being placed on long-term sick leave as it was so attritional. He joined Operation Nightingale back in 2012 on the excavation of a Roman site at Caerwent and has not looked back, gaining a degree in archaeology in 2018 from the University of Leicester (where he is now an Honorary Visiting Fellow), and publishing works on the subject of wellbeing with archaeology. From his perspective: 'Having "time out" for a week or so with like-minded people sharing a mutual interest can only ever be beneficial, so in that regard it added some steps in the right direction to the journey'. The fact that

war. Forrest Guth said that Carl had been 'deeply affected by the war and bore emotional scars. "He couldn't hold down a job" Forrest remembered'.[2] When one reads more about Carl's war it really isn't surprising. He was one of the first into Dachau camp and acted as an interpreter for the inmates who described the horrors of their existence there alongside all that Carl could see for himself. The war, and his involvement in it, however has left traces such as his tag, which, bizarrely, have helped some who have suffered similar experiences in later conflicts (p. 46). Perhaps in telling his incredible story (there could be a book on him, so amazing were his deeds), we will be able to perpetuate Carl's memory, adding a new 'brother' to the famous band. He seems to me in many ways to epitomise the challenges faced by our archaeological participants, and to emphasise why we dig.

Notes

[1] From *Easy Company Soldier: The legendary battles of a sergeant from World War II's* Band of Brothers, by Don Malarkey with Bob Welch (2008). New York: St Martin's Griffin.

[2] From *In the Footsteps of the Band of Brothers*, by Larry Alexander (2010). New York: New American Library, p. 298.

Opposite: I have always believed that 'finds' are important on our digs. Second World War excavations are up there with Roman sites for quantity. © Harvey Mills

Below: Serving and veteran US military personnel laying a wreath on the cross at Albourne Green, 2023. © Harvey Mills

BELIKIN

3 LEGENDS

The convict burials of Rat Island

THE STUDY OF ARCHAEOLOGY is replete with legends and mysterious tales – from the lost city of Atlantis, to the gold of El Dorado. I am pretty sure that every local Historic Environment Record in the UK will have its own collection of folklore, and fantastic tales of possible buried deposits. From the vanished treasure of King John, to buried circus elephants.

In 2019, I was fortunate enough to give a presentation to an archaeological conference in Caen, Normandy, discussing the findings of our *Exercise Joan of Arc* excavation at Bullecourt that we will look at later in this book. The whole premise was pretty daunting, given that I was to speak in my incredibly rudimentary French, which is augmented by as many online translation functions as possible. A room full of native French speakers awaited and, although I felt I could probably bluff my way through the talk itself, questions were altogether more terrifying as a prospect. I knew the word for tank was *char* (and not, as a well-known digital platform would have you believe, *reservoir*) but this was perhaps as good as it got. I cannot tell you how grateful I was that my session was running so far behind schedule that the questions session was removed. Imagine also my chagrin when a later speaker, also British, gave his paper in English; I really need not have worried!

To relax after this, Harvey Mills and I decided to drive to the Normandy coast before the trip

Above: The Age of Enlightenment; a burial at 'Rat Island' with a craniotomy. © Alice Roberts

Opposite: A view from the grave. Burrow Island 2021. © Harvey Mills

A view of Burrow Island from the cross channel ferry as it arrives from Normandy. © Harvey Mills

back to England and to see some of the haunts of Easy Company in 1944 – a place of pilgrimage. From Sainte-Marie-du-Mont, the earliest place of capture and one which boasts the famous picture of Forrest Guth and other luminaries standing in the village square, through to Carentan and the fighting through the town. We also visited Utah beach, one of the main landing beaches of 6 June 1944, passing a large statue of Major Dick Winters along the causeway to the sands. The bronze paratrooper now crouches to the flutter of the *Stars and Strips* and the French *Tricolore*. I have been out to Belgium and France with young soldiers as part of their early phases of military training and a battlefield study. Invariably these visit the old trenches and memorials of the First World War and yet, on several trips, the standard viewing on the coach home is indeed *Band of Brothers*.

The fields of fighting, the cemeteries, the monuments, are poignant places and certainly gave us food for thought as we took the ferry back to Portsmouth. As we arrived in England dawn was breaking, and we slowly passed the huge aircraft carrier, HMS *Queen Elizabeth II,* drawing us to an altogether more modern martial environment. Just as we crept gingerly past this grey leviathan, a small tree-crowned island peered out from the shrouding mists on the left (or should I say port) side of the ferry, like the cresting of a whale. This small tidal island is called 'Burrow Island' and is accessible via its own narrow shingle causeway twice a day when the tides are low enough to permit it. If you are fortunate to take a harbour tour around the Portsmouth naval base you will see the most fascinating historic dockyard (and I can't recommend this area highly enough for heritage buffs) and will also be regaled with a very dark tale surrounding this innocuous-looking piece of land. You will be told that 'Burrow Island' is also known colloquially as 'Rat Island', so named as it used to have a major rodent problem as these small animals gorged on the corpses of people buried there. Some tell you that this was where prisoners of war were disposed of, others that it was the last inauspicious resting place of dead convicts. And it all sounds like a huge urban myth, the sort of tall story that seems to be present on every single Ministry of Defence site in some form or other.

Salisbury Plain itself has had some rather splendid rumours too: German equipment from the Second World War brought over to England by American service personnel and promptly buried when they were told that it was upsetting the locals. I was really not sure that there wouldn't have been a single soldier with the wit to think of selling these items but there you go. Another tale was that a batch of Harley Davidson motorcycles had, Merlin-engine style, been crated and buried on the training area. The story was not unusual, the method of their detection, however, was: crystal-dowsing of a map. The applicant that told us about this find demonstrated the violent swinging of the crystal pendulum whenever it was lowered over a certain area on the east of the Plain. I must confess I was unable to elicit similar movement but this could be a fault in me. Duly encouraged, we went on site where the specific location was marked out and then the turf was scraped back with a machine to reveal some of the cleanest fresh chalk I have seen in the region. In other words, natural geology, and certainly no motorbikes. The oddest one was the rumour of buried mess silver at Larkhill, again on the Plain, to avoid it being looted by an invading German army. Again, I think most entrepreneurs being asked to complete such a task might have found another solution but perhaps this is my cynicism once more.

You can thus probably imagine my delight on receiving a phone call from the Ministry of Defence police who had responsibility for Burrow (Rat) Island to ask if I could come along and deal with the human remains that had been found by a (trespassing) member of the public on this island overlooked by the naval base. I expected to be handed some cow or pig bones when I arrived and certainly not the very obviously human skull in the evidence bag I was presented with. The stories emanating from this site of rodents scurrying around feasting on burials, and that human bones formed a sizeable portion of this island were, in fact, real, and a cursory inspection of the 3 m high 'cliff' face on the island soon revealed many more bones that were gradually being exposed by storms and high tides from the shingle, shell and sand that had entombed them. We needed to do something to recover these remains as archaeologically as possible and this seemed the perfect opportunity for some Operation Nightingale fieldwork.

After a series of urgent emails to who I felt would be the key authorities on this (local heritage experts at Historic Environment Records, the Ministry of Justice for an exhumation license required for the removal of human remains, and various marine policing agencies so we didn't get arrested for visiting the island so close to the Portsmouth Naval base), I put together a team of archaeologists and veterans who would approach the task with gusto. I worried about the effects that exhumation of human remains may have had on team members but all were aware of the project goals and were still keen to take part. By now, our team had evolved from its origins with the Rifles to include (suitably enough) Marines, bomb disposal and Naval personnel and we thus trudged across the tidal causeway to visit the island and the remains that were being eroded. The veterans waded through the muds, keeping a close eye on the time as none of us fancied being stranded there for a further seven or eight hours if an incoming tide cut us off. This was more of a challenge for some than others, especially those with no legs and whose short prosthetics meant that they sunk far deeper into the sands than the rest of us.

The scene that greeted us on our first foray was really rather ghoulish, with numerous burials eroding from what appeared to be rock-cut tombs. Many of these had lost bones to the sea and thus it really was a rescue mission. Traditionally, archaeology is performed in a horizontal plane, with layer upon layer being removed and carefully recorded. This simply was not possible on Rat Island; time was against us with tidal actions and we had no possibility of digging through the almost 3 m of overburden through tree roots down to the remains; it would have to be an approach from the side, working from toe bones to skull. I checked with Jackie McKinley, an osteoarchaeologist, to see if our methodologies would suffice and her advice on taking regular photographs with scales and then dealing with the recovered remains in a laboratory setting tallied with our thoughts. Wessex Archaeology were able to provide digital models from our photographs so this technique certainly worked. Our advice on handling skeletons once we arrived was provided by Nick Márquez-Grant from Cranfield University Forensic Institute, which was co-located at the UK Defence Academy, happily enough for us. In later years Nick's colleague David Errickson would join us for this role, along with Claire Hodson.

The team cleaned up remains in the cliff face and soon we were faced with an eerily jumbled scene with skeletons in small, constrained holes amongst the ruins of the 17th-century Fort James and the rubble of later constructions and installations. Our veterans collected what they could before we made a tactical withdrawal ready to plan for a greater endeavour, as it was clear that a larger project would be needed. Thus was born *Exercise Magwitch*.

Abel Magwitch was one of the key characters in Charles Dickens's novel of 1861, *Great Expectations*. Without giving any plot spoilers, Magwitch was a convict destined for transportation and incarcerated on one of the huge and foreboding prison hulks before he escaped, and we meet him at the start of the book. Although the work is not set on the south coast of England, Dickens was from Portsmouth and there is little doubt he would have been very familiar with these prisons. There were several possibilities put to us at the start of our work on the island, centring on the probabilities that the remains we had found were, as all the local stories had it, the bodies of convicts from the

From left to right: former Royal Marine Dickie Bennett, archaeologist Dr Sarah Ashbridge, forensic anthropologist Dr Nick Márquez-Grant, and veteran Elaine Corner in one of the Rat Island workshops. © Harvey Mills

The eroding graves at the base of the cliff on Burrow Island clearly visible as gaping holes. Our recovery work works against the tide to retrieve remains. © Harvey Mills

prison hulks (old, de-masted, wooden warships now firmly anchored in place) or prisoners of war in the same miserable form of incarceration.

If the latter, we could be looking at many nationalities; after all, Britain was at war with most of the nations on earth in the later 18th and earlier 19th centuries, the dates we suspected for these burials. They could be Russian, German, Dutch, Danish, Spanish, French or several other nationalities, including Americans. Several of the military team members made a few comments hoping that the bodies might indeed be the remains of American soldiers, not through any antagonism (after all, our veterans fought closely with US counterparts in recent conflicts) but rather through a reason of greater self-interest (and delusion).

America takes a very different stance to the British in the attitude to its war dead or times past. In the UK, an understanding of burial in a 'foreign field', or cemeteries constructed close to the point of the soldier's death is well-known. In the First and Second World Wars, such was the scale of death, it was decided at an early moment that the remains of the dead would not be returned home and the origins of what we now know as the

Commonwealth War Graves Commission was created. Even though the Ministry of Defence will undertake as much assessment work as possible to identify and bury remains from these wars if they are found by chance, there is no policy to go and actively seek for the remains of the missing. The situation is the direct opposite in America where there is an undertaking that nobody is left behind. This is the mission of the Governmental 'Defense POW/MIA Accounting Agency (DPAA)'. This unit is based in Hawaii and my team were under the mistaken impression that, should the bodies we had found prove to be Americans from the Wars of Independence or of 1812, they would get to return the remains in person.

Although such a splendid trip was never likely to materialise, the thought that the remains *might* be American was not altogether fanciful; a prison for Americans was established at Forton in Gosport, just a stone skim away across the creek. Forton also held black prisoners from the Caribbean who had fought with the French. Portchester Castle too is visible from Rat Island. This magnificent site was originally an old 'Saxon Shore' fort built by the Romans to assist defence against raiders but we know from excavations that French prisoners of war were incarcerated here too – both from the graffiti they left behind and also their mortal remains. In fact, looking at the military buttons, rosary beads and similar finds was one of the very first jobs I did for Barry Cunliffe, the excavator, when starting as his research student thirty years ago. The archival search for the finds I did back in the 1990s also included opening a brown cardboard box filled with items recovered in what we call a 'field walk': a measured, systematic survey picking items off the surface of a field. This was clearly part of an old cemetery as there were parts of gravestones and even the grinning faded heads of old china dolls. Really sinister – and a perfect box of accoutrements for a Halloween set. They didn't get included in any final site reports.

Part of the joy of undertaking Operation Nightingale is putting the team together, establishing a series of extra events and seeing what other skills are present within the Ministry that we can apply to the project. Ideally all will have fun, gain a training benefit and produce something for the archaeology team that is as cost-effective as possible.

It turns out that we could run a pretty decent archaeological unit within the Department. A new set of maps was provided to us by Daz Smith of the Royal Engineers, a stalwart of Operation Nightingale projects but we have yet really to tempt him onto pre-20th-century sites, and we persuaded a group called 17 Port and Maritime

Regiment to provide a combat support boat, both to move equipment and also to provide a quick exit method should we misread the tides or get carried away (metaphorically) with the interest of the work. This might have been useful in avoiding a soaking given to Alice Roberts and her film crew from the TV series, *Britain's Most Historic Towns*, when just one more film take was needed as the causeway gradually receded. Such trials are, however, as I am constantly told by military participants, 'character-building'. And you can file backfilling a site by hand in that list too.

Then there was the Royal Military Police: we were able to incorporate this project as part of their body recovery training. Rat Island is perfect in providing tricky recovery methods against the clock, just as they might face in operational theatres. Furthermore, they have laser scanners that would assist our recording of the area. When you combine all these military assets it can be a fearsome scene, particularly if you are illegally bait-digging on the island. The individuals undertaking this illicit task were greeted with the kind of boat they would probably associate more with films like *Apocalypse Now* and the Mekong Delta suddenly beaching itself on the island and disembarking a group of soldiers in fatigues. I've never seen people move quite so quickly to escape tricky questioning! With the two British aircraft carriers moored opposite the island, security has certainly

Laura and Kevin of the Royal Military Police sieve through spoil at Burrow Island to recover any small bones. © Harvey Mills

been heightened and even we have been subject to loudspeaker questioning from police river launches as to quite why we are there. It is not a particularly easy answer when you know you should reply on the lines of recovering bodies ...

As part of the training, we all visited the forensics labs at Cranfield University and this knowledge was tremendously useful preparatory work. On the island itself the veterans and archaeologists looked to recover as much by way of eroding remains as possible, accompanied by the most curious aspects of nature as it turned out; a series of furry abseiling caterpillars that had the capacity to administer a rash to anyone that touched them, sometimes in the most peculiar of locations, and a local fox that seemed to have a penchant for the teams' digestive biscuits. This animal looked incredibly healthy and I did rather wonder if begging techniques had been perfected over several years.

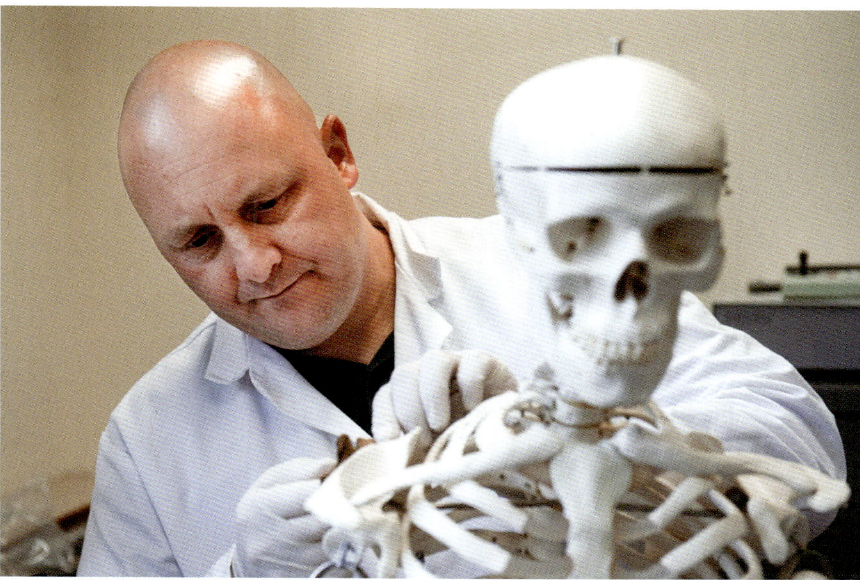

Former Royal Signaller Matt Smith put through his anatomical paces at Cranfield Forensic Institute. © Harvey Mills

The work necessitated several field seasons, such was the scale of erosion and the depths of deposit but this enabled us to bring many different participants to the site and also to invest in the post-excavation side of the work to uncover as much information as possible about the people whose bones we were recovering. We could see immediately that many burials were in what looked to be rock-cut tombs (in fact the pressure of the

After recording its location, veteran Rob Steel recovers a femur from one of the graves. © Harvey Mills

Right: A foot emerges from the sands on the island: the bone is often in remarkably good condition. © Harvey Mills

Below: Initial cleaning of one of the Burrow Island skulls. © Harvey Mills

material above them had consolidated the beach shingles into a solid rocky mass rather than being evidence of graves cut into such hard material). The lower parts of several graves were missing as the sea had claimed foot and leg bones during storms. A walk along the foreshore recovered some of these elements but the chances of reuniting body parts with erstwhile owners was pretty remote without the expense of DNA assessment.

The burials were aligned in an east–west orientation with the skulls at the western end; in a Christian fashion even though the island itself was not consecrated ground. The burials had originally been in coffins, part of the elm wood of these containers still being preserved along with iron and copper nail fittings, although earlier graves were sometimes disturbed by later inhumations. In these cases, the remains of the first burials then formed the material that packed around the new graves. Space on the island was clearly at a premium so not only were old graves cut through but coffins were also stacked one on top of the other. As mentioned, the French prisoners of war buried at Portchester Castle had certain identifying items with them and, at the nearby Haslar Naval hospital, whose burial ground dated from 1753–1826, earlier excavations of the inhumed remains of the Royal Navy also turned up interesting artefacts. Perhaps the most intriguing was the discovery of a skeleton of a sailor who had two coins placed over the eye sockets: a feature more akin to graves you might expect to find on sites of Classical antiquity. These coins proved to be a halfpenny made in Gosport in 1794 and an anti-slavery token proclaiming *Am I not a man and a brother?* The deceased may well have been an abolitionist. On Rat Island, however, none of the individuals took anything with them to any afterlife. We did find a clay pipe bowl depicting a warship of the type from the Battle of Trafalgar, a type popular after the British victory of 1805 and which had been manufactured by a Mr Thomas Frost of Southampton; wonderful serendipity given we could see Nelson's ship *Victory* from site as she now lies as a major visitor attraction in Portsmouth Naval base, but as the find was made in the soil around graves, it could have come from just about anywhere. This being said, several of the skulls did have strange circular holes in the bite of the teeth, made by the regular grinding action of

We tend not to make any special finds at Burrow Island but this image shows several views of a clay pipe bowl made by a Thomas Frost of Southampton in the early 19th century. It depicts a warship of the type from the Battle of Trafalgar of 1805. You can see Nelson's flagship, HMS *Victory*, famously involved in that battle, from the place we found this item. © Harvey Mills

a clay pipe stem when gripped in the mouth by smokers. The very fact that the graves had nothing at all, not a single button, may be significant if these were indeed the remains of prisoners from the old hulks; any possessions or even clothing would have been something to recover by other prisoners to try to make their own existence better in any form they could.

If these were prisoners of the hulks, it is a curious feeling to gaze over to HMS *Victory* and to think it was old warships such as this that formed the place of incarceration and the people we were exhuming may well have known all about the results of the battles fought by these vessels. Returning briefly to Dickens and *Great Expectations*, the hulks were, rather wonderfully, referred to as being a sort of Wicked Noah's Ark and one of the main characters, Mrs Joe Gargery, admonishes her nephew Pip when quizzed about why people were put on these ghastly leviathans; 'I didn't bring you up by hand to badger people's lives out. It would be blame to me, and not praise, if I had. People are put in the Hulks because they murder, and because they rob, and forge, and do all sorts of bad; and they always begin by asking questions'. But questions are crucial and it is always vital that the team asks them frequently. Science can be incredibly useful in all of this.

The teeth of the remains not only revealed a penchant for tobacco, they also can be assessed along with the bones for their stable isotopic compositions to reveal where people grew up and what sorts of diets they had. In the case of these individuals, most had a signature consistent with a British origin although some could have come from the northern European mainland and a diet

Not only was the work of the surgeons clear with the craniotomy, we were also intrigued to notice possible coffin lining material still *in situ*. © Harvey Mills

Dr David Errickson of Cranfield Forensic Institute discussing details of a mandible with team members. © Harvey Mills

based mainly on plant and animal foodstuffs (with some fish) was also seen. Although we couldn't determine the cause of death of these people (smallpox, typhus, cholera, scurvy and all manner of other prevalent ailments of the period could have been the cause and might have left no trace) we were not alone in this. One burial excavated in 2017 had clearly intrigued local surgeons and had been the subject of an autopsy shortly after death. This was illustrated by cuts to the ribs and, more spectacularly, a 'craniotomy' where the top of the skull had been removed. The radiocarbon dates from the site show the probability that the burials were made from the mid-18th through until the earlier 19th century, quite possibly before the 1832 *Anatomy Act* made the provision of cadavers simpler for surgeons of the Enlightenment to investigate anatomical questions. For me, the fact that the top of the skull had been replaced with the burial and the coffin placed in the ground with some dignity perhaps counteracted any pre-suppositions that dead convicts might not be afforded a decent burial.

Although Nick and Dave have done the bulk of the osteological assessment work, an initial phase that has always been enjoyed by the military participants is to go to the nearby headquarters of the Royal Military Police (RMP) at Southwick Park. Not only is the RMP forensic centre based here, enabling the team to lay out and examine the skeletons in more detail on stainless steel benches, but also there is the wonderful D-Day map on a wall of the stately home; the location where Eisenhower made the statement 'Ok, we'll go' (or similar) on 5 June 1944. For those of the team that had also worked on our *Band of Brothers* dig and could pick up the placement of Utah beach, this gave tremendous project connections.

The vast majority of the burials were adult males, but not all. At least one woman has been found and the bones of one baby too and this leads to further questions (apologies to Mrs Gargery) as to just why they were buried here? Were they on the hulks too? Was it simply a convenient place of disposal? There are death certificates for women

One of the early maps of Burrow Island contained an important clue as to the origin of these burials as a 'convict burying ground'. Redrawn by and © Katherine Osgood

on French prisoner of war hulks in this period and indeed an entire ship devoted to women in Plymouth.

Further evidence points to this island being for convicts: a map proclaiming Burrow Island to be a 'Convict Burying Ground', and a tale of the Portsmouth of the 1840s and 1850s published in a newspaper called the *Graphic* on 5 January 1878 called *By Celia's Arbour* are illuminating. The latter proclaims:

> Brave and honest soldier – there is the roll of musketry over his grave – God rest his soul! Down below, creeping sluggishly along, go the gangs of convicts armed with pick and spade. No funeral march for them when their course is run; only the chaplain to read the appointed service; only an ignoble and forgotten grave in the mud of Rat Island.

Although perhaps not forgotten, and indeed perhaps relatively dignified.

One of the skulls from Burrow Island. Over thirty individuals have now been recovered and will eventually be reburied. © Harvey Mills

Above: The burial of the man with the craniotomy had been placed in an elm coffin, which could still be seen in our excavations. © Harvey Mills

Right: Members of the Royal Military Police looking through all the material at Burrow Island. © Harvey Mills

Opposite: The face of Magwitch. Facelab LJMU produced this striking image of the face of the man whose skeleton had undergone the craniotomy. © FaceLab LJMU

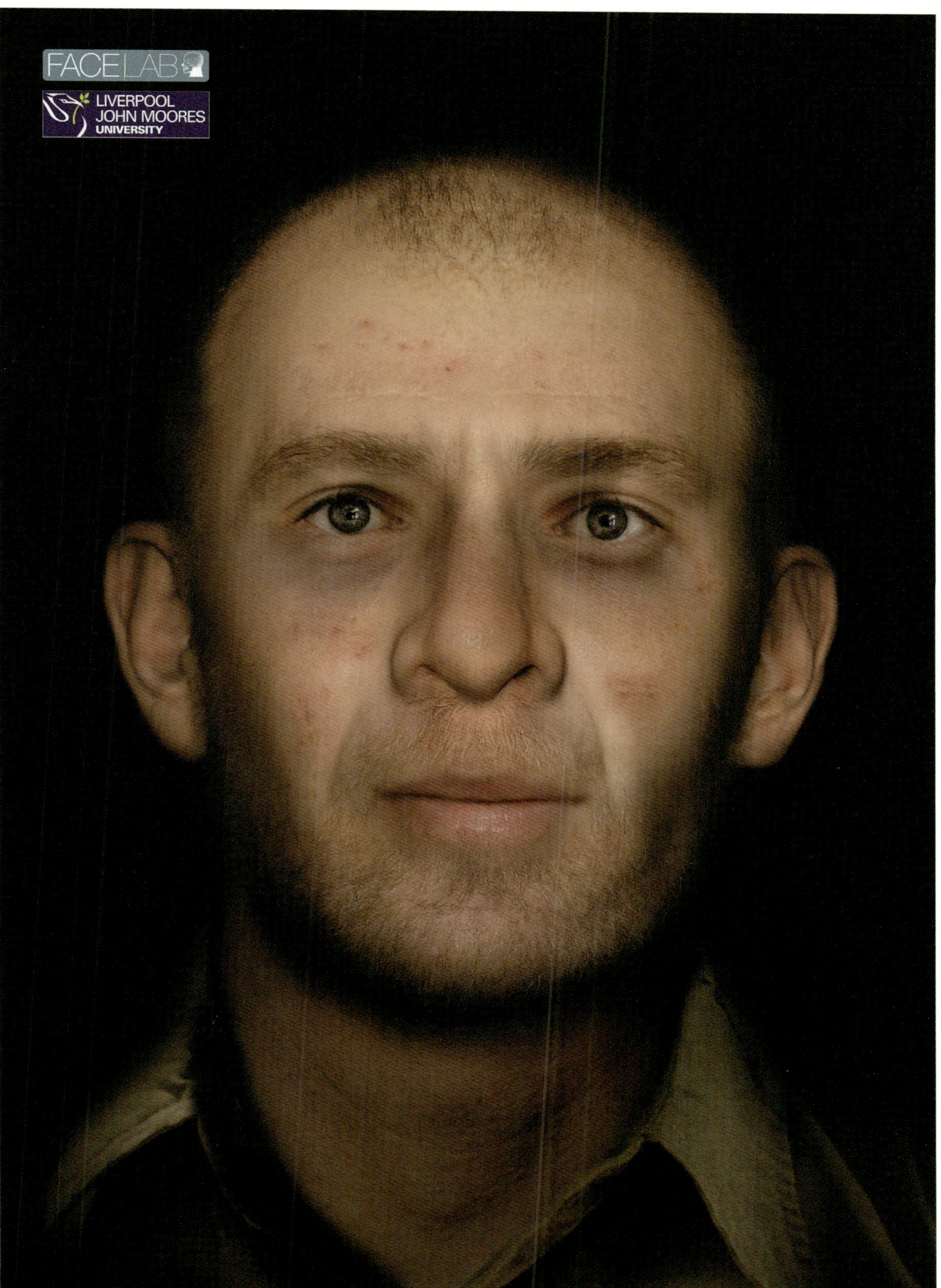
FACELAB
LIVERPOOL
JOHN MOORES
UNIVERSITY

This being said, we have remarkably little opportunity to get to the individual lives of the people buried on the island at this time; you might expect more as, in some cases, it was only around 200 years or so ago. On 17 May 1830, one Charles Morris Jones from Aberystwyth was incarcerated on the *York* hulk in Gosport for the crime of stealing from his employer, a Mr George Shepherd of Abingdon, his sentence being transportation. A report of 7 February 1831 in the *Reading Mercury* newspaper showed that this man, however, never reached the shores of Australia. On 3 February 1831, Charles Morris Jones 'who was sentenced to 14 years transportation, lately died at the hulks at Portsmouth, and was buried on Rat Island'. We will never know if Charles' remains are amongst the almost thirty individuals that we have now recovered from the island and who we will ultimately rebury on a more stable part of the site.

Finally for this site, as we were most unlikely to give someone back their name, we asked Facelab of Liverpool John Moore University to at least let us imagine what one of these poor convicts might have looked like. We chose the man whose remains had been subject to the craniotomy for the team led by Professor Caroline Wilkinson

Jackie Crutchfield (age 48)

Veteran Jackie Crutchfield joined us on Burrow Island and frequently takes part in local heritage events, not always in excavation attire. © Harvey Mills

Rat Island has been the most 'intimate' excavation I have been on so far. It's an honour for me to be able to see and touch our ancestors, without judgement on who or what they were in life. I actually get really excited about going on digs. I personally feel like I'm bringing them back to life (in death) even if it is just for a short time! Day to day I see people on the edge of life and death. I've seen death. I've had my own experience of near death. In my opinion accepting death, seeing death, talking about death (like on excavations) is a good thing as once you accept it you then only die once instead of living your life worrying about death! Hope that makes sense! To die means you have lived. Rat Island is such a small area yet knowing there are so many coffins still buried there is mind blowing. The little we do know about the prisoners, what life was like, where they were from, doesn't really give them all a sense of individuality in death. Some may have died on board ship, some in Porchester Castle, etc., but being able to go along and retrieve/rescue/see these people almost gives them a place in existence again. Our dig was like a personal... 'ceremony' if you like. I find it emotional yet extremely comforting knowing we have helped them in the present. I like to think we have let their spirit go free now. That saying of 'life is so transient, finite and fragile that there is no time to hate anyone' is so true.

In death we become even more fragile so need even more care! Something inside me needs and wants to help people in life and in death and you'd be amazed at how many people I help that are at the end of their life but want to know about our excavations! I'm careful what I say but they ask to see pictures sometimes and I show them ones that are for the public. Others don't want to know so I don't speak about it at all. One thing very personal to me about going to Rat Island was the drive there and the view from the island. Portsmouth/Gosport and especially Southsea are what you would call triggers for me. Spent a year and a half in and around those areas with a person that attacked me. I would only go there occasionally. Seeing all places, navy bases, pretty much everything, really was a reminder for me. The trip to Rat Island with you all was the first time I had driven that way for five days in a row! It was a massive breakthrough for me doing that!

to examine. The results were astonishing, and we really felt we were gazing into the eyes of Magwitch. It would not be the last time we made use of this technique. We also made use of the scanner that had generated the data to produce this reconstruction to compete a 3D print of the skull which we could take to presentations, schools or history festivals without being in breach of a million and one ethical considerations. Following its initial print, the skull was painted in part by a veteran and in part by me to make it more photo-realistic; it does surprise people when you tell them it is made of plastic. Funnily enough this technique is even more intriguing to some of the team as it is broadly similar to methods used to create their prosthetics; scanning the element that is removed before printing it out in titanium (rather than plastic) and replacing it on the living body. We have at least two participants whose own skulls were repaired in just this manner.

By 2019 we had done so much work on the island in partnership with the Military Police that it had been incorporated into part of their body recovery training: its title of 'Redcap Recovery' given by the then officer in command, Ryan Parmenter. This team worked really well with our veterans (perhaps with a little nervousness at the start given that a few of our military participants had, shall we say, other dealings with the RMP during their careers) and gave the 'redcaps' a chance to hone their skills in an archaeological environment, which was, perhaps, less pressured than work with remains they would have to undertake as part of their military role. Since Rat Island, I have even bumped into Military Policemen from this task as part of my normal day duties and it has proved to be the perfect induction between teams.

Lots of our participants live around the Portsmouth area, one legacy of it being such a large Naval base, and this certainly makes for easier organisation as they can commute from home to the site; at least as far as the causeway anyway. This might change the overall bonding dynamic, but this model still works and we can achieve great things. One of these veterans, Jackie Crutchfield, formerly in the artillery amongst other units, was clearly very moved by her participation on Rat Island and told me why this site was so important to her, especially as she now works as a carer; a duty she performed throughout the pandemic.

Over the years it had become clear to me that, although it was a real concern at the start, working with human remains was not necessarily a problem for the Operation Nightingale participants. In fact, as Jackie points out, they can see these remains with a different perspective to that of the archaeologist. Perhaps even more incongruously, taking them to a battlefield excavation also seemed to work, and thus the potential for utilising both might seem ideal. This leads therefore to Bullecourt. A battle of 1917 with, on the Allied side, British tanks fighting alongside Australian infantry, who knows perhaps the descendants of some of those incarcerated on the Portsmouth prison hulks who were successfully transported over to Australia, unlike the poor unfortunates on Rat Island who died before they could be moved.

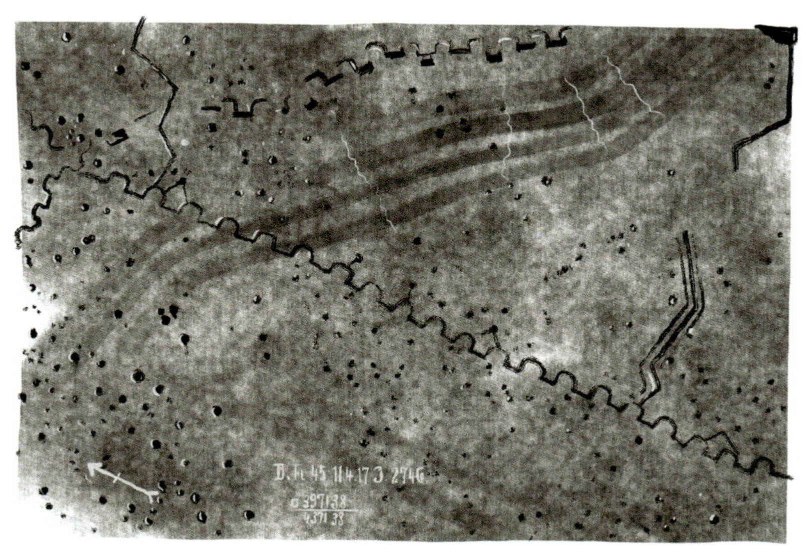

Above: Drawing up lines of battle. The Hindenburg Line 1917. © Alice Roberts

Opposite: Still life from Bullecourt. Some of the many tank finds we made on site. © Harvey Mills

4 MUD, BLOOD AND GREEN FIELDS BEYOND

Digging for tank 796 and traces of the First World War

FROM 1914 TO 1918 the First World War ravaged vast areas of the world and resulted in the deaths of millions, with lives ruined across the globe. It was industrial in nature, with huge quantities of materiel being produced and expended, much of which still remains in the soil of the battlefields today.

In 2014 a few of the Operation Nightingale team travelled to Belgium to assist in some field-work undertaken in advance of a pipeline being inserted. The route was around the city of Ypres – a name that will forever be synonymous with the First World War. Archaeological studies of this era are relatively new, after all, materials were only deposited just over 100 years ago and some still debate whether these are indeed 'archaeological'. For what it is worth, my strong view is that they *are*. These are very much the traces of human lives, deaths, habitation and recovery and thus certainly fitting an archaeological narrative. I am probably close to the truth in saying that the military archaeology projects are those which engage the

An iron harvest: a roadside in Bullecourt. Excavations of First World War sites come with their own special hazards. © Harvey Mills

military veterans most and are the easiest to recruit participants for.

In addition to the pipeline work, a couple of us were based at a site called *Irish Farm*. This had been a British cemetery during the war but with the remains being moved afterwards to a new location across the road and to another cemetery: *New Irish Farm Cemetery*. The former location was being redeveloped as part of an industrial estate and our remit was to make sure that the site was examined for any archaeology and human remains before building work commenced. We saw traces of the farm and there were indeed remnants of the burials of soldiers, some incomplete (scraps of uniform and the occasional bone), others more-or-less intact. All the remains were recovered in readiness for reburial in the adjacent cemetery.

In the evenings, former Royal Marine Dickie Bennett and I were staying in a small town to the south called Messines at a place called the 'Peace Village'. Messines was a town I knew well as I had worked there for several years, leading a team of volunteer archaeologists with my colleague Martin Brown, looking at a battle of 1917. We got chatting to Dave Moutter, an ex-British soldier who now worked on bomb disposal on these building projects, and he mentioned a site over in France that he was very interested in: part of the Battle of Arras of 1917, the site of Bullecourt. This was thus the origin of one of the bigger Operation Nightingale projects, an excavation that eventually was codenamed *Exercise Joan of Arc*.

Our excavation team wanted to look at the final location of the British tanks that took part in the attack of 11 April 1917. These were pretty well all destroyed and the subsequent attacks by British and Australian infantry on the village of Bullecourt itself was a costly failure.

There were some contemporary maps of the location of destroyed tanks and later historians (both official and otherwise) have also attempted to confirm this but we felt that we could use archaeology to add to our understanding. It was a gamble, after all, much of the remaining armour was removed immediately after the war as salvage by the Chinese Labour Corps and the local farmers probably completed the job. If you go around many parts of northern France and Belgium today you can still see recycled war materiel being used in agricultural regimes: railway tracks and screw pickets for fence posts, concrete bunkers as sheds. Add to this the fact that tanks retain a fascination and most villages seem to hold a museum of rusted relics of the conflict, including tank parts, then how likely was it that any Bullecourt evidence remained *in situ*? The splendid museum in Bullecourt itself is a repository of lots of tank fragments, scales of a gigantic man-made beast now lying supine on a floor like a colossal hunting trophy.

There is also the constant reminder of danger, with ordnance frequently found lying in the fields or placed at the side of the road for French bomb disposal to collect: the so-called 'iron harvest'. This danger is genuine. The farmer known to everyone in the village of Bullecourt and who we have all grown to love, Didier Guerle, has himself been the victim of such 'friendly fire', ploughing through an unexploded phosgene Livens shell and poisoning himself as a result. It was a very close call and one which he chooses to commemorate by utilising the offending (and now inert) cannister as a water trough for his chickens. He is probably the only farmer I have met who also has a wall made out of exploded shell cases, great for a safety 'show and tell' at the start of each excavation.

Not all ordnance is immediately recognisable either, especially when one is looking for large pieces of tank that may bear a passing resemblance to projectiles. Step forward Harvey Mills! On one of the initial site walkovers to see what was on the surface before we conducted surveys, Harvey was calmly brandishing something he thought might be part of a tank exhaust system and asked Dickie Bennett for his opinion. Dickie blanched and told

A target in 1917, our target of 2017. This is a German postcard of tank 796 after its destruction in the first Battle of Bullecourt in April 1917. Image in Public Domain

Farmer Didier Guerle (centre) discusses our work with two visiting Australian officers. Bullecourt is a site of pilgrimage to many Australians. © Harvey Mills

him to put it down very quickly and carefully: this was a Stokes mortar, unexploded and potentially *very* dangerous. Harvey duly obeyed and there was a happy ending. Dickie, a former Royal Marines Sergeant, had of course encountered fear on operational tours but this was an experience of similar jeopardy! Lo and behold, when we all walked past the Bullecourt Museum there was a huge banner on the wall outside the entrance, with an image of Australian troops sitting by a large stockpile of these objects. The Stokes mortar now features prominently in safety briefings.

The Mark II tanks used at Bullecourt are probably the most photographed from the Great War as these were the first examples the Germans captured. Thus they appear on film, on photographs, and in sketches – all a useful starting point for any investigation. There is wonderful German air photographic coverage from just a couple of days after the battle, even to the extent of revealing the routes taken by the tanks as their tracks scoured the fields. There is even a large collection of postcards of these tanks, with images of German soldiers posing around their newly captured trophies and cards sent back to relatives in Stuttgart or Berlin. You can still find these cards in online auctions (often labelled as *Cambrai*) and there are indeed images of our excavation target. Good luck in buying one of these postcards as you'll be bidding against one of our stalwart veterans, Jack Robson, who must have one of the best collections in Britain compiled as part of his research for our programme!

As such this resource is almost unheard of for archaeologists. We made use of these resources and then threw geophysical survey (magnetometry) into the mix to try to pinpoint a suitable location for an excavation trench. One location had been ploughed so we were able to walk over the field to look for items on the surface to see if a spread of material hinted at a tank below; we were not expecting to find a Neolithic handaxe but the joy of archaeology is its unpredictable nature. Armed with all this information we were able to approach the French authorities for permission to excavate. The aim was to try to verify the final points reached by the tanks in the battle of 11 April, based on our studies, and to see if anything remained. Our two chosen targets were both 'male' tanks, armed with two 6-pounder naval guns (the 'male' element being a none too subtle acknowledgement of sticking out appendages), tanks 796 and 797.

Why though *Exercise Joan of Arc*? Well, the name captured many elements; a nod to perhaps the most famous (from an Anglocentric) French military figure and thus our hosts; the fact that this has an association with armour and so a nod to tanks; and then to one of the finer military puns of the First World War. The Australian 48th Battalion fought at Bullecourt and indeed had some dugouts cut into the railway embankment that still survives and has become very familiar to the dig team. Battalion headquarters were dug into this covering mound too and, during the fighting of 11 April, tank 797 trundled back to this site to ask the Australian officers what they should do next. To paraphrase, the reply on the lines of 'move elsewhere' was given as the presence of this tank was now drawing artillery onto the headquarters. The 48th Battalion was commanded by Lieutenant Colonel Ray Leane from South Australia, a veteran of Gallipoli. There were many other Leanes in this unit: his brother, three nephews and others. In fact, there were so many Leanes that it was jokingly known as the 'Joan of Arc' Battalion as it was 'Made of All Leanes' (Maid of Orleans). Ben Leane, the Battalion Adjutant and brother of Ray was killed at Bullecourt and a nephew, Captain Allan Leane, mortally wounded.

As this was the first such permit given to fieldwork of this nature in Bullecourt, we were given a 5 × 5 m area to examine for both locations in the first year and were thus a little nervous when our first turf was removed to strip the site; it was a large field and we were putting two very small trenches into it with a big team that could become bored quite quickly if nothing was found. As with all our fieldwork programmes, we had planned 'educational' elements, such as visits to the Bullecourt Museum, the 'Deborah' tank museum at Flesquières, the Wellington caves at Arras or the trenches at Vimy Ridge, and it helps if you are staying in a city as beautiful as Arras. However, a fortnight based around visits to museums and cemeteries really would not have made up for a lack of archaeological discoveries in the eyes of the team (or, indeed, its director).

Imagine the nervousness therefore when the trench – over the site we felt to be the best guess for tank 797, close to the railway embankment – was opened and revealed ... a shell crater. The large metal signal we could see on our surveys had been given by a screw picket, a First World War invention that looks like a large corkscrew

The Bullecourt team visit the display of an original Mark IV tank (the Deborah) at Flesquières. This tank now has its own museum. © Harvey Mills

with eyelets through which you could thread your barbed wire entanglements. These items obviated the need to hit a post with a hammer or mallet to drive them into the ground, potentially attracting enemy attention. It was an interesting enough find, but not a tank. We had one trench left, in a pasture field on the edge of the village. This was supposedly where tank 796 had broken down. Commanded by 2nd Lieutenant Hugh Skinner in 1917, this tank had worked up to enemy trenches when it encountered a large shell crater but promptly broke down before it could reverse away. As the Germans were now able to bring artillery up to the immobile tank and start shelling it, Skinner decided to get the crew and the guns back to the Allied trenches and this successful rescue saw him awarded a Military Cross. The crew survived and this was no small accomplishment given that 52 of the 103 tank crewmen in this battle were killed on this day.

Our maps suggested that this destroyed tank had later been used as a machine-gun position by the Germans and, indeed, appeared on both photographs and film in the German archives. The geophysical survey was inconclusive as there was so much metal in the area around this part of the Hindenburg Line trench network. Nevertheless, we marked out the small square that we felt might yield some results and, with a degree of trepidation, began to mattock down through the topsoil.

We soon encountered more shell craters, perhaps rather unsurprising given the moonscape that was Bullecourt in mid-1917, and our first features were pieces of very heavy, curved corrugated iron known as 'elephant iron' that probably once served as the structural elements of a German troop shelter. There was a great deal of ordnance too, certainly enough to keep Dave and Florian (our bomb disposal leaders) busy. These finds really make for easier archaeology as, unlike the handaxe we had seen in our field walking, they are all date stamped – oh, and with a place of manufacture too. They are small time capsules of information and are incredibly useful indicators of different activities when looked at by relevant experts. Just as there are specialists in Roman coins and medieval

The moment of truth as the team measure out the proposed area of excavation and hope the 'desktop' research will pay off. © Harvey Mills

Left: Former infantryman Rob Steel regards the interior of a German infantry troop shelter. © Harvey Mills

Below: Success! A link from a tank driving chain emerges from the soil: we were in the right location. © Harvey Mills

pottery, an ammunition expert such as our colleague Mark Khan can tease a real narrative from a small tube of brass.

Already, therefore, this was proving a more productive area than the first trench and I was soon able to relax completely as our first demonstrable piece of tank was found. This item resembled a rusty figure of eight, if a bit bent and twisted, and was part of a large chain link which drove the tracks of a tank in rather the same fashion as the wheels of a bicycle. The tank memorial at the site of Pozières on the old Somme battlefields makes use of these chains as fencing around the monument, held up by inverted 6-pounder cannons as bollards. If nothing else was excavated, we had at least found a small element of what we wanted. Fortunately, more was to follow, and this piece was altogether more spectacular. Two long, slender metal runners linking a number of flat slabs ran into the edge of our excavation trench (as all the best finds on almost all excavations seem to). These were uncovered and cleaned by two of our veterans, Rob Steel, and Pete Cosgrove, formerly of the Royal Tank Regiment and thus someone who had major links of ethos with this site. Pete's story is extraordinary and worth reading at some length.

Left: The intricacies of our tank track found at Bullecourt. © Harvey Mills

Clockwise from top left:

Sometimes you lift finds out of the ground delicately within a block of surrounding soil. Other, larger, finds call for different techniques. © Harvey Mills

The completion of our excavation of the length of tank track. © Harvey Mills

Tantalising traces of the original paint scheme were still present on the track: with red primer and 'Racing Green' top coat. © Harvey Mills

The team gently expose the tank track and 'grouser' from tank 796. © Harvey Mills

Pete Cosgrove (2nd Royal Tank Regiment, age 40)

On 21 November 2009 I was wounded by an IED while driving a Viking Troop Carrying Vehicle serving with Egypt Squadron, 2nd Royal Tank Regiment while coming to the end of a six-month tour. At the time I was in the lead vehicle protecting a Combat Logistics Patrol to Sangin, Afghanistan. We moved through Gereshk after it became light and turned into the desert heading for Sangin.

I don't remember the bang; all I remember was the feeling everything was caving in on me and then the massive wall of dust began settling over me, and then it hit me, the sudden pain, knowing I had been hit in the legs as I couldn't feel them. My vehicle commander was lucky just to have been bounced round the turret and was able to get out the wagon and pull me out. It was a horrible feeling as I felt very alone and dazed laying in the sand even though my commander was OK. I had a vision of the Taliban coming over the nearest sand dune, guns blazing, thinking we had just driven into an ambush like in the classic WW2 films.

Luckily that never happened, and our Troop Commander and the medical Vikings were up with us. The blast had caused damage to my legs with the left leg and foot being far worse and the right leg badly bruised. Even though I had just been blown up there was still a sense of comedy, which the British Soldier over the years likes to rely on to get them though the worst situations, as one of the first things I asked when I came round to reality was that my iPod was still in one piece! Then this was followed by our medic nearly putting the wrong end of my morphine pen into me, nearly causing them to get the shot. Apart from that the medic did a brilliant job on me and made me comfortable as we waited for the medivac helicopter. The morphine helped take the pain away as we waited, but very soon the laughs and the jokes became that of sadness and feeling I had let people down and screwed up, then followed by wondering what's going to happen next in this life-changing episode of my life. All these feelings going a hundred miles an hour in my head as they put me on the stretcher and got me onto the helicopter to Camp Bastion to be operated on.

Once I came to in Bastion, I found out my left leg was broken in three places and had shattered the majority of my left foot with the possibility it could be amputated. Luckily one of the surgeons at Bastion believed it could be saved and did what they could till I was medevac'd to the UK and began the long process of recovery, having a series of operations at Selly Oak in Birmingham and rehabilitation at Headley Court, and follow-on operations since leaving the Army in 2013 as sadly I was medically discharged, as I was unable to carry on my career as a Tank Crewmen due to my injuries.

Perhaps his military career was at an end, but Pete was just starting his Operation Nightingale story. His link to the tanks made him the ideal candidate to examine any finds we were making, recognising many of the artefacts through the many hours he had spent reading about tanks or trips to the tank museum at Bovington in Dorset in the south of England.

I made the decision that we should extend the edges of this trench simply to enable us to reveal the full length of this item and am glad I did. This was a section of the original track of a Mark II tank –

Peter Cosgrove, then of the Royal Tank Regiment, in theatre before he joined us on our excavations at Bullecourt. © Peter Cosgrove

we presumed that of 796 as that was the only tank that reached this location, and we were slap bang on top of the position at which we thought it had been destroyed. I think it is safe to say that the team was pretty thrilled, especially as we had received a fair deal of scepticism on there being anything left on this battlefield that was tank related. These things are always worth a punt.

Peter takes up the story:

From a very young age I became a bit of a history buff and was mainly interested in military history, being brought up on a healthy diet of museum visits, air shows and classic war films and collecting militaria. So, hearing about the tank dig and meeting Richard while on rehabilitation at Tedworth House, who explained the role of Operation Nightingale and Dickie Bennett's Breaking Ground Heritage with their intention to carry out a dig to find the remains of a Mark II Tank this was certainly right up my street, and was certainly something I wanted to get involved in being that I was a Tankie and we would be looking at the role played by those early tank crews which I had an interest in. So using some of my own knowledge on the subject could possibly help with the team's project.

Plus, I had a relative who had served in the Tank Corps in the last year of the Great War, who had previously seen action in France since 1914 as an Infantryman with the Royal West Kents and had been wounded during the Somme offensive, resulting in him being sent home for treatment and recovery and transfer to Tank Corps. So, it really felt it could be a real chance to do some hands-on history.

There was always that possibility that we may come across human remains since the numbers of missing and unrecovered dead from both sides was extremely high from the Great War. At the time I was so focused on the track recovery and worried about the live and dud ordinance that was around us that I had not thought that this would happen, thinking any remains would have been recovered during the post-war clean up.

So, when one of the team spotted what looked to be remains under the track, my heart started to pound a bit, and then faster, and I could feel something wasn't right inside me, just like that day in Afghanistan. I had to walk away for a bit. I began thinking that they had been driven over or that they were the tank crew and it wasn't 796 that we found and it was a different tank that had been lost sprang quickly to mind. Now that flight-or-fight feeling start going inside me and I had to go and for a walk and do something else to keep my mind off it as I began to remember some bad memories.

Pete went off, clearly very distressed. This was ghastly for the rest of us too; we are meant to be providing an engaging, enriching, cathartic experience for all of the participants and yet here was one of our team for whom the reverse seemed to be the case. While we have always been incredibly keen to avoid such eventualities, to be cognisant of the many and varied potential triggers for team members (and to try to minimise the potential to encounter them), we do plan for their possible occurrence and mitigation. Pete went for a walk with Kayleigh, our 'Hidden Wounds Team Leader' from Help for Heroes, who was part of the team. Chatting with him, she brought him back to Bullecourt in 2017 rather than 2009 in Afghanistan. And then we noticed him gradually getting closer to the excavation, eventually being able to sit close to the edge of the trench while the team exposed more of the remains. A pause in the action while we informed the local mayoress and police of the discovery (a legal requirement in France), followed by the Commonwealth War Graves Commission coming to site and permitting the work to continue, was just the respite we needed.

I went off to do some walking round the fields to see if there were any surface finds to keep my mind off it and to compose myself as I felt like a right idiot in front of

The police arrive on site to verify that the remains we have found are from the First World War. © Harvey Mills

everyone at the time and started to beat myself up and needed to get a grip of myself. We certainly knew this was the spot of 796 and that that Skinner's crew got out and to safety and that the tank had been captured and may have been used as observation post by the Germans.

So, what were these remains doing there? And now I was intrigued as the track had been removed and a new task was at hand and I needed to get back over to the dig. In my mind I was telling myself this was what you see on TV and grew up with watching and now I had the opportunity do something like this for real and I was about to blow it. Once back at the site I was told we now had to stop digging and wait for the local authorities to arrive until we could do anything else, which looked to be the following day, which would mean us looking after them overnight as word had spread around the village and we had crowds arriving on the site. Plus grave robbing is rife on the Western Front battlefield and I personally wasn't going to see them robbed, so volunteers were asked to stay overnight on 'Stag' and look after them.

Peter sitting on the top of the trench watching the excavation of the remains of two German soldiers. © Harvey Mills

Now the last time I was 'on stag', it was a cold night in Afghanistan in the middle of the desert with an enemy out there in the night. Now this was a different situation and these Kameraden needed to be looked after, so volunteering, and with locals kindly helping us with sleeping bags and tents since we were not prepared for this outcome, was certainly worth the long night and little sleep in this foreign field to make sure they could be recovered and given a proper burial and laid to rest with their Kameraden.

Once we were allowed to carry on, I wanted to get in there and recover what remains we could since it was our last working day on the site, with the guidance from Richard and his team who showed me how to do so. This helped me fight a demon because the last time I held body parts was in Afghanistan when we lost from my unit young Josh Hammond who, at the age of 18, was killed in action by an IED alongside the CO of the Welsh Guards while in a Viking. That day he was killed I spoke to Josh and we were joking and he was telling me some really cheesy jokes which he was good for and a real morale booster. The IED that got him had been planted on a stretch of road that I had driven over that morning when it had not been made live. That thought will always stay with me. But most of all was the day after as the troop I was in was held up on a stretch of road beside a river and we were held up by the enemy and IEDs, but that evening Rendezvous with the rest of the squadron our Viking was tasked to a broken-down Viking back to Bastion but also to take some remains recovered of young Josh, with the Sergeant Major handing me a small bag. That was very much a lump in the throat moment and that drive back I will never forget.

And that was what I was thinking as I handled these remains of these German soldiers. I began to think of the discussion and jokes with Josh that day and started in my mind having a chat with these Germans. Asking who were they, what unit they were from, what were they doing here, which part of Germany or Austria were they from or what were they doing before the war, their home life, things like that? It must sound strange to the outsider reading this but at the time I felt I had some kind of soldierly bond, having served our respective countries, though in very different conflicts. Sadly they paid the ultimate price, along with members of my own family during the same conflict but there is me living with consciences of war like many of their Kameraden and the Allied soldiers who suffered the effects of the Great War long after the guns fell silent.

After we had finished on that last day, I left the site with a real buzzing feeling, and felt we had achieved something amazing, something that I thought I would never get a chance to do in my lifetime. Finding the part of 796's track and other items made my week out there, though finding the remains was emotional and brought the reality of war home again to me. Recovering those remains, in that short time, made me happy to think these soldiers we found could be remembered in a decent way and have a proper burial even though we may never know their names. The feelings I had that week and leaving on the last day and coming home from the dig was a big sense of achievement both physically and mentally, being able to overcome those demons which I was hiding with the help of a great bunch of supportive people who are friends today. If I got the chance to do it again, well, let's just say my wife Victoria wouldn't be able to stop me!

So: perhaps a triumph snatched from the jaws of disaster? As Kayleigh told us, sometimes it is, in fact, good to face one's terrors rather than always trying to avoid them.

Peter completes the excavation and subsequent recovery of the remains of the two German infantrymen. © Harvey Mills

The week we had out in Bullecourt was an amazing experience. The first couple of days we thought we weren't going to find anything because attempts had taken place soon after the end of the war to clean up the area. We were finding the usual items commonly found, such as ordinance, buckles, buttons and so forth, but the breakthrough came in the form of that small part of the tank track drive mechanism from 796. Being able to identify it as tank track, once we began to clean away the earth, was a wonderful achievement for us all, which was a main goal of the project.

This special find, which we had to remove from the excavation trench by lifting it with a tractor, was accurately drawn on to the trench plan and photographed before it was taken off to our finds room for further cleaning. This yielded further information, some red primer paint still adhered to the track and, on top of it, green paint. Given that all the First World War tanks in the many museums have been painted and repainted hundreds of times, there is still a degree of discussion and debate about original colours. Harvey was able to photograph and identify this green colour as being a specific pantone: 560C or 'British Racing Green'. This might seem to display astonishing hubris given that the top speed of such a tank, on a good surface and with a fair wind was 4 miles per hour. I rather think that this colour was present because the vehicle had been made by Fosters of Lincoln and their traction engines were generally this colour. Whilst not suggesting the entire tank was this colour (although it might have been) it was a fun discovery and certainly further justification of such fieldwork were it needed. I also had a wry smile when Sir Peter Jackson produced his astonishing colourised film of the 1916 classic, the *Battle of the Somme*, entitled *They Shall Not Grow Old* in 2018 complete with tank in British Racing Green.

As we drew towards a close, we were satisfied that we had achieved many of the project aims and were engaging in cleaning the site area that we had exposed beneath the tank track. Lieutenant Skinner had managed to extricate the crew of tank 796 and we had thus approached the 2017 excavation in the knowledge that we would not be encountering the remains of a missing tank crew. But this was the First World War; industrial in scale both in terms of material and production, and also in the scale of death of participants. And here it was that we faced perhaps one of the single biggest tests of the whole programme.

We were thrilled to have found such an identifiable piece of tank in such a small trench. Phil Kimber, a Royal Air Force Regiment veteran had been given the task of the site cleaning and he called us over to look at something he had found. The item was standing proud of the light soil and, on closer inspection, had a tell-tale honeycomb look where it was slightly damaged. This was bone, part of a pelvis, and we were thus face to face with the war in its most fundamental form. Although we had briefed all the team that this is always a possibility on excavation of such sites, nothing could really prepare Pete for this eventuality; a discussion is very different to encountering remains for real. This transported him straight back to Afghanistan.

Pete was correct that there is a challenge on such sites – that the remains can be looted if left unguarded overnight – in a sense killing them for a second time as you would remove any chance of future identification. The small items found as part of military equipment reach paltry sums when sold but can be the difference between a name and a grave to an 'unknown soldier'. To this end, on each occasion we have encountered human remains, we have asked of the team who would be willing to camp out next to them, to provide a guard to ensure the integrity of the site. And almost without fail every veteran has volunteered, in spite of any physical ailments from which they are suffering and for which a night in a tent might not be something that their doctor would suggest as sensible. For this is a bond of kinship, no matter the conflict or nationality. Those who have fought will empathise with such victims from the past in perhaps a way that a non-combatant archaeologist just won't. I hope that we are creating similar kinship and bonds within our archaeology too.

At Bullecourt in 2017 I thus asked for volunteers to guard the site overnight and Pete was one of them: sitting around a fire (again that leitmotif) and chatting. The kindness of the French villagers in supplying everything our group needed was truly heart-warming too. The next morning, Pete was ready to continue and asked if he could once again join in with the archaeology. This he did, with huge reverence, until the job was complete, and we had recovered all the remains ready for their return to the Germans and subsequent reburial. Their equipment showed us that they were Prussians, young men who were not officers and had been armed with stick grenades and pistol ammunition, perhaps hinting at them being machine gunners. This might fit with a wartime Australian map which showed the defunct tank being used as a machine-gun post. It is, of course, just as possible that the tank served as a convenient burial marker reference.

The recovery of the remains of these two German soldiers after 100 years in the ground effected another form of rapprochement. The farmer, Didier Guerle, is an incredible character, a kind and generous soul who nonetheless has family stories of the village being occupied by German soldiers, not once but twice. In 1940, his father housed two British soldiers briefly on their way to Dunkirk, one was killed on this journey. German troops then stayed on part of the farm (but, as Didier tells us, in far less salubrious accommodation). Perhaps unsurprisingly therefore, there is a local collective scar and yet when we found the bodies of these two long-dead men, it was Didier who offered to hold onto them before the Commonwealth War Graves team collected them. As we came to his house the following morning, we found that Didier had placed his own wooden crucifix on top of the two boxes of remains, which he had placed respectfully in an isolated part of his farmhouse. Didier also asked that we gather to have a minute's silence as a team to remember the fallen of all sides, although the fact that his sheep succeeded in breaking out of their pen at this very moment and started running along the street rather broke the solemnity of the moment!

Back then to the UK, and almost immediately I was into another project, this time based at the headquarters of the charity Help for Heroes at Tedworth House in Tidworth on Salisbury Plain. The use of this former stately home as a recovery centre for the wounded is part of a long tradition; certainly the First World War saw many treated in such locations, the impressive grounds and fine buildings all perhaps aiding recuperation. Our programme, funded by the National Lottery Heritage Fund, was to build a wooden tank of First World War vintage. We had seen numerous examples of so-called decoy tanks of this period being used and it was fortunate for us that we had found bits of a real one in Bullecourt so we had something we could look to replicate in timber. The plan was to have this vehicle on wheels so we could take it to schools or history festivals. Andy Robertshaw of Battlefield Partnerships was to lead this for us. As the historic advisor to Steven Spielberg for his adaptation of the Michael Morpurgo book *War Horse*, Andy was well placed (in spite of being 'killed' in the film!). Initial plans were to make this wooden beast at 1:1 scale (and, if so, I rather think it would have turned up in Andy's next film venture: working for Sam Mendes on the film *1917*). This, however, would be a lot of wood, would have required an even bigger trailer to transport it, and would have been almost impossible to move around a school playing field and thus a decision was made to err on the side of caution and make a 2:3 scale model instead.

This was a real boon as it opened up heritage to those based at the house, and also a project for those for whom excavation was perhaps not going to be a realistic option. Pete was also able to be part of the build to add to his tank work of the year. We have several team members for whom making

Two German soldiers found at Bullecourt, 100 years after they were killed in action. © Harvey Mills

model kits is a passion (Pete included) and their results and attention to detail are often astounding, not every model builder has the attention to detail of taking soil from the actual site to incorporate into their dioramas; our Bullecourt modellers did! The wooden tank was simply a very big model kit with all the inherent challenges that this presented. It was also rewarding to see former soldiers who had spent a fair proportion of their military careers working to fix Challenger tanks now applying their skills to a tank model. It was completed on the morning of that year's annual Chalke Valley History Festival near Salisbury in Wiltshire, which was a relief as we had booked a place for it to accompany our talking to the general public about our fieldwork in France: complete with toy carrier pigeon and Pete dressed in the costume of one of his Royal Tank Regiment forebears. The tank has now visited several schools and charity fundraising events as well as history festivals, and certainly gained many more miles on its tracks than the original ever did.

One regret we had was that we had ordered the paint before the dig, hence a dusty brown rather than our Racing Green! This practical work also served to demonstrate the benefit of work that could be done slowly, over long periods of time, and with the need for follow-up elements; our tank would need repaints, repairs and embellishments just as real ones do. It could be used to assist educational and outreach programmes as well, requiring different skillsets from our participants. A seed was therefore sown which we were to harvest years later at a site called Dunch Hill.

Clockwise from top left:

Planning a tank build with the veterans. © Harvey Mills

Del, a former soldier with the Royal Electrical and Mechanical Engineers, working on some of the wooden tank tracks at Tedworth House. © Harvey Mills

Our wooden version (2/3 scale) of Bullecourt tank 796 on display in the fields of the Chalke Valley History Festival. © Harvey Mills

As a final aside from 2017, I noticed that one of the contributors to this volume, Dickie, was working away on the wooden superstructure of the tank and had a very noticeable tattoo on his right arm of a First World War tank. This seemed to be part of a pattern, with Rob Steel and his Roman centurion (and indeed eagle with SPQR) tattoo digging Roman ditch features at the Midden, and Wally (whom we shall meet later) with his skulls.

Archaeology of the First World War may seem, on the face of it, to be a bit peculiar, surely we know everything there is to know from the contemporary writings, from the photographs, from the films? I think this is only partly true, not everything is written about; manuals are not always followed; records of things are not always kept; and, of course, propaganda can always distort an historic narrative. We can definitely gain new insights and thoughts on battles, of developments, of lives through the remains themselves: the story of our tank and its colour scheme, final moments and re-use for example. With no veterans of the war surviving we can still encounter elements that made their lives more bearable – the rum jars, the camp coffee, the brown sauce – and bring back their landscapes. I have read that one veteran claimed it was smells that gave him flashbacks to the war; the smell of a butcher's shop, a wet autumn morning, brown sauce. Our veterans too have such triggers from senses, be it the sound of a helicopter, the taste of certain food or (as we discovered taking samples from animal teeth for isotopic signatures) the smell of drilling into bone.

There are so many myths surrounding the First World War that archaeology is, in fact, vital in helping to correct false stories. As an example: many people think they know all there is to know about the Battle of the Somme; of 60,000 British casualties on the first day (1 July 1916) and of soldiers sent into battle with almost no training whatsoever. This is such a falsehood; training was often in incredible detail. We have excavated a small set of trenches at Perham Down on Salisbury Plain, built to replicate a set of German trenches in the Somme region (the chalk geology is identical). The set appears in plans and air photographs but was no mere schematic; these were deep, almost 2 m/6 ft in places and spread over many hectares. They were revetted with timber, had corrugated iron roofs for the shelters, and even braziers to keep out the cold. The latrines were dug as per the manuals and used (yellow chalk and a pungent aroma: I'll leave it there), whilst screw pickets held barbed wire. The plans even detailed the actions of the units who would attack (the Middlesex and Essex Regiments along with elements of the Rifle Brigade); where and when they should move; how the artillery would support; and where they should take any 'prisoners'; the local church was to be used. We found parts of grenades and many fired rifle cases with dates appropriate to training for the forthcoming Somme campaign. The training took place over half a year before the Somme action and thus these were no mere raw recruits. This was an army being forged.

One cannot escape the fact that, for the Middlesex and Essex Regiments that were at Perham, those early days of July 1916 were a disaster, one can even see soldiers from the former in the 1916 propaganda film *The Battle of the Somme* (a production included by UNESCO on the Memory of the World Register, such is its importance) attacking German positions after the Hawthorn mine has been detonated, only to be repulsed and many killed. Within our Perham trenches we also found a carved chalk block. On close scrutiny in the post-excavation rooms, with photography and other techniques, this was seen to have the words 'Liverpool Reg' carved into it and a design that was part of the badge of Lord Derby, the aristocrat who raised the Liverpool 'Pals' Battalions in 1914. This unit faired comparatively well on the first day of the Battle, supported, as it was, by French artillery. We have seen no written record of them training at Perham Down; this small object opens new worlds therefore. Archaeology really can add texture and insight.

Not only do military participants on these First World War projects enjoy themselves, they bring a fresh eye to some of the events, as some of the components we are excavating are familiar to them. As I write this, fighting continues in Ukraine and I have been conscious that many of the images taken from the air of various defensive positions would not have been out of place in field fortification manuals of the First World War. Reversing this, soldiers of today can recognise terrain and topography and how they might use it now, in probably the same eye as an infantryman of the past. An example of this comes from Dickie at the site of Mametz Wood on the Somme. On looking at the trenches on the edges of this much written about Somme woodblock under the gaze of the Welsh dragon statue, Dickie looked up and down the short valley and told me that, had he been here in 1916 defending the wood and the trench on the edge of the covering trees, he would have placed a little protruding trench called a 'sap' from the front line. This would have enabled any defenders to fire a machine gun across the length of the valley, forcing any advancing soldier to walk through a reaping scythe of lead. Lo and behold, when Peter Masters undertook a geophysical survey of this precise area what did he find? A small sap ran directly from the German fire trench. Such thinking brings assistance to the archaeologist: I would never have thought of this.

I can't leave Mametz without recounting another story. They do say that you should never meet your heroes. Well, this golden rule was well and truly broken when, in 2016, an Operation Nightingale team took part in an excavation at Mametz for BBC Wales to commemorate the contribution of the Welsh 100 years before. The actions of this unit are well known in Wales and the 38th Division extraordinary. The war is often taught around the writings of the war poets and this is not necessarily a good thing; not everyone was writing verse in the trenches and many that did perhaps had not the greatest talent. But this division? Goodness me, some of the finest writers of the war fought at Mametz: Siegfried Sassoon (known as 'Mad Jack', won a Military Cross here, only to throw the ribbon away in protest against the war. Later in life he moved to Salisbury Plain where he wrote poems referencing the archaeology); Robert Graves; and David Jones whose masterpiece, the epic lyrical poem *In Parenthesis*, focuses on this battle. I had been asked to assemble some veterans to help the excavation alongside some old friends of mine. This was duly achieved and two of them were Welsh veterans of wars of the 21st century. Matt Smith, a signaller, and Ant Cook, an infantryman, were part of the team, both passionate rugby

Still life from Bullecourt. The equipment found with the remains of a German infantryman in a frontline trench in France. © Harvey Mills

supporters and very proud Welshmen. Can you imagine their feelings when one of the greatest names of Welsh rugby, former Captain Gareth Thomas, was announced as the presenter of the programme? Gareth is a superstar for a thousand reasons and it was a colossal relief to find him to be utterly charming, generous and kindness personified. He threw a rugby ball around with the veterans (incredibly appropriate given the number of Welsh rugby internationals that fell around these woods in 1916) and didn't make a single comment at the Newport/Gwent Rugby shirts that Matt, in devilment, wore each day in spite of the rivalry with his own Cardiff team. I tried this tactic too with a Bath shirt and Gareth admitted he enjoyed playing against Bath as they were a proper side, much to Matt's chagrin. He has never announced this, being far too modest, but that year was a Rugby World Cup year and Gareth was much in demand for commercials. Indeed, brewers *Guinness* secured his services and Gareth donated the entire fee to Operation Nightingale. Gareth told me that he was looked on as a Welsh hero but didn't feel he was; these guys are heroes, he told me, pointing at the veterans working away and with the woodblock and ghosts of the Welsh lads of 1916 in the background, astonishingly moving and generous – a wonderful man.

The results of our first season at Bullecourt were such that a return was an imperative, and charitable donations like Gareth's ensured this would happen. We went back to the same field and opened up a far larger area, full of shell craters this time and detritus from 1917. The team lowered soil levels in the area that had yielded both the tank track and the two German soldiers and this clean soon revealed what looked like an ostrich egg; unmistakeably the top of a third skull. It seemed as though this third, of only partial remains, was laid on top of a length of expanded metal; it looked like a sort of stretcher made from a type of chicken wire. Whether this scene was one of the remains of a comrade being recovered by two colleagues who were, in turn, killed or simply a

Scanning the Bullecourt skull in readiness for a facial reconstruction. © Harvey Mills

The skull and facial reconstruction by Facelab LJMU of the German soldier from our 2018 fieldwork. © Harvey Mills. © FaceLab LJMU

jumble of human remains we will never know. The scene of the third individual's inhumation were uncannily reminiscent of the types of Iron Age burials of the last centuries BC, of partial human remains, you get in this area, parts of the so-called 'Arras Culture'. He was an older man and his skull was well enough preserved for Isabel Burton, our German physical anthropologist from Facelab, to scan the remains for a facial reconstruction. This extraordinary technique really does play well with the team, almost giving this German an identity once more, and certainly helping us to picture him in his final moments,

The physical anthropologists on our team could tell us that, from the fusion of his bones, the third German was in his thirties or older. It seemed from the wear of his teeth and a circular gap in the bite that he was a pipe smoker, like many of the men on Rat Island. There was nothing with our German soldiers that would have enabled the men to be identified and so all three were reburied as unknown soldiers in Metz.

Across the site there were excited calls as team member after team member found large pieces of metal that were associated with a tank (almost certainly 796): more chain links, cogs and sprockets, a piece of engine gear that the veterans nicknamed the 'dirty blancmange' by dint of its peculiar shape. A small piece of metal with the letters '..EWC..' was also recovered. I could only think of one word in English with this combination initially; 'Newcastle'. Well, the 6-pounder cannon of this tank were made by a company called Armstrong Whitworth based in, you guessed it, Newcastle. This was one of the data plates of the tank's guns. Other finds included a small oil tap (one of only two surviving from a Mark II tank in the world, the other being the Tank Museum in Bovington), the head of a hammer (which I like to picture being liberally used in both exasperation and desperation by the crew when the engine broke down) and enough components of the tank to at least compose a very rusty engineer's manual. We think we have retrieved about one tonne of the tank, of its original 28 tonne weight. One other splendid find was a fired casing from a 6-pounder tank shell; an item with its own story as it demonstrated (thanks to date stamps on its base) the real speed and efficiency of British munitions work and logistics supply by this point in the war, and also that the tank had certainly gone down fighting. This case was carefully excavated by ex-artilleryman Paul Barnsley (who had uncovered the third German), and by John, a former officer in the Royal Engineers.

For John this had been a first excavation with us and had been designed, in part, to provide him with a period of respite. For him, however, the artefact was not the most poignant element of the excavation. This arrived in the form of an Allied boot. The decaying leather object still held the bones of a soldier's foot and we showed this to the Commonwealth War Graves team who were there to collect the remains of our third German. Quite rightly they told us that this individual may well have survived the loss of the foot and thus these remains would not be reburied in the grave of an 'Unknown Soldier' (DNA assessment is not possible when there are hundreds of thousands of possible candidates, especially as we could not rule out a German having been wearing these Allied-pattern boots when they were hit). John had specifically asked us if he could work on this part of the site, to excavate and clean this boot, this foot. He, uniquely on this site, was a man who

Above: One of several 'transit clips' we discovered on the excavation sitting in the end of the 6-pounder shell case to demonstrate how they fitted. © Harvey Mills

Below left: John (Royal Engineers) and Paul (Royal Artillery) on the discovery of the fired 6-pounder tank shell. © Harvey Mills

Below right: An Allied boot, an Allied foot, an Allied casualty. © Harvey Mills

A 'scant remains' grave erected by the Commonwealth War Graves Commission in a military cemetery by Bullecourt. The final resting place for 'our' foot. © Harvey Mills

could express empathy and shared experience; he had himself lost a foot and an eye in an explosion. Operation Nightingale really does have some unusual connections. The boot was taken away with reverence and is indeed now buried in a War Graves cemetery. The epitaph simply stating:

> Here lie the mortal remains of some of those who fell locally during the 1914–18 war and whose identity is unknown: Known unto God

A very neat inscription: this 'scant remains' grave can and will hold other small, isolated bones as they are recovered from nearby battlefields. All were once parts of a human being and are treated with respect. The words will be appropriate whatever the nationality and whomsoever they were a part of. As things are, we know that there is 'just' a foot in the grave, but more bones will follow. Our team will continue to visit the site so long as the project exists, or the participants go to France. Paul, the veteran who excavated our third German said:

> I returned to Bullecourt with my family to show them the battlefield and the work I had been involved in especially being part of the team that recover an unidentified German soldier in 2018. I have read many books about the battles and hope to return to Bullecourt soon. Engaging with Op Nightingale has got me where I am today. I am now working and retraining to become a carpenter and moving on with my life.

From the Gulf War and Bosnia to more tranquil fields.

We have been keen to make Operation Nightingale available to as wide a group of beneficiaries as possible, including veterans of other nations, and Bullecourt enabled us to put Australian, British, French and German team members on site a century after their forebears had been trying to kill one another. Jan, a non-commissioned officer with the German air force, the Luftwaffe, was with us in 2018. Just before the digging season had begun a German historian, Rob Schäfer, told him about the dig and he managed to join us. For veteran of Afghanistan Jan Kirchner:

> I would say that I do have to struggle a bit with flashbacks from time to time, the participation helped me to know that I am not alone. As I was during my tour in a multinational team, I did not

Right: Jan Kirchner, formerly of the German Luftwaffe, and now an Operation Nightingale veteran too. © Jan Kirchner

have comrades in Germany to whom I could relate about my time in Kabul. Furthermore, after taking part in Operation Nightingale, I was contacted by a British psychiatrist who did some work with the veterans and Breaking Ground Heritage. The exchange with her helped again to sort out some ghosts of the past.

Throughout the projects we have seen the importance of friendships and bonds between individuals, most of whom have never met one another before even if they were all in a foreign country at the same time with the military of different nations. We tend to say a few non-denominational words around all our excavations when we have finished, especially when human remains have been encountered. Such moments seem especially charged when the timescale is closer, the proximity perhaps adding weight. So, it was at Bullecourt in 2018 when we asked Jan to say some words. And it was this that was perhaps the most memorable moment for him:

> I spoke some words to them and although I had no idea who they had been, I felt a very emotional connection to them. That is something which I keep very dear for me, because that made clear that death is the end, but as long as we feel for those who are gone, they are not forgotten.

He concluded by commending

> the British charm and humour. The spirit within the group was extraordinary, I was there only a couple of days, all the others were way more experienced and closer together. But I did not feel left out or something like that, the bond of war experience and of interest in the wartimes of the past made us get together. Being the 'Fritz' amongst a lot of 'Tommys' was wonderful. Of course, there are some differences between the British and the German Forces. But 'Brothers in Arms' is no empty

The team get together at the end of the project to say a few words for the fallen. The contribution by our current German veteran, Jan, was incredibly moving. © Harvey Mills

'Scotchy'. An Australian veteran of Afghanistan removes some screw pickets from the trenches occupied by his fellow countrymen 100 years ago. © Harvey Mills

slogan ... The connection between the past, the war between Germany and Great Britain, and the present, German, British, Australian and further veterans now as friends and allies, that had a very deep impact on me.

One of our Australian team members concurred with Jan. Scotchy, the infantry soldier we met earlier at Aldbourne, felt that when it comes to the camaraderie on site:

> This is the most important part of the dig to me. There isn't many experiences in your life that come close to the level of mateship earned in the Military. What I can say is the week you spend on a dig comes close. It's a bit of hard work in the hot sun or the rain, camping out with your mates, sharing stories with fellow veterans, discovering history, learning from archaeologists and having a beer at the end of the day. It encapsulates elements of the military but in a setting that allows you to relax and focus on one thing – Digging.

In the years I have worked with the military it is clear how tight these bonds are. How shared experiences across both nations and generations provide bonds and understanding. As a civilian I will never quite be part of this, nevertheless I, along with team-mates and fellow Ministry civilians Phil, Alex and Guy, can play our part in bringing the archaeology to these people and facilitating further friendships. I think respect both for the sites and the participants is key for me. I was gratified when Rob Steel, one of the veterans told me that:

> I have been on several sites now but I would have to say work on the Hindenburg line at Bullecourt was one of my life highlights, it was an incredibly interesting, professional and fun excavation. The site was approached in an incredibly safe, insightful, caring and ethical manor given the nature of the site and its links to WWI casualties and death. Everything and everyone was treated with the utmost of respect and everyone helped each other, bringing together a very good and successful team that accomplished its aims time and time again and has been a privilege to be a part of it.

Given that Rob was a sniper in the army and has since gone on to collect a degree in archaeology from the University of Winchester, become a member of the Chartered Institute for Archaeologists in the UK, worked as a professional for several years now and harbours big ambitions for experimental archaeology (which we'll see later), I'd take this as a battle honour for the archaeologists of the team!

We have been back to Bullecourt on other occasions, on excavations with the Royal Military Police, our veterans and other volunteers and it will always hold special memories for the project, becoming almost a place of pilgrimage and certainly somewhere where lasting friendships were made. With the farmers, with the villagers, with the local military and police who provided wonderful evening barbeques for the team. Each time we have been, we have encountered human remains. Bodies and parts of people killed in war and yet, perhaps bizarrely, the site has helped people who have suffered trauma in more modern conflicts. Perhaps the unofficial regimental motto of the Royal Tank Regiment of *From mud, through blood to the green fields beyond* (and hence colours of brown, red and green on their ties) might also serve amply for the progress of our participants.

With the knowledge that conflict archaeology was a successful and engaging sphere of our discipline for the team, we decided to look at another element and, unusually for archaeologists, to look upwards to the skies rather than to the ground.

Above: A peaceful pastoral scene that was once the torn ground of trenches. © Harvey Mills

Left: No longer marching. The *idée fixe* of 'boots' is a thread throughout our First World War projects. © Harvey Mills

5 TALLY HO!

Archaeology and the Battle of Britain

ARCHAEOLOGY OF THE AIR. It seems a strange concept and, of course, it's only when items fall out of the skies that one can consider them things that can be excavated. In the United Kingdom, the Ministry of Defence is 'responsible' for the *Protection of Military Remains Act* (1986); anyone wishing to examine or uncover a site of a crashed military aircraft needs a license administered by the Joint Casualty and Compassionate Centre within the MOD. For a while, I had wanted to see how such sites might be approached archaeologically, what one might be able to record, what it would tell us (if anything)? Such an approach might also be able to show non-specialist archaeologists that dig the sites of crashed aircraft what they could achieve academically with relatively little cost. From the perspective of Operation Nightingale, I also thought that such sites might be really interesting for participants; meeting ethos and also perhaps a degree of nostalgia for anyone who had made *Airfix* model aircraft kits in the past!

As with sites of the First World War, there is a proximity with excavations of the Second World War that adds a different dynamic to sites, after all, you have a chance to work on a site with someone

Above: Vapour Trails: the Battle of Britain 1940, after Paul Nash. © Alice Roberts

Opposite: A Hurricane in the livery of P3700 growls over our dig site, wonderfully evocative. © Harvey Mills

Excavation in progress at the theatre in Stalag Luft III in Zagan, Poland. © Crown Copyright

who can actually remember the event happening, with someone who was involved, or a next of kin that lived with the results. A case in point is Stalag Luft Three (III) in Żagań, Poland. This was the site from which the famous 'Great Escape' was made in 1944. Allied airmen held in this camp dug a series of tunnels christened *Tom*, *Dick* and *Harry*, with the latter being used in March 1944 to enable 76 prisoners to escape. All but three were captured and 50 were executed as a result.

I was fortunate to be part of an archaeological team there in 2011, the year we started Operation Nightingale, with my friends Professor Tony Pollard and Dr Iain Banks of Glasgow University, and others, in an attempt to locate tunnel *Harry* and a mythical tunnel, *George*, that had supposedly been constructed below the theatre in the camp. Both were found. I worked on *George* and was astonished to see a structure lined with wooden boards, with electric cables and ventilation pipes made from old milk tins linked together. The team found the wheels of an escape trolley and, most incredibly, parts for a radio made by the prisoners from materials scrounged from around the camp. The most extraordinary thing was that the man that made these radios, Frank Stone, was there with us as we excavated. How often in archaeology will you be alongside the manufacturer of an object you dug up?

Another veteran, Alfie Fripp, was with us too. He was one of the first men captured in the Second World War, becoming a prisoner of war in October 1939 and incarcerated until 1945. Alfie had been held in Stalag Luft III prison and I asked him how he felt that a bunch of archaeologists were excavating part of his life story, almost as they would with very ancient history. He said that he was between reticent and ambivalent at the start but, as he saw progress and the attitude of the team, he decided it was a very good thing, not least as it would help perpetuate the memory of those who had been imprisoned and those that were killed. I think that the serving members of the Royal Air Force with us as part of the dig team felt very much the same. This is why I mention this story even though it was not an Operation Nightingale project; the power of the near-present to engage and tell stories of people with similar narratives, hopes and fears.

Our first exploration was to accompany a team looking at a crashed British Stirling bomber in Sussex to locate the engines. Next step, having got a taste for how I might run such a site, was to assist a metal-detecting search of a crashed B24 Liberator near Lyneham in Wiltshire, augmenting the work with a geophysical survey by Peter Masters and a small amount of excavation too. This showed how popular working with these types of sites was and thus the next stage was to find a site on land owned by the Ministry, to apply for a license ourselves, and to throw a raft of archaeological techniques at it. It was worth noting that if any finds are made on such sites, they are still *technically* under the ownership of the MOD. The excavator has to provide a list of items as part of their report on proceedings and then, unless the RAF Museum wants them (very unlikely), the items become the property of the finder. The last thing I really wanted was a shed full of small pieces of rusted aircraft and so we also needed a finds strategy to deal with any items; to find a use for them.

People who have an interest in these crash sites know a lot about them, their histories, and the personalities involved. I frequently comment that if they knew as much about Roman coins as they do about the different components within a Spitfire, a professorship might not be out of the question. Many of them have dossiers on each crash site and indeed know some of the eyewitnesses to events. The importance of people assembling all this information was made clear when I asked contacts about possible crash sites on land owned by the Ministry of Defence, a fair likelihood I thought given the nature of the Department's work. Low and behold, there was one close to home on Salisbury Plain and it was that most celebrated of entities, a Spitfire from the Battle of Britain of 1940.

I was given an approximate grid reference and some fading yellow–brown photographs of the site, with some trees, helpful for location, in the background. This was the starting point for a more scientific survey to see if we could find where this Spitfire, P9503, had hit the ground. We knew that the airframe flew with 609 (West Riding) Squadron, whose logo was a pair of crossed hunting horns and the motto *Tally Ho*, and thus *Exercise Tally Ho* was established; a tribute to the motto rather than, as the army members on site believed, teasing the Royal Air Force and any upper-class stereotypes.

We were able to find a narrative of the crash that occurred on 27 October 1940. The Spitfire, piloted by Pilot Officer Paul Baillon, was brought down by return fire from a German aircraft crashing just to the south of Upavon airfield, in fact within a short walk of Chisenbury Midden and adjacent to the Iron Age site of Lidbury Camp. Paul Baillon bailed out successfully and was able to file the following combat report:

> I followed the leader into a separate quarter attack and opened fire at 500 yards closing to about 70 yards with a 5–6 second burst. Oil spurted over the whole of my windscreen and I broke away to the right. I climbed for a few seconds and as the cockpit became filled with oil and fumes, and my

Squadron Leader Alfie Fripp, formerly incarcerated in Stalag Luft III, watches excavations of the theatre building in which he acted a part in *The Merchant of Venice*. © Richard Osgood

> visibility forward was nil, I bailed out. The machine landed one mile south of Upavon aerodrome and was completely destroyed. I landed nearby uninjured.

I think the aircraft 'landing' was something of a euphemism.

During excavation work, the team was shown a letter written by Paul to his wife Peggy, in which he recalled the episode:

> I had a bit of excitement today when 3 of us went up after a lone raider. We found him and went into the attack in turn from the rear. I had to turn away after firing at him continuously for 5 seconds because my oil tank must have caught a bullet from him, and, as oil spread right over my windscreen reducing forward visibility to nil I felt I had to do something about it and broke away.
>
> I went on for a bit, climbing all the way, and I came to the conclusion that I couldn't possibly land the machine because I couldn't see a thing in front of me; so I decided to jump for it – which I did with great success… it was all very exciting for a first engagement, especially coming down by parachute which really was not at all unpleasant.

Several of our excavation team had made parachute jumps themselves, one of them forced to do so by enemy action. Most of them seemed to have actually quite enjoyed the experience.

So we knew the aeroplane had dived down into solid chalk, that it may well have caught fire, and we believed much of it had been recovered after the crash. Would there be anything left for us to research? The aerial photography was sadly inconclusive, it would have been wonderful had the site been pinpointed by a member of the Royal Air Force in early photography of the Plain; after all, famous archaeologists such as O.G.S. Crawford cut their air photography teeth as members of the Royal Flying Corps or Royal Air Force and their central flying school was located within view of the crash site. The answer would instead be provided by geophysics.

Georgia Kelly was undertaking her archaeology thesis at Reading University and she worked with her colleagues to undertake an initial survey, after which we brought in Peter Masters from the University of Cranfield. As mentioned previously, Cranfield is co-located with the Defence Academy at Shrivenham and thus was another of these opportunities to draw together various resources available to us. I took Peter to the site and he spent hours walking up and down, bleeping away with his magnetometer. The result was wonderful; something that if you'd seen it on a petri dish would have been most alarming, a very livid-coloured blob in the middle of a more soothing hued background. It showed clearly that there was something large and metallic to investigate.

Having booked that part of the Plain and some fine weather to accompany us, a team of volunteers was put together to excavate the crash site, focusing on this central area that we felt could be the impact point. Military trucks descended on the scene with the ability not only to lift anything really heavy from the ground, should that be needed, but also to move equipment to the dig – not just the items you might expect on an excavation but also essential personal equipment like one of the team's electric wheelchairs. We have always worked on the basis that the team members are able to make their own decisions on their capabilities and for this dig George Pas was going to be a key player in the finds tent to catalogue and clean what we hoped would be the series of interesting and engaging artefacts we would uncover. This tent was one of those olive-green military tents you see on training exercises, musty-smelling and very hot in the sun. They are easy to put up, however, and serve well on digs as they are pretty robust, probably the reason that so much army surplus seems to fall into the hands of archaeologists. In fact, on many Operation Nightingale digs I have noticed that the only ones wearing camouflage clothing are the archaeologist or civilian supporters, the military veterans choosing something from their new world. We had another large logistics tent called a DRASH on this excavation, which served as a command tent, with the ability for us to put up information boards and the suchlike within it. There was also a glitter ball affixed to the roof – to this day I am still not altogether sure of the rationale behind the appearance of this item.

The digging could now begin and, given the rich quality of the grassland, the turf was going to be removed by hand. De-turfing is an unpopular task when it forms part of military orders for digging trenches and yet there seemed to be a surprising willingness to embark with mattock and shovel when rich rewards were possible. The fact that the weather was good helped too, I always admire commercial archaeologists who excavate in all weathers to meet pressing deadlines. An early engagement with a frozen site and the requirement to part-defrost the ground with a brazier before excavation could commence was an important education for me that this would not be my life. I always try to dig in the warmer months – not that you can necessarily guarantee this on Salisbury Plain. The topsoil was very thin here and so it was not long until that gorgeous squeaking sound of trowel on chalk could be heard as the team cleaned the excavation area. In conjunction with this, metal detectorists worked around the site, flagging the 'noise' of metallic readings which might help indicate the spread of material outside our chosen excavation trench and hence a possible direction of the crash.

Our team was our usual mix of archaeologists and wounded veterans with a few serving military personnel adding their assistance. Perhaps not surprisingly we had more members of Royal Air Force and Army Air Corps on this one too. Added to the whole experience was the presence of one particular guest and team member: Rosemary Baillon. Rosemary was Paul's daughter and she

The impact crater of Spitfire P9503 with the indentations in the chalk being an almost perfect cross-section of the aircraft. © Crown Copyright

Darius Smith (staff sergeant, Royal Engineers, age 50)

Darius Smith (Daz) of the Royal Engineers.
© Darius Smith

I joined the Army in August 1989 aged 16 years old and completed numerous tours of Bosnia, Kosovo and Afghanistan, leaving the Army in March 2018, at the rank of staff sergeant.

My first involvement in Operation Nightingale was nearly ten years ago. An RAF friend told me about a *Time Team*-style project where they would be digging up a WW2 Spitfire. Without hesitation I volunteered to help wherever I could. I've always had a fascination for vintage military items, so this was like a dream come true. I attended the dig and liked it far more than I thought I would. But why was this, why did I like it so much? The answer to this question was answered when I left the forces in March 2018, after 29 years' service, I knew it would be a wake-up call for me no longer serving in the Army.

I've seen many ex-forces personnel find civilian life far too hard. And very sadly a few have taken their own lives as the jump was simply too much. I was determined this wasn't going to happen to me. When I attend digs now, I feel back at home again. The banter, debates, socialising, and probably most important is being around injured service people. I love helping others. Physical injuries are often obvious for all to see, but PTSD in all its forms is often blind to many. I often hear others talking about their military antics. Incidents that no normal person should have to witness.

Personally, I don't talk about things I've seen. We all cope with PTSD in different ways, and there is no wrong way to act when you realise you have PTSD. Do I have PTSD? Yes.

It started with things I saw in Bosnia. It then raised its head again after my tours of Afghanistan.

I never talk about it in the open as it makes me feel emotional. I also have a view that anyone who has served long periods of time in war zones will have PTSD. It's not normal to attend repatriation parades twice a week. Nobody should see the frequent death of colleagues as routine. It's not normal, it's far from normal. My involvement with Operation Nightingale helps me stay in touch with who I really am. Darius 1989–2018 is who I am. 2018 onwards ... I'm pretending to be me in a world of civilians.

had never met her father. Her mother, Peggy, had been pregnant when Paul was killed just a few weeks later in November 1940. For Rosemary, like Alfie and Frank we met earlier in this chapter, this site had personal memories and links, all the more extraordinary as Paul had never got to see his daughter. I'm sure many of us have visited places important to our immediate antecedents and for Rosemary this must have been a week of mixed and powerful emotions.

This was also the first excavation for someone who has now become a bit of a project stalwart, as long as the digs relate to the events of the 20th century: Darius Smith (Daz) a Geographic Specialist with the Royal Engineers and the person who made the maps for our work at Rat Island.

The final moments of Spitfire P9503 might well have been enough to induce traumatic memories, perhaps even PTSD, for Paul had he survived the war and yet uncovering these events through their material traces was cathartic for those who came to site. The excited chatter between diggers accompanied the scrape of trowels and bleeps of metal detectors in an archaeological symphony as the work progressed. Intriguingly, our chosen excavation trench location area seemed to contain a high percentage of the metallic readings with the flags marking material illustrating the dig site as being the epicentre of a near-vertical crash, with the shock wave of debris not extending too much further out. In fact, the competed excavation revealed just how vertical this crash had been with a near-perfect cross-section of a Spitfire. We even noticed that the 'pitot tube', an item used for measuring the air speed of the aircraft, was projecting vertically from the chalk, in the correct location (the port wing) and that we could also discern the impact of the machine guns through the corresponding pits in the bedrock, as well as the concertina of engine, cockpit and fuselage, wing leading edges. This complete silhouette of the aircraft as it hurtled into the unyielding ground not only showed that the impact had been from a vertical dive but also justified the use of careful archaeological techniques.

The finds were coming thick and fast, keeping the tent team very busy and requiring constant referral to their Spitfire manuals. It is incredibly useful that such reference works exist, and also that parts are frequently stamped with a '300' prefix for the Supermarine company and sometimes with the part of the aircraft itemised too. We thus retrieved propeller balance weights, the fuel gauge, a gun mechanism, the cockpit clock, a flap selector, a turn and bank indicator, switches, fasteners, datum lines, information plates such as 'radio transmitter' and 'Folland Aircraft Hamble' amidst many other items. Ammunition was also there in some quantity, hence justifying the presence of our bomb disposal personnel. This gave us a small snippet of detail about the armourer's composition of projectiles: ball rounds, armour piercing and all with a date and place of manufacture.

The finds tent was the workstation for another new veteran, Elaine Corner. Not only has Elaine moved on to organise volunteers to participate on

Above: One of the data plates from Spitfire P9503. © Crown Copyright

Left: Investigating the engine: pinpointing finds from the Merlin engine of Spitfire P9503. © Crown Copyright

our programmes, she has now rejoined our team, but this time beyond the finds tent and onto site itself to excavate a 7th-century burial.

We camped around the site in the evening, telling stories around a campfire and, one evening, watching the film *The Battle of Britain* adjacent to the crash site of one of the protagonists. It is quite a noisy film with, unsurprisingly, many explosions and the sounds of machine-gun fire. Quite what the Gurkha unit on a night exercise close to the site made of it I am unsure but no flares were launched and we weren't attacked with Kukris, so all was good. There also seems to be a beer associated with most of the projects and this was no exception, with several bottles of *Spitfire* being donated to the team for the film evening. This story was repeated with the excavations at Aldbourne. I had been filming the *Digging for Britain* coverage of the first year of this dig with Alice at a studio near Swindon and noticed that there were bottles of *506* beer from the Ramsbury Brewery (very close to Aldbourne) on display: Easy Company and the 'Band of Brothers' being part of the 506th Parachute Infantry Regiment of the 101st Airborne. I mentioned this and the connection to our dig to the studio owner who also owned the brewery! A case was provided for the team and I put them in my Spitfire artefact-free shed for delivery on the second season of the project.

Further to these sites being unusual, we also recovered lots of corroding aluminium of Spitfire P9503. What to do with this? Most digs have a retention and disposals strategy (just ask any director of a Roman pottery kiln or tile site) and for me this material could be used without affecting the integrity of the archive. My solution was to ask a company, TMB Artmetal, to make small pin badges of the Spitfire for the team (they had used the brass of shell cases from Mametz to make poppies on another dig); not what you'd normally do on a dig but there was a lot of this material and it was corroding with a limited chance of conservation and no real desire of curation. The results were beautiful too, shiny and sleek like an

Elaine Corner (Royal Electrical and Mechanical Engineers, age 54)

I first became interested in archaeology as a child, watching the excavation of the Jorvik Viking site in York. I never had the opportunity to do any archaeology until, following my medical discharge due to a motorbike accident which resulted in my leg being amputated below the knee and back injuries, I was told about Operation Nightingale by my case manager at Step Together Volunteering. I went on my first dig in September 2013 excavating a WW2 Spitfire crash site. I mainly worked in the finds tent and found it really exciting to see what emerged from the lump of mud and metal I'd been handed. It was great being back with veterans and serving personnel, with all the banter I had missed since my Medical Discharge.

Elaine Corner of the Royal Electrical and Mechanical Engineers. © Elaine Corner

original Spitfire. In so many ways these are not normal digs!

The final object to be recovered was the item that probably yielded the biggest signal on the geophysical survey, part of the reduction gear of the Merlin engine. This was heavy, and the local press on site were keen for me to hold it up, trophy style, for their photographs. Not a problem, except that lots of photographs were wanted and at various angles. My arms were giving way by the time I was able to put it back down. Lots of the finds were also examined using an XRF machine. This stands for X-Ray Florescence and is an excellent, non-destructive, and immediate method of measuring the composition of an item which might be manufactured from several different types of material, thus requiring differing and careful conservation techniques. This is achieved by measuring the secondary X-rays (fluorescent) emitted by a material when they are subjected to a primary X-ray. Chemicals have specific signatures, like a fingerprint, which can be measured. Of course, this also works for your prosthetic limbs and other surgical components placed into your body, as the veterans demonstrated to me, gleefully. Medical-grade titanium was demonstrated, much to everyone's relief.

Although Pilot Officer Baillon had successfully bailed out of the stricken aircraft, there were still a few traces of those last desperate moments. The team excavated the pilot's harness strap end, flying helmet microphone plug, the Bennet connector from his flying helmet, and the oxygen mask strap tightener. All of these would have been quickly unfastened by Paul as he made to get out of the aircraft as speedily as possible.

The associations of one's senses to the material one is uncovering works really well on the excavations of the Operation Nightingale project, each archaeologist having tangible connections to their work. Perhaps these modern sites give us something extra. Proximity enables more experiences. For example, I have been told by friends who have excavated a post-medieval cemetery that they have encountered distinct smells on this work – I would imagine rather unpleasant ones. Smell *does* feature on our excavations of 20th-century sites too; there was a distinct aroma when the amber-coloured chalk of the latrine pit of the First World War trenches at Perham Down was uncovered. On our crash sites, we have a lingering smell of fuel on some of them when areas around the engines are exposed. One uses one's touch and sight all the time on digs but smell also has its place.

Reading a book on history is wonderful, but touching the elements involved – holding hands with the past – is extraordinarily evocative. Artefacts hold stories and memories and if they are of a loved one or relative you never met, the magnitude of emotion is on an altogether higher level. Picture yourself on an excavation of an

The grave of Pilot Officer Paul Abbott Baillon in Bayeux, Normandy. Paul was the pilot of Spitfire P9503 when it was shot down in 1940.

A dig with a view. An important consideration of project designs is the location of the fieldwork. A landscape like this, Lurgashall in West Sussex, is so therapeutic. © Harvey Mills

aeroplane flown by your father, whom you never met. You are watching the excavation of a moment of great terror for him (even if he survived) and watching a team of servicemen and women gently uncover traces of these events. One of them shows you a handle that was used to release the perspex canopy, enabling your Dad to bail out and escape the stricken aircraft. This one item was essential in ensuring that his life was saved; had it failed to work he would have been killed. He had touched it; you can touch it. This is something so removed from excavations of prehistoric, Roman or medieval sites that I always find it incredibly profound and moving, a real justification for the archaeology of the modern.

On sites, I am sure most of us try to put ourselves into the lands of those that came before, to look at their experiences, to think of their emotions; their lives; their worlds. To view things as they did. Amidst the debris of this crash site were some large thick pieces of armoured windscreen glass. This sat at the front of the canopy of the aircraft; it was something Paul *had* to have looked through. And Rosemary could look through it too now, sharing a view of the world through the same prism as her father. I will never forget that moment, nor will all

those military participants on the dig or, for that matter, all the other diggers. Rosemary was given a small piece of this glass.

Almost exactly a month after his first crash, on 28 November 1940, Paul was shot down and killed over the English Channel by the then leading Luftwaffe 'ace' Helmut Wick, who was himself shot down moments later in scenes reminiscent of Paul Nash's extraordinary 1941 painting *The Battle of Britain*. Paul's body was later washed ashore on the French coast and is buried in the Bayeux War Cemetery. If you are ever in Bayeux looking at the incredible tapestry, or undertaking a visit to the many museums, go and visit Paul, spend some moments with him knowing his story. Paul was 26 when he was killed.

The dig finished with a flypast of a Harvard trainer – the type of aircraft in which Paul had learned to fly – organised by one of the Operation Nightingale participants who was a Hercules pilot in the Royal Air Force. We then moved onto the post-excavation phase or report writing, cataloguing and thinking just what to do with the finds. In spite of the disposal of one piece of glass and some corroded aluminium, there were lots and lots of other items that needed a home. The likelihood of deposition in a store in Wiltshire was unimaginable; certainly the shelves in the archives at my base would not have been suitable. So a different solution was sought to avoid my garden shed being clogged up.

The first stage involved my taking all the items into my daughter's school and laying them out in the shape of a Spitfire for the pupils' study of the Second World War (complete with utterly adorable 'evacuee' costumes including teddies, labels and cardboard gasmask boxes). This was great on so many levels, with the fact that the aircraft was manufactured locally, with women to the fore. It flew from a Hampshire base (Middle Wallop) and crashed whilst intercepting a raid on a local town (Andover). It was the sort of history lesson I used to love and my daughter got past the initial embarrassment of parental presence to enjoy participating. The children seemed to enjoy this method of engaging with the past and so I was pretty comfortable with my decision for the final repository of the finds: Ratcliffe College in Northampton, Paul Baillon's old school.

I had been chatting with Dominic Berry, the Head of Art and Design at the school, and had been delighted that he could join the veterans on the dig, meeting up with Rosemary too. Dominic had the wonderful idea of engaging his pupils in art, science, mathematics, history, technology and many other educational aspects through the medium of building a replica Spitfire at 1:1 – not just any Spitfire but Spitfire R6631, in which the school old boy, Paul, had been shot down and killed. Our discussions led to a decision that we should change this project to a study of Paul's other aircraft, P9503, and that any artefacts we recovered would be incorporated in all the studies and any builds.

Some months after the completion of the fieldwork I duly visited the school with Rosemary and one of the archaeologists on the team, serjeant Paul Turner of the Rifles, and we presented everything to Dominic and the Ratcliffe Spitfire Project. This programme had so many facets, with veterans visiting the school as a part of it, that I think we really achieved a maximum for the crash site, along with publishing our results for others to see how such excavations could be run. Historic England use our project as an example for other applicants who wish to look at aviation archaeology. Dominic told me that 'There are a great many young people out there now who will always remember their part in the project and talk about it for years to come'. The project won an award for Heritage at the Ministry of Defence 'Sanctuary' Awards, which was presented at the Department's Main Building in London. A short scramble from this building to the North Bank of the River Thames sees the location of the Battle of Britain Memorial. And amidst the armourers loading the guns, the women building the aircraft and plotting their flights, and a series of running flight crews, is a roll of honour of inscribed names of all those pilots deemed to have flown in the Battle. Paul's name is in a short column below one of the most famous of fliers: Douglas Bader.

Based on the Spitfire success, we turned to an excavation of the main workhorse of the Battle of Britain – a Hawker Hurricane that had crashed at Saddlescombe Farm, West Sussex, on 9 September 1940. This site met many of our requirements in creating a project: a peaceful, beautiful location, the strong likelihood of finds, and the opportunity for an evening campfire. The location was, however, on the National Trust Estate so discussions took place with Tom Dommett of the Trust to assuage fears he may have had of such a dig. This aircraft was a veteran of the fighting of 1940, flown by several 'aces' and successfully shooting down an enemy aircraft when it was moved to one of the most well-known Allied squadrons – 303 Squadron – that of

Our three Polish veterans on site in 2015 looking for the traces of the Hurricane from the famous 303 Squadron. Left to right: Łukasz Juźwiak, Emil Maluk, and Łukasz Zub © Harvey Mills

Taking off on patrol from RAF Northolt at 17.25 hrs. Met a large formation of about 40 Ju.88s escorted by a large number of Me109s and Me 110s. Combat taking place at around 17.50 hrs. Flt/Lt. Kent shot down a Ju88 which was seen to fall into the sea. He also went on to damage a Me110. Sgt. Frantiszek destroyed an Me 109 and a He. 111 before having to crash land in a cabbage field next to Downs Hotel 1.5 miles from Woodingdean, Brighton, his Hurricane being hit in the radiator, fuselage and port wing.

The pilot of Hurricane P3700: Sergeant Kazimierz Wünsche. Courtesy of the Wünsche family

Hurricane P3700 before it was shot down; it is a strange feeling having contemporaneous photographs of the item you are looking to excavate. © Wojtek Matusiak

the free Polish forces. This was 2015 and, by now, Operation Nightingale had been operating for a few years. We wanted to see how well this would work with veterans of another nation and thus, on discussions between our team and the Polish Embassy in London, three Polish soldiers joined our excavation; Łukaz Juźwiak, Łukaz Zub and Emil Maluk.

On Monday, 9 September 1940, our Hurricane, piloted by Flight Sergeant Kazimierz Wünsche had taken off from RAF Northolt on the outskirts of London to intercept a large enemy formation. The operations diary records the final events of the aircraft (see above).

The plan to find the aeroplane followed our Spitfire model, walking over the ploughed field to see if there was any material on the surface where we thought it had crashed (there was) and then Peter Masters working his geophysical survey magic to produce a very clear plot of where the largest amount of metal was – almost certainly the impact point. With the plot and the grid reference he provided we were accompanied by two experts in this sort of air frame, Paul Coles and Andy Saunders, and marked out an area we would dig by hand. This time we would be watched by two members of the pilot's family, his daughter, Grazyna Gasiorowska and granddaughter, Joanna Gasiorowska-Brundle. Having all these veterans on site as well as expectant family members adds an altogether different form of pressure to a site director! As with the Spitfire I need not have worried – *Exercise Huragan* (the Polish for Hurricane if you are wondering) proved just as successful.

The gentle soothing sound of mattock, shovel and trowel was accompanied by chatter in Polish and English, reminiscent of the famous scene in the *Battle of Britain* film where Polish pilots pretend not to understand commands in English prohibiting their attack on Luftwaffe aircraft. 'Repeat please!' being shouted in turn by each

Hoping that our measurements of trenches will tally with the geophysical survey results. © Harvey Mills

Łukasz Zub (12th Mechanised Brigade, Polish Army, age 41)

In August 2015 I was asked if I wanted to take a part in an archaeological project organised in the UK. Having no experience in excavation but knowing that the project was aimed at veterans and the artefact was strongly linked with the history of the Polish military, I didn't hesitate and said yes.

To me the most valuable part was the fact that we were working on something that is a part of world's history. The Battle of Britain had a significant impact on the Allies winning WWII. Moreover, Sergeant Kazimierz Wünsche was a Polish pilot of the legendary 303 Squadron. That means he was a Polish hero and I had a possibility to touch things that had last been touched by him before we dug it out. Awesome feeling.

Polish infantryman and part of the P3700 team, Łukasz Zub in Afghanistan. © Łukasz Zub

The magic of finding part of the Merlin engine of P3700. © Harvey Mills

I asked about what he felt to be his favourite moments on the project and whether archaeology had been beneficial. He replied:

I think there were three such moments: the excavation of elements of the cockpit (radio adjustment panel), as this was something that the pilot had direct contact with; the excavation of the propeller hub as the biggest part of the plane; and meeting Sergeant Wünsche's family.

With regards the importance of archaeology he felt:

It is difficult to point out its exact effect on my recovery, but I know it has a healing power. An unforgettable experience. I hope similar projects will be run soon in Poland.

Pole as they dashed off to engage an enemy. Of course, we watched this scene later one evening on the dig. This was also one of the earliest excavations where our project put soldiers of different nations together; this had worked well in military operations and it was lovely to see the mutual respect and teamwork in action in an archaeological project with a shared goal. Often the silence of concentration on the excavations is palpable, only interrupted by the sound of scraping trowels, thus it was as our three Polish soldiers worked carefully alongside former British military medic, Mark Mortiboys, to expose the area of the ammunition boxes within the scant remains of the crumped aircraft wings.

Łukasz was right to highlight the huge and heavy propeller hub that we found at the base of the crash crater (the items producing the biggest signal on Peter's geophysical survey) as it still had remnants of the wooden propellers surviving within it. There were hundreds of other finds too, from ammunition to keep Mark Khan happy, through to the cockpit gyroscope, Merlin engine valves and pistons, crankshaft counterweights,

Our largest find, the propeller hub from the Hurricane. This now lives at RAF Northolt, the station from which it flew in the summer of 1940. © Harvey Mills

Mark Khan, our on-site ammunition expert, examines the composition of the ordnance belts of P3700. © Harvey Mills

and reduction gear. I think we all liked the Morse code tapper too as something that Flight Sergeant Kazimierz Wünsche had touched and, to top it all off, a tiny spanner used by the mechanics and presumably dropped in the cockpit and lost, in the expectation that nobody would ever find out.

Local National Trust volunteers plotted in the crash crater and its contours for us, showing that the final moments had been very similar to those of Spitfire P9503 – a near vertical crash. Our dig had taken place just a few days after a major disaster at nearby Shoreham air show. This meant that our proposed flypast of a Hurricane was more distant that it might otherwise have been. However, the growl of the Merlin engine flying over the South Downs conjured images of the summer of 1940 and the valour of Polish airmen.

I leave it to Flight Sergeant Wünsche's daughter and granddaughter, Grazyna and Jo, to tell us about him.

Grazyna Gasiorowska (daughter of Flight Sergeant Kazimierz Wünsche, 303 Polish Squadron, RAF) and Joanna Gasiorowska-Brundle (his granddaughter)

Kazimierz Wünsche served with the 303 Polish Squadron based at RAF Northolt from 1940. During the Battle of Britain he was credited with 4½ kills and two 'possibles', but on 9 September 1940 he was shot down over the South Downs. He bailed out of his Hawker Hurricane with burns and leg injuries, but returned to active service the following year. For his service he was awarded the Distinguished Flying Medal, Distinguished Flying Cross, Croix de Guerre and Virtuti Militari (nr8829). Following the end of the war, Wünsche returned to Poland with his young family and took up a position as a flying instructor. But because of his service with the Allies, the communist government treated him with suspicion and put him in the reserve. He eventually became one of the founders and pilots of the Polish Air Ambulance Corps. He died in Warsaw in 1980 at the age of 61. As the daughter and granddaughter of Kazimierz Wünsche, we will be forever grateful to the Operation Nightingale Team, Andy Saunders, the National Trust and the tenant farmers of Saddlescombe Farm who helped to excavate the Hurricane last year [2015]. It gave us the opportunity to see the plane for the first time in 75 years and know that the last person who touched it before us, was our relative.

For Kazimierz's daughter Grazyna this was an opportunity to celebrate the memory of her father and finally tell his story with pride. For his granddaughter Joanna this was an emotional experience to learn about her family history and feel connected to a man who died when she was just a few months old.

Contemplating the past and departed family members with Grazyna (centre) and Jo (right), the daughter and granddaughter of Kazimierz Wünsche. © Harvey Mills

British readers may be familiar with quite a few of the sites in this book, and that is a good thing, resulting from a conscious decision. From the beginning we wanted to make sure the result of the work reached as wide an audience as possible, with articles in the popular magazines *Current Archaeology* and *British Archaeology*, lots of public talks, a strong social media output and that most powerful of all: television. Our first televisual adventure was with the incredibly popular series *Time Team* at 'Barrow Clump' in 2012 and several of the team, such as Phil Harding and Jackie McKinley, are now regulars on our sites. BBC's flagship programme is *Digging for Britain* and the presenter Alice Roberts is a friend as well. We had filmed the Hurricane excavation for this programme as something a little unusual but nonetheless important and we felt a television audience would be interested in the findings of such a site conducted archaeologically. I did rather wonder what this would look like, but Daz had worked incredibly hard to restore the shine and lustre to the propeller hub until it positively sparkled. All Daz's techniques were effective and the items looked splendid on camera.

Kazimierz Wünsche flew from RAF Northolt

and close to the main gate of this base today is a memorial to the Polish airmen, under the watchful gaze of a spread eagle that is perched on top of a column that has 303 Squadron emblazoned upon it. Within the base is a museum to the Poles and also Building 27 – an Operations Building from the Battle of Britain and now a 'Listed Building' protected by law. It is here that all of the finds now live, viewable by the public. Some 75 years after being shot down, this Hurricane had returned to its old base.

The team has looked at other crashes, including a German Messerschmitt BF110 at the idyllic location of Lulworth on the Dorset south coast. The views from this site in the summer haze up the cliff to Flower's Barrow and over to a turquoise sea as the breeze caressed the fire-coloured plants of the grassland could not have been further removed from the maelstrom of 1940.

The site was adjacent to the coastal path within the Jurassic Coast World Heritage Site and the spectacular location is an attraction for many members of the walking public. The dig team fielded many questions from interested holidaymakers and locals, one of whom was an eyewitness to the crash as a young boy. Such tour guiding is a useful skill to learn for all participants on the project, and one particular couple were especially memorable. A pair of Orthodox Jewish visitors walked past the excavation and quietly asked us what we were excavating. This was, of course, a Second World War airframe, part of the war machine of an utterly insidious regime, perpetuators of the Holocaust. They calmly thanked us for telling them about our work and slowly walked down the hill, lost in their thoughts until they disappeared from our view. I am struggling to think of a stronger demonstration that objects are not entities without meaning, that they are loaded and come with stories and narratives and that they are agencies of power in their own right.

Our project has been designed to encourage the development of the participant wherever possible, be it through use of a skills passport, through increasing responsibility on sites or just

Success as the propeller hub is moved to the trench edge ready to be transferred to a vehicle and taken away for conservation.
© Harvey Mills

by providing opportunities that enable friendship groups to form beyond simple excavation participation. With a finite number of sites on Ministry of Defence land, and a limited budget of course, it is always heartening to see others pick up the torch and to run projects that enable the team to continue their work under an 'Operation Nightingale' banner and meeting these aims without my having to be there. Another piece of aviation archaeology took place at Holme Lode in the Fens of East Anglia in the east of England in 2015. This work was a project directed by Stephen Macaulay of Oxford Archaeology East and included another geophysical survey by Peter Masters with illuminating results. The search was for Spitfire X4593 and the aim was to recover material and to employ archaeological standards to record the crash. The excavation opened a large and very wet area, which revealed a crash crater around 70 cm below the ground surface.

As this team dug down, they could see the traces of the 1940 efforts of the Royal Air Force team to recover the body of Pilot Officer Harold Penketh who had been killed in the crash. Wooden boarding had been used to line the crash crater and shore up the site for this work and the backfill of the operation even included parts of an RAF-crested plate. Soon they located airframe material left behind by the recovery team of 1940: part of the engine, fuel tank components, the pitot tube, ammunition and the pilot's headrest.

At over 2.5 m down, the archaeologists found a large part of the cockpit area, which included the pilot's flying helmet within the wreckage, then his cigarette case and his watch. This was followed by some elements of the pilot himself. Work stopped and this discovery was reported to the Coroner and the Joint Casualty and Compassionate Centre within the Ministry of Defence – done by the book. That evening, a Spitfire flew over and a small gathering was held at the edge of the site, including team members whom we worked with on our digs: Paul Turner, Peter Masters, An Osborne, Richard 'Perce' Percival and Peter Atkinson, among others. The remains were recovered and have since been reburied in a War Grave, with a memorial stone to Harold on the crash site:

> Pilot Office Harold Edwin Penketh, Born 2 May 1920, Called to a Higher life 22 November 1940. *A Fine Young Man*.

Stephen's team retrieved the propellers of the aircraft and then recorded the crash crater in three dimensions, over 6 m deep in places, to produce an accurate digital model of the site, a first for this sort of work and an exemplar of how to approach such sites. The dig had been very important for Harold's family, also for the archaeologists and for our team. It is really gratifying when veterans are able to go and participate in other projects that are not run by me (or Phil, Guy or Alex in the MOD team) as this shows continuity, an investment in the project and its values and ethos. It emphasises the fact that the wider industry supports such an approach.

Have these digs changed our understanding of the aerial battles of 1940? No. Have they changed the lives of those who fought in the 21st century? Undoubtedly.

6 FACING BEOWULF

Excavating remains of Anglo-Saxon England

THE END OF ROMAN BRITAIN in about AD 410 heralded many changes; in buildings, fashions, material culture and many other elements. The archaeological record reflects this and there are far fewer sites of the Anglo-Saxon period, the early medieval, leading to it having been called the 'Dark Ages' in the past. Yet there are still traces and the main training area of Salisbury Plain is a case in point. Recent discoveries include dwellings, a so-called 'Sunken Featured building' (the clue is in the name) at Tidworth and several stray metal finds such as a spear at Breakheart Bottom on the west of the Plain. Most notably, however, there have been excavations of several cemeteries in recent years, at Bulford and Tidworth as part of the Army Basing Programme, which was designed to build houses for military families returning from Germany; these remains were uncovered as part of the planning process. These sites contained the bodies of hundreds of individuals, often with items reflecting their lives in the 6th and 7th centuries: copper alloy workboxes, cowrie shells, spears, knifes, combs. The numbers are enabling us to 'repopulate' the landscape with lots of information about people from those years, their lives and diets. Operation Nightingale has also been incredibly fortunate to examine three such sites, one in

Above: A button brooch from Barrow Clump, depicting what appears to be the snarling face of a warrior in a helmet. © Alice Roberts

Opposite: The panoply of arms, 7th and 21st century, with Rifleman Jake Watts modelling the more modern equipment. © Crown Copyright

Following the track through the grass to the last barrow in the cemetery at Barrow Clump. © Harvey Mills

Gloucestershire and two around the Plain. The latter were Avon Camp and our most-excavated site of all: Barrow Clump.

The veterans are familiar with their Regimental standards, with flags proclaiming various battle honours. The faded flags, when retired, flutter like old dishevelled moths from the gnarled beams of various British cathedrals but bearing names familiar to most: Waterloo, Somme, Normandy. From an archaeological point of view, Barrow Clump would certainly feature on any heritage equivalent. Barrow Clump is a site of many periods from the Neolithic onwards, its earliest manifestation with flints and a buried land surface. There was once a cemetery comprising Bronze Age burial mounds on this hillside, some 4000 years ago, but these have largely been ploughed away to leave just the one barrow: Barrow Clump. Surrounded by a ring of beech trees, this tranquil site is a calm grove on the edges of the training area of Salisbury Plain, the tree bark carved with the names and regimental badges of soldiers that have passed through on exercise. It is also now home to that most industrious of creatures: the badger. These beautiful animals are expert excavators but dreadful with their recording strategies and can thus play havoc with an archaeological site.

Barrow Clump was, quite reasonably, on Historic England's first ever iteration of the *Heritage at Risk* list because of these burrowing animals. In 2003 and 2004 a team led by Dr Jonathan Last from English Heritage examined part of the site to establish the exact nature of the animal damage and to consider how much still survived: was it even worth trying to protect? The answer was, avowedly, yes. Not only had much of the prehistoric layering survived but Jonathan uncovered something that nobody had been expecting, a 6th-century cemetery site. Finds included a silver spoon, horse bridle, amber beads and, in the very first grave encountered, a glorious 'great square-headed brooch' with gilding and twisting designs and stylised human faces. It is not uncommon for such early medieval/Anglo-Saxon sites to utilise earlier burial mounds as places to bury their dead but this site was extensive and needed protecting.

Over a large number of years I tried various non-lethal methods of keeping the badgers away from the burial mound but, for a number of reasons, they were without success. During the autumn of 2011, when we had just started Operation Nightingale, I received a phone call from a woman called Sarah Russell who worked for Landmarc, a company that was repairing the fencing at the barrow. She asked me if I wanted to collect the 'spear' that they had found lying on the barrow surface. I went to the site with Steve Winterton and Alex Bauer, riflemen on work experience with me, expecting to collect part of an old fence. On arrival, however, this was palpably an iron spear of the 6th century. It was also accompanied by several fragments of human bone, all unceremoniously ejected from the burial site by the new animal residents.

I was crestfallen; what on earth could one do to protect this really important site? We got Alex to continue his work experience by doing a technical drawing of the spear with help from Wessex Archaeology's drawing office staff while I pondered the issue – and then decided that the only way to deal with the rapidly declining archaeological resource was probably to excavate it, thereby we would at least have a record before everything was jumbled up and destroyed. Tentatively I approached English Heritage's Inspector of Monuments for the area, Dr Amanda Chadburn, and put this forward as an idea and one which I could use as a major focus of attention for Operation Nightingale, then in its early days. We were incredibly fortunate that Amanda saw the merit of this and, subject to a good project design and funding, said she would agree to our application. *Exercise Beowulf* was thus born. Choosing names for the digs is always entertaining, especially when you see them on the MOD's Daily Range Summaries alongside real military exercise names such as *Druid's Dance* or *Wessex Storm*, and it is a challenge to try to find a name even vaguely relevant that will pique the interest of participants too.

We thus began at Barrow Clump in 2012 and I have now spent about half a year of my life with veterans on this magical, healing location with them making wonderful discoveries that have really added to our understanding of the time period. I mentioned in the introduction to this volume that we began the overall programme working alongside the biggest of the infantry regiments, the Rifles. I used to visit their Casualty Officer, Lieutenant Colonel Mike Smith, in their headquarters in Winchester, Hampshire, on a regular basis. There was a board on the wall there indicating recent deaths in action and casualties too and the scale was pretty overwhelming. The regiment really embraced the potential of archaeology as an aid to recovery. After calls to various battalion quartermasters and transport units (MT as it is known by the military), a site

A golden sun illuminates the burials lying below a track to the side of the burial mound. © Harvey Mills

camp was established around the Clump in the summer of 2012 and the first season of excavation could begin, with soldiers camping outside the trees. This looked like a mini-Glastonbury Festival at times and was indeed once reported to Range Operations as an illegal 'rave site' by a concerned member of the army.

One of the keys to the success of these sites is the appointment of suitable contractors to support you – with staff that are good at archaeology but also sympathetic and engaging. We could not have wished for better at Barrow Clump as Wessex Archaeology, in particular Phil Andrews and Dave Murdie, were appointed. Both are incredibly experienced archaeologists and used to working alongside one another; Phil is a leading expert on Anglo-Saxon archaeology, having directed a great deal of fieldwork at Saxon Southampton (*Hamwic*), for example. Indeed, he was responsible for the excavations underneath the football stadium in that city, which still retains a portion of the cemetery under the pitch to this day – blamed by some in the city for the poor results of the team in their new ground until a 'pagan priestess' was brought in to bless the stadium and to remove the curse present. Dave had worked with Phil on that site and discovered some wonderful gold and garnet objects, a recurring theme as Dave always seems to make good finds on the digs. I'm sure a deal of this is down to the fact that he is an incredibly skilled and thoughtful excavator. So Phil, everyone's favourite 'Uncle' and Dave, one of the most entertaining raconteurs you'll ever meet (Phil once missed his last bus home waiting for the punchline of a Dave story) were thrown into the mix and Barrow Clump could begin.

Whilst the site was being stripped of turf in readiness for excavation of the deposits below, some of the team visited the Wiltshire Museum in Devizes for artefact familiarisation with the curator David Dawson. Their display, based largely on the archaeology of Blacknall Field in nearby

Phil Andrews photographs the excavated burial of a 6th-century female. © Harvey Mills

Pewsey would, we hoped, provide suitable parallels for the team as they worked to recover information. We also hoped to be able to provide the museum with something of a headache by making lots of finds in our time on site. Indeed, Corporal Steve Winterton ('Winno') spent much of the six weeks on site, and indeed the following two years, telling anyone that would care to listen that he wanted to find a sword, in spite of frequent gentle comments by Phil that such finds were really pretty unusual.

As the tracked machine slowly tracked onto the mound and stripped away the covering soil it seemed to some that no features or graves were present and that it would consequently be a *very* short dig, not the six weeks we had envisaged. Winno was the most doom-laden of all on site, mischievously suggesting that Phil would end up in a hole of his own if no burials were encountered (Phil's introduction to the phenomenon of 'banter' that is still much talked about). This fear quickly disappeared, however, as the tell-tale dark soil fills of features within the bright white chalk soon appeared, ditches, postholes and, of course, grave cuts. The honour of excavating this first grave went to Winno and Rifleman Laurence Savage and, although there was no sword, the excavation had begun in earnest.

One of the subsequent burials that was soon exposed was allocated to Rifleman Rowan Kendrick and this turned out to be one of the more important graves on site. Rowan, or 'Kenny' as everyone calls him, had been in 1st Battalion the Light Infantry and later 5th Battalion the Rifles.

> After suffering a mental breakdown in service, I was tasked with working in the stores on rear party while the battalion went on tour to Afghanistan in 2012. One of the other soldiers on rear party, Rifleman Lawrence Savage, was asked to gather a small group of soldiers to take part in an archaeological dig in Caerwent, Wales with Operation Nightingale.
>
> His next mission was Barrow Clump.

Kenny had spent several days on this grave under the expert tutelage of Dave Murdie, revealing both the male skeleton and the grave goods placed in the grave. I asked Kenny if he was bored with this work and he replied that, on the contrary, he was concentrating so hard to make sure he did everything correctly that he was exhausted at the end of the day and that he was sleeping properly for the first time in years, since Afghanistan in fact. Well, this concentration clearly paid off. The burial was one of the more complete on site and the individual was accompanied by a 6th-century spear *and* the most exquisite drinking vessel. The latter was made with bands of bronze decorated with small dots holding together staves of yew wood, which still, miraculously, survived more-or-less intact in spite of being in the chalk for 1500 years; one of the very best preserved examples in Britain. We all held our breath as this was eventually lifted by the on-site conservator

Rifleman Rowan Kendrick (Kenny) with a chum.
© Rowan Kendrick

and placed into a suitable container. It all held together, and you can now visit this glorious item in the Wiltshire Museum in Devizes, now a part of the collection that we had visited at the very start of the project. This fact is, quite rightly, a source of pride for Kenny and he told me that he would take family members to see the artefact, happy in the thought that he had given something back to the country; to this day I find that statement pretty humbling given all he had already done in his military career.

It didn't end there though; Kenny has now completed ten years as a professional archaeologist, having left the army. He mentioned that his career advisor at school told him he wasn't clever enough to be an archaeologist (a genuinely shocking statement in so many ways) and thus he joined the army. Well, he should perhaps take that individual to Devizes to see this small and beautiful object he found or, alternatively, invite them to the British Museum. If you climb the stairs there and walk through various rooms until you are face to face with the Sutton Hoo helmet in the Early Medieval Galleries, you will find another link to Kenny. For within Raedwald's squinting range (if this is who was buried with the Sutton Hoo helmet and all the other treasures) is a photograph of the Barrow Clump burial: bucket and spear included. The caption in the display case reads:

> *Man buried with a small bucket and a spear, from the Anglo-Saxon cemetery at Barrow Clump, Wiltshire. © Wessex Archaeology, burial excavated by Rfn Rowan Kendrick, 5 Rifles.*

It's impossible not to visit, to undertake a form of pilgrimage, whenever I find myself in the British Museum and I know others, probably Kenny included, do too.

The cemetery had been placed into the pre-existing Beaker period and Early Bronze Age burial mound – a monument that had already been there for the best part of 3000 years when

Burial of a 6th-century male with a drinking vessel and spear, excavated by Kenny. © Crown Copyright

the Saxon bodies were being buried. The elements of this funerary mound were still present, with the turf mound of the Beaker monument visible along with a number of prehistoric cremation urns, still with remnants of their ashy filling. The most noteworthy aspects of the earlier monument were the ditches; a big circle that ran around the mound itself, with steep sides and a smooth flat base that were tributes to the industrious predecessors who laboured with antler picks, bone scapulae and similar tools to create an architectural marvel, and all without the support of the Royal Engineers with heavy digging equipment. This was something that certainly generated a respect from those military veterans who were all too aware of the pain of having to dig a foxhole on Salisbury Plain, let alone something of this scale. A number of our 6th-century burials were placed within the ditch of the prehistoric barrow and some into what is called the 'berm': a flat area between the barrow ditch and the mound it surrounds. The mound itself was, however, free from later graves. When we were looking at the spatial patterning of the burials we noticed that one area in the ditch had a high concentration of male burials with shield bosses, the central iron elements that survived from a shield. Mike Kelly, one of the riflemen, who had been partially blinded in one eye during actions overseas, postulated that this could represent a form of shield-wall for the afterlife, protecting others buried beyond them. It was a neat theory and shows that it needn't be academics that come up with ideas about deposition; this was Mike's first dig with burials after all.

Not everyone is a 'natural', it has to be said. We were given some able-bodied assistants by the army to help the archaeologists to shift some of the heavy soil above the areas we wanted to excavate. At one point, one of these helpers called over one of the professionals to assist with a particular area. In retrospect this was suspicious and the soil he wanted moving was a little bit too loose. Nonetheless, when the first mattock hit this area there was a sickening crack accompanied by much giggling from said soldier. The mattock had knocked into the plastic skeleton he had spent an inordinate amount of time burying at this location rather than getting on with his real job. The Halloween item was duly exposed and then removed. The joke will, however, always be with this soldier as, unbeknownst to him, around 25 cm below his stunt replica was a *real* burial, complete with shield and spear. If he had spent less time on his practical joke his few days helping us at Barrow Clump would have been altogether more rewarding.

Finds from the Clump in the Wiltshire Museum, Devizes with 'Kenny's Bucket' to the fore. The staves of yew wood are all original. © Harvey Mills

The first season of Barrow Clump was also our first foray into national television, in the form of the last series of the much-loved *Time Team*. Its stars seemed happy; Phil Harding was back in his beloved Wiltshire and Helen Geake was on a 6th-century site that was perfect for her. It was super that Raksha Dave and Tony Robinson could join in too; though the latter was treated to a very soggy rendition of *The Last Post* by the buglers from the Rifles; it was quite a wet digging season. We could also showcase the equipment available to us, being a military project. Peter Buxton, the surgeon commodore when we were on site, also has an archaeological post-graduate degree and was thus able to get a mobile X-ray unit to site. Material from the grave cuts could be scanned

Time Team at Barrow Clump, Sir Tony Robinson (left) with the author. © Crown Copyright

instantly and I dare say that many professional field units would be envious of this capability. I should add, I suppose, that we also used this in a studio with Alice Roberts and *Digging for Britain* some years later but the system broke down as it was too hot in Dorchester Museum! Surely not hotter than an Iraqi summer? It redeemed itself as we assessed a particularly long seax (a single-edged bladed weapon) some years later.

Time Team were very responsive to our programme aspirations, such as the desire to have several little cameos throughout the project. Phil has some really impressive connections and was able to bring a barrel of beer from his favourite *Hopback* brewery to the site. It was called 'Saxon: the Rifleman's Ale' and had supposedly been made with ingredients that would have been available to a brewer in the 6th century. It was certainly a great deal more palatable than the special brew put together by our Royal Logistics Corps chefs, which utilised the juice in the ration tins of fruit on site, together with yeast. This brew was, however, lethal as I believe several members of the television crew found to their cost. A more traditional extra for the programme was getting one of our team, Winno, to try to cast bronze that would be consistent with the jewellery we had been discovering on the site: small square-headed brooches, button brooches, disc brooches, pins. He undertook the challenge with gusto, pumping bellows to obtain the relevant heat. However, these experiments are not guaranteed to succeed and sometime into his casting, the crucible holding the material exploded. Given that Winno was on the project as a result of an explosion in Afghanistan that had curtailed his military career, this was another moment where we all held our breath – he looked up again with a beaming smile however.

Not all the finds were wildly exciting, we did find a part of the extensive badger sett that was filled with old ration tins, such as processed cheese (known by some as 'cheese possessed'), the result of a badger that seemed to have had an attraction to shiny objects of modern vintage, the Saxon items not being good enough for them!

Barrow Clump was very much about people facing challenges, setting their own limits and, in many cases, overcoming them all while accomplishing incredible archaeology. As someone leading the work and witnessing the huge progress being made in all departments this truly was awe-inspiring. Just one example: from an early age it was drummed into me that one of the things an archaeologist must *never* do is to sit on the edge of the section, it is a form of professional sacrilege and always results in admonishment. In an early week at the Clump I noticed that there were a sneaky pair of legs I could see perched over part of the site and so I went to administer some swift justice. When I arrived, however, I could see that I had been looking at the complete picture; it was *only* a pair of legs. The owner, Tyler Christopher, had removed his prosthetics and perched them proudly against the trench edge as he manoeuvred

Tyler Christopher (The Rifles, age 38)

We lost quite a few lads when we went out to Iraq as a result of shootings and IEDs, then in Afghanistan we lost another lad in our Company. It was on 13 August 2009 that I was patrolling in Afghanistan and got injured myself. I was thirteenth in line, so there were plenty of people in front of me – I thought I'd be safe. We went out and I stood on it [an IED], but I didn't know what I'd stood on to begin with.

The first thing that went through my head was that we'd been shot by artillery and the impact was right where we were. I slowly started to try and move and shouted to the man to the right to check he was OK. I did the same to the man in front. At the same time, I was trying to stand up and nothing was happening. My arm wasn't working either. That's when I realised that I wasn't alright.

The lads that came to do first aid couldn't get to me at first, they couldn't get closer because another IED had been exposed, but eventually we got back to camp where a helicopter picked us up. I ended up losing both legs above the knee and damaging my right arm, it was broken in two places. I also had some internal organ injuries. At the time I couldn't feel anything – I was in total shock. (https://www.pilgrimbandits.org/always-a-little-further-tylers-story/)

Tyler Christopher, ex of 4 Rifles, in his military days. © Tyler Christopher

Tyler is utterly indomitable, now farming in Wales as well as playing sledge hockey for Great Britain among his many other life adventures. Tyler's humour and laughter are also infectious, though when I saw him taking two femurs from the burial he had worked on with him to the finds tent in his wheelchair I did rather wonder if there was going to be some sort of macabre joke about missing body parts about to be played. I was relieved this didn't manifest. Tyler said that, 'The digs helped me with my mental health. Opened me up to talking to strangers. Got me back outside working with a team. Just really loved being outside with all the others on the digs.'

The team uncover one of the many graves cut down into the chalk at Barrow Clump.
© Harvey Mills

himself into a more comfortable position to excavate the feature he was working on. This was pretty humbling and certainly curtailed any grumbling we had on site about poor weather or long hours, as this man simply got on with things, no matter what life threw at him. Tyler had been injured by an improvised explosive device (IED) whilst serving with the Rifles in Afghanistan in 2009, losing both of his legs along with sustaining other injuries.

We ended our first year at the Clump swordless but content that it had been a fascinating season, and in the knowledge that there were two more summers ahead. This turned out to be slightly pessimistic as we returned on five other occasions.

Our second season was a glorious warm summer and this tended to fit the pattern of all our summer digs, apart from the open day in the last year which saw a downpour of biblical proportions just before the visitors arrived leaving the burials looking like a ghoulish parody of Millais' *Ophelia* with skeletons in graves underwater. Liberal deployment of site sponges solved the problem but the work was never as clean as it had been. By now we were able to see the progress of some of the soldiers involved. Both Kenny and, later, Rifleman Savage ('Sav') could attend site as professional archaeologists with Wessex Archaeology. The team was joined by serving soldiers from the nearby 4th Battalion of the Rifles, assisting our veterans and wounded. This longstanding military presence on this site was emphasised both by the tree carvings and also by some of the finds that were coming up. Mark Khan, who had worked at our air crash site, was able to add an astonishingly poignant story to our 6th-century grave goods with a find from the uppermost layers. Here we had found an old service fork from the mid-20th century. On its handle a service number was stamped: 821579. Mark was able to trace this to a specific individual: Gunner James Moderate. James was an air defence gunner who was captured by the Japanese and subsequently murdered on 5 March 1943. He has no known grave and is commemorated on the Singapore memorial to the missing.

In times past, archaeologists may not have paid much attention to such modern elements that lay above the more traditional archaeology that they were interested in – this was not going to happen on our site; the veterans, quite rightly, would not allow it. Other items conveyed their own particular martial ethos: a set of parachute soldier's wings surmounted with the Queen's crown was excavated and this meant a lot to paratroopers on the dig – people like Steuart Bowman who had spent much of his time working on the prehistoric cremation burials here in the first year with expert Jackie McKinley. Steuart or 'Gandalf' as he is affectionately known by the team, given his resemblance to a certain Middle Earth wizard, is someone who really thinks on site, always keen to put forward interesting theories and someone who takes great care with his work. For us to ignore a cap badge like his would not have been right: furthermore it was something that sparked a lot of interest and conversation on the open days not least because paratroopers on the doomed *Operation Market Garden* had flown into Arnhem from sites very close to the Clump in 1944.

Back then to the assistance provided by the serving members of the Rifles. As this was the local battalion, we also saw reunion of friends on site. Robert Walters ('Wally') was working with his old mate and former colleague in 4 Rifles, Tyler. They were excavating a burial methodically, gently revealing the bones held in the chalky soil but disturbed both by badger claw and tree root. Fortunately, the skull was still pretty much intact and while they worked, I noticed two things about Wally in particular. First, he was taking quite a few photographs of the skull of this burial and, secondly, his own arm was festooned with tattoos of other skulls: a sort of Iron Age 'Roquepertuse' skull cult made flesh (an extraordinary site in France with human skulls displayed in niches cut into stone uprights). Chatting with Rob about this he told me that the existing ink represented fallen comrades but that he was thinking of getting another to represent the burial he had worked on, an altogether more positive experience and hence all the photographs. It was another moment which emphasised to me how important the project was and how privileged I was to be able to work on it.

So, to our third and final year at the Clump, 2014 – at least we thought it was going to be. Each year seemed to produce its own highlights and succeeded in upping the ante of discoveries made. This was, of course, perfect for maintaining the levels of expectation and excitement amongst the dig team and to ensure engagement in the project was never a challenge. By 2014 some of the veterans had now started their academic

Veteran Steuart Bowman reverently excavates the remains of a child. © Harvey Mills

studies under such luminaries as Professor Simon James at the University of Leicester and it was the turn of Sav to be on site as a professional employee of Wessex Archaeology. He picked up archaeology in a way that showed he had natural abilities, garnering praise on his flint identification from Phil Harding no less! Sav's skills led him, later on, to develop training packages for new archaeologists, passing on his knowledge to others.

Something else that he clearly embraced, and included in his training ideas, was the whole phenomenon of 'Health and Safety' on site and, from this point onwards, Sav could rarely be seen without lurid high-visibility clothing, at great odds to the camouflage of his previous employers. Neon oranges and yellows were to the fore and this was certainly of value when an armoured column had some challenges with their map-reading, being a kilometre out, and suddenly emerged at the small track besides our excavation. To be fair to them, it must have seemed a little incongruous on the training area. Sav stood in front of this column like a Day-Glo pastiche of that famous image of the individual in front of the tanks in Tiananmen Square and explained the project to the lead driver, who thus realised their error and the vehicles slowly growled away.

A special find: the Visigothic brooch discovered by former signaller Matt Smith. © Harvey Mills

This excitement over, we could return to the excavation work. Matt Smith, whom we have mentioned at Chisenbury Midden, was working on a grave very close to another being excavated by former Royal Marine Dickie Bennett who had joined us for the first time with his daughter after Help for Heroes had highlighted the opportunity. Matt and Dickie soon struck up a friendship, though this was certainly tested by rivalry; not that between their respective military units but, rather, by the quality of the finds they were recovering from their particular features. Both were finding beads of vivid colours, of glass, of amber and their gleeful discussions on the lovely jewellery they were uncovering was probably a million miles away from the sorts of conversations they might have had in their Mess in the past. I'm not going to state which individual came out on top in this competition as both are friends. What I *can* say is that Matt's burial produced a wondrous crossbow-shaped brooch made of iron and with stripy bands of brass extending along the length of its body. This was a type of brooch of late 5th- to early 6th-century date and usually found in southern France or northern Spain and associated with the Visigoths. Heavily corroded and with lumps of chalk adhering to it, after conservation this item seemed even more precious. It is only the second such brooch to be found in Britain (the other being from Kent) and the first to be recovered from a grave context. Was the person wearing it a Visigoth herself? This question will have to wait, although we have examined the isotopic signatures of the teeth from the earlier years (yielding signatures to illustrate that the majority of people had grown up on the chalklands) we still need to assess

The three blades of Barrow Clump: two swords and a seax above them. 'Winno's sword' is at the bottom. © Harvey Mills

whether the brooch owner was part of the Gothic migrations or perhaps simply a local woman who enjoyed some of the more exotic jewellery items of the time. A bit like Matt and Dickie!

As this year drew to a close, we had one final grave to excavate. Winno was the man for the job. As he was digging away, he came across a long thin, straight, piece of iron. It couldn't be could it? After three years of telling everyone on site about his desire to find a sword, had he done so? Steve came over to Phil and me to tell us what he thought he had discovered, and we walked over to his trench area. By this point Phil had had three years of experience of military humour and as he peered into the grave cut he looked up at Winno and told him, sympathetically, that it was part of a tractor. Very shortly after, however, he started chuckling and confirmed that it was indeed an Anglo-Saxon sword!

Winno's jaw dropped and he told us that his heart was pumping at such a rate that 'I've not felt like this since I was mortared by the Taleban' – a line that has never been delivered on *Time Team*. It really was a thing of beauty too – pattern welded and with mineralised elements of the wooden scabbard still preserved, the sword was complete with 'sword bead' and gilded bronze decorations to the scabbard. Winno was too nervous to speak at his own wedding but certainly not so reticent to talk about this find to anyone who would listen, and he has even helped give presentations on his archaeological work since.

Another veteran whom we first met as part of Operation Nightingale at Barrow Clump was Jeanette. Jeanette Flitney was a bomb disposal officer with the Royal Logistics Corps. Anyone familiar with the fighting in Afghanistan and Iraq will be aware of the pressure on these soldiers, the constant threat of IEDs, the suicide bombings, the casualties. I had known Jeanette before Operation

Jeanette Flitney (bomb disposal officer, Royal Logistics Corps, age 57)

I was at Tedworth House [the Recovery Centre run by the charity Help for Heroes] for a short stay, as I was not able to leave my house on my own or do anything other than lay on the sofa. A very nice lady who was looking after veterans and organising activities persuaded me to go with her to Barrow Clump for a couple of hours. We ended up staying for the whole afternoon and I really enjoyed it and felt very relaxed at the site and with everyone. So I asked if I could go back the next day; the rest as they say is history.

Jeanette has now become a project stalwart and can often be seen concentrating with trowel in a muddy hole or taking part in post-excavation scientific assessments. Each of the team face their own challenges. Many dislike the sounds of gunfire, be it artillery or rifles, and this makes organising excavations on a military training area a little more tricky. The sounds of helicopters too are frequent on the training areas and can be very distinctive, the pulsing percussion of the twin-rotors of a Chinook in particular. For some, such as Dickie Bennet, this is a positive sound; the noise of going home, of exiting a firefight. For others, it is a direct association with conflict or indeed of bodies of friends and colleagues being brought home. Nonetheless, if you factor this potential into the risk assessment and have a strategy to deal with this then that shouldn't preclude such sites. Jeanette's strategy for drowning out the sound of gunfire was to listen to loud music through headphones. I quizzed Jeanette on the various excavations she had taken part in and what was special for her.

I enjoyed Barrow Clump the most as it was so varied: from pottery shards, bone fragments to full skeletons with grave goods. I also had the opportunity to learn from Jackie McKinley about bones and cleaning a skeleton. The area was great for allowing an individual to work as a team or individual. But the support I was given at all sites from fellow veterans and most of the staff made me feel safe and able to keep coming back even when I had a setback. Barrow Clump was so good because we were all staying in the same area and able to support each other in the good and bad things. Military people, no matter what service (including the civil servants), have a very unique sense of humour which isn't always understood by people who have not served. So being able to let off steam and talk about things with fellow veterans/serving soldiers was very beneficial. The act of uncovering something in a safe surrounding and with people that you feel safe with is very therapeutic.

I think the banter on the digs is very important for the advancement of the individual. It feels like we are still in the military family but with a safety net as everyone knows that we have issues still to deal with. This means that on the whole people know how far to go and when they need to be more careful and understanding.

I also enjoyed being peaceful on site and being able to work through my own thoughts and feelings whilst carrying out the seemingly repetitive task. Removing earth carefully from around an item, although seemingly repetitive, is not – it is doing a task that is calm, controlled and allows the mind to feel less frazzled. Excavating skeletons and graves made me think about life and all its ups and downs. Barrow Clump showed me that even in death there could be respect and peace. The graves were cut with such care and all the dead were placed with love and respect. I gradually learnt that even though there were explosions or gunfire around me I could concentrate on what I was doing, and I would be safe.

It has helped me a lot. It gave me an outlet when I was most alone. I could go to an excavation and know that I was with people who understood and who would look out for me. That I could be involved as much or as little as I needed/could cope with. It allowed me to start feeling I could get out of the house and be active, that I was not worthless. As I did more, I felt more confident to be able to get out of the house and to be able to participate in activities. It was the start of my being able to join in with people and it also helped me with my interaction with men, which had been difficult due to issues in the military and my PTSD. As I did more I found that I was able to learn new things, and retain them. That I could start to help others and enjoyed some more of the external social activities.

Nightingale, meeting her on a Ministry of Defence training session, so it was a bit of a shock seeing her again on this project.

The burials were special; they often indicated the love in which the individual was held and the care with which they were interred. As we excavated, it was important to see the ethical stance of the team as they excavated; with care and respect and sometimes also while talking to the remains they worked on. We were careful to make sure that all the participants were coping with their tasks given that dealing directly with the dead in this fashion would seem an obvious trigger of distressing memories. And yet they managed well; the recovery of child burials was probably the most pressing as many of the men and women on site would empathise with the position of a mourning parent and also could reflect that these individuals had not lived a full life. I think perhaps the distance in time helps.

As a curator of the archaeology for this area it was useful to continue work at the Clump in later years too (in part when further graves away from the designated area of the Scheduled Monument were unearthed by badgers) and these later, shorter, forays revealed more pottery than all the other summers put together. The furthest south-west cremation burials from the 6th century were found as well as a complete pot in a grave, excavated by Jayne (a volunteer) and John Hughes, a former Argyll and Southerland Highlander. We worked in later November and December when the frost crackled the ground. My friend Lisa Miller worked on site too, I have known her since university days and her brother Mark Mortiboys had joined us as a veteran participant on both the Hurricane excavation and also at Rat Island. She worked with Briony Lalor to uncover a female grave with disc brooches and amber beads that glowed with a fiery look when held up to the watery sun of the winter mornings. My daughter Katherine also visited the dig with her friend Rosalie. We discovered just in time that they had managed to set fire to one of the old, mostly dead, beech trees on site by poking

The first intact pot we recovered from the Clump, accompanying a male burial alongside an iron spear. © Harvey Mills

Above: A dig camp site in November.
© Harvey Mills

Right: A female burial at the Clump, with disc brooch, tweezers, pin and beads visible.
© Harvey Mills

Paul Ewins and Paul Barnsley uncover a grave. © Harvey Mills

a dead leaf-filled cavity with a glowing stick taken from the embers of the campfire, thus avoiding a rather embarrassing call to Range Operations. In spite of fire risk, I think it has proved important to have families on site, to support participants, to remove any fears of attendance and sometimes to change the overall dynamic to a feeling of community.

A track at the side of the Clump also had graves below it and, by excavating this specific area, we were able to determine how detrimental the route, used by armoured vehicles and tractors, had proved to the underlying archaeological deposits. Any ceramic vessels below the tram lines created by tyre or track had not fared especially well, but the graves were mostly different. On occasion we found skulls a matter of centimetres below the ground surface that had not been crushed or even cracked. This was important information for my management of the Plain and at the same time an astonishing opportunity for the veterans. Our final Saxon foray here saw the discovery of a second sword, this time by an American Air Force veteran Jason White, who now works for Cotswold Archaeology. The grave was completed by one of our old artillerymen, Paul Barnsley, and he found the grave to have a large spear, metal belt and large pin. Paul had earlier completed the excavation of another male burial that included a very large single-edged bladed weapon known as a seax. When we first saw it we wondered what the artefact might be, teasing Paul that it might have been used in the weaving process for knocking weft. Nonsense, he said, this object 'cut people's heads off!' He *was* correct in that it was a weapon but we'll never know the history of the item. I have long wanted to find a female burial accompanied by a weapon or a male with jewellery, but it didn't

A so-called 'deviant' burial of a male not placed into a grave cut with any obvious reverence. © Harvey Mills

happen at the Clump. Finding weapons in a burial doesn't equate with the person being a 'warrior' but it does make for a good juxtaposition with our veterans and certainly led them to make easy comparisons with roles in life and to put them into thinking archaeologically.

There is really a wonderful, ethereal, atmosphere at the Clump. I think the trees and the noises generated as the leaves are rustled by the breeze, and all the other elements of nature, help. Tyler could often be seen listening to the birdsong there (indeed trying to attract particular passerines to his area of the excavation) and the countryside is incredibly important to him; perhaps explaining his transition to being a farmer these days. There was also a resident family of buzzards nesting in the trees above us. Initially this was endearing but, after six weeks, the sounds of a chick screeching in a manner akin to a poorly oiled wheelbarrow wheel (for which it was occasionally mistaken) was a little less therapeutic.

The site has enabled soldiers and their young families to camp together, to paddle in the nearby river, to enjoy a hog roast, possibly in scenes similar to those witnessed at the nearby Neolithic site of Durrington Walls or the feasting that went on at East Chisenbury in the Iron Age, creating bonds. On one occasion when we camped up there, we had a night-vision monocular with us and the children went spotting animals with it, though it soon became a piece of star gazing equipment. The peace of this site on a still summer evening with woodsmoke drifting through the tree branches and happy chatter below will stay with many of us.

Archaeologically the work achieved so much too: we have advanced the geographical boundaries of 6th-century cremation vessels; added a Neolithic (and Beaker period) story; recovered a cemetery; recorded antiquary trenches; placed the Visigoths in the landscape (perhaps); removed the site from the *Heritage at Risk* list; assessed the effects of vehicle tracks over archaeology; and all whilst having huge fun. Another key element is that this work is all published in a monograph. Barrow Clump remains the biggest publication thus far, a site largely 6th century in date but stretching into the 7th and perhaps even very early 8th centuries too.

Our engagements with the early medieval period did not, however, stop with Barrow Clump. Two sites saw us focusing on the 7th century: one, at Avon Camp, was on Ministry of Defence land while the other, at Cherington in the Gloucestershire Cotswolds, saw the team more in rescue archaeology mode. A metal detectorist, Chris Cuss, had worked his way across a number of fields on this site and was rewarded with some metal items that were clearly Anglo-Saxon in date: a silver gilt sword pommel and buckle. Rather than digging them out, he did precisely the right thing in reporting them to the Portable Antiquities Scheme. He then recruited the support of archaeologist Toby Catchpole at Gloucestershire Council who was able to locate more and to plot some of the finds. The work was not completed, however, and the site was pretty vulnerable as it lay just below the surface and would have been ploughed away in a couple more seasons.

Katie Marsden, who had worked with us as a finds specialist at the Clump, now worked for Cotswold Archaeology. She asked if we could establish an Operation Nightingale project to deal with the threatened site and we were able to gain a grant from the Bristol and Gloucestershire Archaeological Society to make sure we could. *Exercise Shallow Grave* was established and I was delighted to learn that, in their support of the work, Cotswold were providing an old friend of mine, Matt Nichol, and his colleague, Chris Brown, to direct the work.

The burial that Chris Cuss had found with his

The fields of the Cotswolds welcome us to *Exercise Shallow Grave*. © Harvey Mills

Cleaning the top of the excavation site is both laborious and crucial in revealing features cut into the bedrock below. © Harvey Mills

metal detector was of real importance, perhaps not of the same tier of status as the so-called Prittlewell Prince, a 6th-century burial with a panoply of grave goods excavated in Essex in 2003, nor the internationally renowned finds of Sutton Hoo in Suffolk, but perhaps not too far removed. With this burial of a young individual were the glass sherds of a 'cone' beaker (shaped like an ice-cream cone), parts of a bronze vessel (possibly a cauldron or bowl), an iron shield boss, two iron fittings from the bottoms of spear shafts, known as 'ferrules', and a sword. There remained the potential for other items and this, alongside the fear of ploughing and the deterioration of the bones as they had been exposed to the elements, made speedy work an imperative.

We were camping again, and we were faced with a major problem from the outset: where on earth to watch the very final episode of *Game of Thrones*! Lots of the dig team were big fans of this television phenomenon and, fortunately, coverage was such that a laptop attached to a power source in a motorhome on site enabled this challenge to be overcome. Archaeology should never get in the way of your other life priorities.

All our work was again accomplished without the use of machines, in part as the remains were so close to the surface. We were therefore reliant on a good geophysical survey and that the mapping for the site provided by this, and also by Chris's memory of his detecting results, would be accurate. Thankfully both were.

We began by exposing some features that were probably the beam-slots that held a Roman timber building, now long decayed. As with many structures of the later Roman period in this country, we found the tiny burial of a child in the floor layers of this building. Much debate has taken place as to why this practice occurred; perhaps it reflects the high mortality rates of later Roman Britain and the lack of citizen status until one reached a certain age. I rather think that such a tragedy might be something that families wanted to commemorate by having the body of their child close to them at all times, still within their home. This wasn't a fancy villa of the type found locally at Chedworth or Cirencester (*Corinium*) with mosaics and hypocausts but rather a simple dwelling reflecting how most of the rural farming populace lived in the 3rd and 4th centuries AD.

The team soon also located the main target of the burial area, carved into the limestone bedrock for which the Cotswolds are so famous, and saw a small and poorly preserved femur. The area was, again, just below the surface of the field with some limestone slabs present across elements of the inhumation. Further trowel work adjacent to the bone revealed an item that glinted in the May sun as it was exposed for the first time in 1500 years: a complete glass bowl. Although broken, all the fragments of this green-tinged vessel, shallower in nature than a the small, almost hemispherical, bowls known as palm cups, were in place. We also found further shards of the cone beaker seen in the earlier dig. Finding glass vessels in Saxon graves is not especially common; finding two is very rare.

The ferrules from the spear shafts were noted as having been at the head of the burial rather than at the feet; an unusual burial practice and perhaps one more akin to Frankish fashions. Towards what remained of the skull of the skeleton was a blackened area with several small dark metallic items of silver. This was going to prove incredibly difficult to excavate and so a block of soil with these gilded silver elements within was carefully lifted and then X-rayed by Pieta Greaves of Drakon Heritage in readiness for her to micro-excavate in a lab setting. This X-ray showed fluted strips and loops, similar to sword scabbard mouths or even to decorations felt to be part of a lyre from the very rich burial site in Prittlewell in Essex. We think that this was probably the remnants of a

Left: The glass dish from a grave in Cherington excavated by Katie Marsden. © Harvey Mills

Overleaf:
As we camp out on site the setting sun gave Harvey just the moment to capture this encapsulation of the excavation. © Harvey Mills

Briony Lalor expertly excavates the female burial at Cherington. © Harvey Mills

drinking vessel but it is not easy to tell. There were also lozenges of gilded bronze and, in the pelvic region, a small iron dagger and a series of bronze studs that were probably decorative fittings for the belt that held this knife. Reinforcing the idea that those buried with weapons such as swords were not necessarily 'warriors', this burial seems to have been of an individual aged between 7 and 11 years, most probably 9–10. This child's burial indicated status for sure, and an expression of power too, but martial? Most unlikely. If, as we think, this may well have been a late 6th-century inhumation, it is impossible not to consider a statement in the *Anglo-Saxon Chronicle* (a partly retrospective national chronicle of events begun around AD 890), that the Battle of Deorham (site unknown but in the local region somewhere) took place in 577 between the Britons and West Saxons and that the cities of Bath, Gloucester and Cirencester fell to the Saxons on this date. If this is accurate in any way we really were digging in a hinterland of the so-called Dark Ages.

As with so many of the digs we seemed to have been blessed with fine weather and evening showers were always incredibly welcome. Matt Smith had, by now, progressed to running much of the administration. Progression is really important on the digs, be it being able to complete more components in a 'skills passport', having the confidence to supervise new participants, or to ensure camp administration would meet military standards. There will, however, always be a space for people to return, and to meet old friends.

It is crucial to find interesting features for the participants to work on, whichever site we have chosen to excavate. Making finds always helps too. Thus, this burial was fascinating and met the 'Barrow Clump standard'. Adjacent to it was another shallow grave, of an individual lying on their back and accompanied by a spindle whorl, an antler toggle and a series of amethyst beads of varying hues of violet. Such beads are a good indicator of a 7th-century date and thus our small cemetery may have been in use for a period of time.

Our burials at Barrow Clump had been pretty gender specific where identifiable – men with weapons, women with jewellery – and we wondered whether this would be the case at Cherington too. Initial examination of the remains with the amethyst beads pointed to a potentially male burial, which would have been particularly interesting but longer-term studies showed that this inhumation was that of a woman. One day I'm sure that we will find an exception to this pattern.

Kindness seems to be forthcoming on so many of our projects and it is delightful that these acts are so varied in their form. On all our projects relating to sites of the 6th and 7th centuries, we have been pleased to welcome 'Weorod', a group that specialises in re-enactments of this time period, not simply showing fights of the age but rather looking at all manner of aspects of the period: costume, crafts, trade. In fact, our results have assisted this group as they can see the methods used to create items, while Weorod's collections of artefacts are all based on real archaeological examples; our Barrow Clump bucket being a case in point.

The Cherington site was our first experience of amethyst. It wasn't to be our last. On the morning of 12 June 1982, the British destroyer HMS *Glamorgan* was hit with an Exocet missile during its deployment in the Falklands War in the South Atlantic. Fourteen of the ship's company were killed. Sean Cahill was one of the survivors and had worked with Phil Abramson and Alex Sotheran on Operation Nightingale projects in Otterburn in Northumberland. His first excavation on Salisbury Plain was in 2021 as a member of the *Exercise*

Julie and Wayne from the re-enactment group 'Weorod' adding their expertise and colour to our fieldwork alongside showing their reconstructions in costume and weaponry. © Harvey Mills

Clockwise from top left:

Graham Moore of the Royal Air Force concentrating hard as he excavates at Avon Camp. © Harvey Mills

Jackie McKinley delivers a masterclass on the recovery of human remains to team members. Being able to draw on such expertise is a huge boon. © Harvey Mills

Phil Andrews watches the mechanical excavator remove the topsoil to reveal the archaeological features below, here a circular ring ditch of the main barrow. © Harvey Mills

An expanse of chalk holding so many memories of Salisbury Plain past. © Harvey Mills

Ring Giver team, which was exploring our next 7th-century cemetery at Avon Camp. The site had been found during archaeological evaluation work in advance of the possible construction of a new museum for the Royal Artillery. The museum project was, however, abandoned but news of the discovery of the cemetery had got out and, in my view, it was vulnerable to potential looting; I had been getting reports from the Ministry of Defence Police of such activities during the lockdown periods of the COVID-19 pandemic.

Sean not only excavated his first human skeletons at this site, but he was interviewed as part of the *Digging for Britain* filming of the excavation. Following screening of the programme, I saw lots of messages on Twitter and Facebook enquiring how Sean was now getting along. Very well was the answer. Sean himself highlighted what was important to him:

> Realising that I am not the only veteran suffering with similar symptoms of PTSD and gaining back my confidence. Immediately prior to my involvement with Op Nightingale, I spent three years caring for my terminally ill father, who passed away just prior to my volunteering through Breaking Ground Heritage, and as a consequence I had little contact with other people, so I really appreciated having social conversations with other people of similar backgrounds. I say without exaggeration that my involvement with BGH/Op Nightingale has given me a new lease of life and purpose. After the death of my father I could not see a future and could only see, possibly, progression into alcoholism and depression. Although I still have bouts of doubt and depression, which are getting less and less, I am now studying at university with a reason each day to 'crack on.'

At the University of Bradford, where Sean was now studying, he was almost certainly the most archaeologically experienced of his peers reading for a BSc. In fact, he was able to gain a dispensation from a part of his university training excavation requirement as he had already signed up for year two at Avon Camp with us! This sun-baked summer of 2022, with the savage solar reflection from the chalk (during the hottest temperatures on record in England), made for an incredible contrast with the wet blanketing of the dig in Orkneys, which Sean participated on immediately having finished on the Plain.

Some of the team that had experienced the recovery of historic human remains on Rat Island joined us at Avon Camp in 2021: another Falklands veteran Julian Pitt, Bridie Baines of the Royal Military Police, ex-submariner John Bennett and former Navy medic Lisa Randall. This was going to be a challenge for them as we were going to do things far more traditionally from an archaeological perspective than we did on Rat Island (see Chapter 3): working top downwards and horizontally. They would be required to draw plans, profiles, take photographs, levels and samples and all the other things needed for working on burials. They would all be learning from Jackie McKinley and thus, if you can meet these standards, you'll be fine on any dig.

This time we were able to use a machine to take off the topsoil and reveal that wonderful white chalk canvas into which the chocolate brown features of the archaeology are cut. We revealed a large circular ditch that had a central rectangular grave, set on the highest point of the landscape. We think this is significant. The 6th- and 7th-century cemeteries are sited on high points where they are visible from settlements in the river valleys, such as Figheldean and Ablington, both of which were already established and mentioned in the Domesday Book of AD 1286. Avon Camp is visible from Barrow Clump and there may well be links between the communities that placed their dead in these locations. Adjacent to the circular ring-ditch was a series of rectangular grave cuts.

At one point we thought we might have had a prehistoric feature; there was certainly prehistoric pottery and a Bronze Age barbed and tanged flint arrowhead in the fill of the central grave but, in lower layers, we found a skeleton with an iron spear and knife, clearly not Bronze Age! This was another Saxon grave and the prehistoric elements simply emphasised quite how material of previous periods was lying around in the general topsoil used to fill the grave.

If the competition for excavation highlights in the last year of Barrow Clump was between Dickie Bennett and Matt Smith, Avon Camp was a battle royale between John Bennett and former Fusilier Chris Burdon. Both are prominent in our work on roundhouses at Dunch Hill but this site saw them working together for the first time. Salisbury Plain and Stonehenge are interlinked so the Avon Camp excavation really is part of that whole story of the local landscape: 5.7 km (3.5 miles) lie between the two sites.

Each time one of the two protagonists made a discovery, the other seemed to follow and there was a constant pressure to keep up with the pair of them with the recording: photography, finds bags and drawing. In the Army corner was Chris with his star find being an antler comb, which had segments cut to form teeth and joined with a central antler spar held in place with iron rivets: fragile, delicate, beautiful and timeless – a functional item and most precious too. The gauntlet had been laid down!

For the Navy, John struck back with a quite incredible assemblage including silver ornaments, amethyst beads, a silver ring, an iron knife, a Saxon coin or *sceat* that had been perforated for suspension, and a collection of glass beads: a black pyramid example, blue and yellow and a Roman 'melon' with a lead core. If this wasn't enough, we thought he had also found a series of beaver teeth representing part of a necklace. These would be a typical find for the 7th century, as would the *sceat* and the amethyst. On closer examination, however, these 'teeth' turned out to be small fragments of cowry shell fashioned to look like teeth. At nearby Bulford a complete tiger cowry shell, possibly from as far away as the Red Sea,

Professor Alice Roberts discusses one of the graves with former submariner John Bennett. John has since begun his archaeology degree. © Harvey Mills

had been excavated accompanying a 7th-century burial but ours had been fashioned to form smaller components of a piece of jewellery.

On our return to Avon Camp in 2022 we uncovered a second burial within a ring ditch (and probable mound), finding a further adult male with no grave goods. While the patterns of burial largely followed those we had witnessed in the 2021 work, in 2022 we thought we had seen a couple of graves that were surrounded by shallow brown rectangles – the possible remains of a mortuary house or structure placed over the burial area. The one we excavated had the remains of an adult male at the bottom, arranged neatly on the chalk, with around 60% of an adult female thrown on top of him. Future scientific studies will assess whether these two individuals were related and will also address the outside chance that these burials are Roman. This was certainly a debating point amongst the team, including Darren Culley ('Daz') from the Royal Air Force, who had really been thrown in at the deep end with this piece of excavation work. Most of the other burials will not be radiocarbon dated as their grave goods are so well-placed chronologically but, as there was nothing accompanying these two individuals, further assessment of their date of burial is needed.

Camping on site in 2022 was spectacular; against a backdrop of frequent displays by the Black Eagles aerobatic team from South Korea and the regular parachuting practice of the Red Devils display team. Not only was it warm, but some of the Plain was alight following live firing into the artillery impact areas. This led to smoke and flames and was accompanied by sunsets of which the painter William Turner would have been proud. This combination did rather give the site the feel of looking into Tolkien's Mordor: I was rather relieved that the only ring that appeared on our site was with a series of blue beads, an antler comb and another Saxon *sceat* rather than their being ominous portents of any fellowship.

The second season on the site revealed another 26 or so burials; it was difficult to be precise on the exact number of individuals as some of the graves held parts of several people – one of the graves contained at least four individuals but there might have been more. The graves, cut deep into the chalk, varied in depth and some were much longer than others; the bodies within them were

Above: Royal Fusilier Chris Burdon in theatre. © Christopher Burdon

Left: Chris Burdon, now a guide for English Heritage at Stonehenge as well as an archaeologist and veteran. © Harvey Mills

Clockwise from bottom left:

Veterans watch on as one of the graves at Avon Camp is recorded. © Harvey Mills

Avon Camp 2022: Air Force, Navy, Army and archaeologists on site. © Harvey Mills

Chris Burdon recording the burial he has worked on at Avon Camp. © Harvey Mills

A double burial at Avon Camp in 2021 with a male at the bottom of the grave and a female above him. The latter had two pieces of marcasite with her. Further multiple burials were found in 2022. © Harvey Mills

sometimes crammed in, sometimes with much more space afforded.

My only slight regret with all the work on these early medieval cemeteries is that we have yet to find a single piece of garnet. Why the sadness? In the Sutton Hoo treasure and the Staffordshire Hoard (as well as at St Mary's Stadium, Southampton) mentioned earlier, there were objects that included garnets and the sites were broadly contemporaneous with Cherington and Avon Camp. These deep red gemstones had travelled some distance and, it is thought, might even have come from the Indian sub-continent. One excellent source is Afghanistan; how incredible would it have been if the finding of artefacts that hailed from an area in which participants had experienced their greatest and most effecting traumas actually helped their recovery? Witnessing the thrill of John, Chris and Sean as they excavated items of a similar vintage was still a wonderful experience demonstrating how working with the dead can help the living: the most astonishing, incongruous, counter-intuitive actuality.

Kenny and Tyler, riflemen who had both worked at Barrow Clump, also came to visit us at Avon Camp in 2022, the first time we'd seen them in a number of years and the former stayed to dig for a week, being probably one of the most experienced diggers on the site. Although the wellbeing components are assessed more formally, and to recognised scales, I have also sent round questions to the team about the key elements for success. The answers vary but there is one element that occurs consistently and appears in almost all returns: friendship. Kenny and Tyler are friends; their return is like a family member coming back and this is one of the things I most enjoy on the sites.

Having cautioned against the equation of a burial with a weapon being, necessarily, that of a warrior, the very first burial in 2022 did appear to have a clear cut wound to one arm, shearing off part of the elbow region while the arm still had flesh on it: the result of work by a sword or seax. The individual also seemed to have an older and partially healed wound to the skull and, to complete the story, one hand was situated by the pelvis even though the forearms were on the chest and wrists up to the chin. There were no items with this person, no sword, no shield, but their bones told a story.

No amethyst beads this year but some spectacular finds and it was the turn of Sean to make some of the major discoveries. One grave he worked on

A single grave which held at least five individuals. There were four skulls in the grave (two visible here) and the remains of a child at the top. © Harvey Mills

Harvey put together a montage of all the different burials from Avon Camp, Salisbury Plain in 2022.
© Harvey Mills

Top: One thing you are likely to get with 6th- and 7th-century burials is a series of rather beautiful grave goods. This was just some of the assemblage in 2021 with amethyst and glass beads, silver rings and parts of cowrie shells. © Harvey Mills

Middle: The third disc in the child's necklace found at Avon Camp in 2022 was intriguing. This image shows several views of it. It almost looks as precise as a watch mechanism with several pierced holes, a covering of silver and Saxon interweave designs. Does it depict a cross too? © Harvey Mills

Bottom: The child's grave excavated by Sean was cut deep down into the chalk with very neat sides. The small human had been buried with a beautiful necklace that included a couple of glass beads (shown here) and a series of copper alloy discs and perforated Roman coins. © Harvey Mills

with Hannah from Military Intelligence had a female's skeleton with an iron buckle, two knives and a whetstone; the most tactile of items with a smooth polished surface and grittier rougher edges. It would still have worked in sharpening knives or shears today. At the northern edge of the excavation was a small, deep grave cut. Beautifully dug down into the solid white rock with steep sides and a flat base, this grave was far more substantial than some of those created for the adults even though it was for a much smaller individual, a child of around 2–4 years of age. As with the burials of many youngsters, not much by way of bone survived; the bones are small and paper-thin, decaying away to nothing. We were left with portions of the skull, and legs: remnants of both femurs and a tibia. What was striking was the clear love that had gone into this burial. And this was certainly not lost on Sean who talked to the child as he worked. This small person had been provided with an exquisite necklace. It had a bead of blue glass that matched the colour of the sky when you held it up. Another was of more coloured glass and then there were two perforated late Roman coins (the latter are quite commonly found in Anglo-Saxon graves). Finally, there were two discs of bronze with suspension loops bearing traces of the original colour which had not turned to the familiar blue-green of corrosion products. The second of these discs had

Many archaeologists will be familiar with this: the deployment of a tarpaulin to provide shade for the photographer to work their magic.
© Harvey Mills

four precise circular perforations and traces of a Saxon interlace patterning; with the eye of faith (almost literally) one could make out a rough cross on this item. Was this therefore evidence of the early emergence of Christianity which really took hold in England in the very late 7th century? Almost emphasising the importance of this last disc was a thin fragment of silver, which Sean realised matched the second of the bronze discs for patterning and perforation – one could be superimposed on top of the other, which would have made the item even more precious.

Two of our volunteers, Kathy and Carlos (who usually never finds anything, so this was a real turn up!), found a further comb, lots of beads and a tiny, perforated cowry shell but I think it may well have been Sean's year for luck. The Saxon finds were spectacular but the human remains themselves will be informative too. We can look at the isotopes from the teeth, as mentioned, giving us information about their diets and places of origin but, most excitingly, the Crick Institute will examine the ancient DNA signatures to establish whether any of the people at Barrow Clump were related to those at Avon Camp, or indeed to other recent local excavations – a fascinating prospect and one which the veterans really want to know more about. On every site it is worth emphasising how the excavations and resulting stories are about people and their shared humanity with us as excavators. We have shared the landscapes and also hopes, ambitions and worries.

I called the Barrow Clump programme *Exercise Beowulf* in a nod to the early medieval, to treasures in barrows (and hopefully not dragons) and one of the all-time great stories.

Opposite: A possible rectangular mortuary enclosure surrounds a grave that held the remains of two individuals: under an incredible sunset, which was one of the joys of the 2022 field season at Avon Camp. The view looks out towards the artillery impact area of Salisbury Plain. © Harvey Mills

As with our First World War sites, the team always gathers together to say a few words when we have encountered human remains. Avon Camp. © Harvey Mills

7 LOCKING THE HOUSE

Finding and reconstructing a Bronze Age roundhouse

FROM THE VERY FIRST PROJECTS at East Chisenbury Midden we realised how valuable re-enactment and so-called 'experimental archaeology' could be in adding colour to our excavations and providing a very visual method of explanation about the sites to our participants. Imagining how structures and features may have looked when complete rather than simply the traces left behind after, in some cases, several thousand years is incredibly useful. It can also assist with testing theories of structural format, use and construction methods of objects and the effectiveness or otherwise of building styles. Other benefits of this part of archaeology are that anyone can make suggestions on how to build the structures, which can be tested, and also that the work is generally undertaken in the open air and needs an investment of time to succeed. As we shall see, these latter elements proved crucial during the periods of the COVID-19 pandemic from 2020.

Experimental work can take many forms; we have mentioned pot-making and food at East Chisenbury, and the Saxon objects and costumes

Above: A room with a view. Our roundhouse at Butser Ancient Farm. © Alice Roberts

Opposite: Caroline from Pario Gallico serves up a Bronze Age feast to the team who are clearly eyeing up second helpings. © Harvey Mills

of Weorod at Barrow Clump and Avon Camp. We also had other highlights that both inspired and fascinated our veterans: blacksmith Ian Thackray using traditional smithing techniques to make a knife in the same style as that found in a grave at Avon Camp, and Drs Jackie Mulville and Susan Greaney challenging our teams to make a palatable menu from foodstuffs present in the Neolithic. The results were extraordinary, and so removed from any prejudice one might have of bland, colourless gruels being the staple of the Neolithic as to really challenge views on how people might have lived in the past.

Experimental work also can make use of real skills that our participants have (even if they don't realise it at the offset); of lateral thinking and problem solving, or artistic talents, of guiding people around the results of their endeavours. It really can inspire them; we met one of the team, ex-sniper Rob Steel, at an open day at the Ancient Technology Centre on Cranborne Chase in Dorset, in the south of England. Clearly the time spent in a smoke-filled roundhouse had a lasting effect on him in that he really aspires to create a 'not for profit organisation aimed at helping all those suffering mental health with the use of experimental archaeology'. His ambition is laudable and I really hope that this book will one day be on sale in the shop appended to his project site!

Dunch Hill is a later Bronze Age settlement site lying close to an area used predominantly to train drivers on the east side of Salisbury Plain and is one of its richest areas of archaeology. Many years ago, it was included on a list of *Heritage at Risk* by Historic England resulting from the fact that part of the very large Scheduled Monument was being ploughed. As this was on the Training Area, it was a relatively simple task for me to request that this ploughing consent was removed. The fields in question are a palimpsest of prehistoric archaeology, with field systems, linear ditches and burial mounds all making their mark in the chalk. During the conflict in Afghanistan we were able to gain permission to place a series of containers at the edge of this landscape to act as proxy for a village through which soldiers could train. The burial mounds were included as a 'cultural site' to add complexity and, hopefully, awareness that the subjects of 'heritage' and 'culture' are of genuine importance.

There is a stone track that runs across Dunch Hill towards the driving area and when you drive along it you get views of the wonderful prehistory in the area; with the Bronze Age Barrows of Silk Hill and Goat Wood right up to all the elements of Dunch Hill itself. What you might not appreciate, however, is that this track runs directly over the top of some precious and important archaeology too. Over twenty years ago, when the track was first put down, Phil Andrews led a Wessex Archaeology inspection of the route to consider what excavation might be needed, if any. In so doing, he and his team found the remnants of four Late Bronze Age roundhouses, surviving as circular arrangements of holes, in which had once stood the wooden uprights of the house. My feeling was that it was highly unlikely that the road had exposed the entirety of the settlement and I was keen to examine whether the military training and the preceding ploughing regimes had removed all other traces of this village. There are so many Bronze Age monuments across the Plain that it is a real curiosity that Dunch Hill is pretty much the only collection of houses of this date that we know about.

All the plans were in place for a field season to look for a house outside the Scheduled Area and then news came of the spread of a very serious virus which affected the entire globe: Coronavirus. With all the anxieties and uncertainties of the ensuing periods of 'lockdown' and changing restrictions on movement and meeting other people, it was tough for anyone, let alone those with underlying mental health challenges. We were incredibly fortunate that much of *Exercise Roundhouse*, our plan to locate a Bronze Age structure at Dunch Hill, fell between such restriction periods even though

A large tracked artillery vehicle (an AS90) moves past the excavation site. The track on which it is driving had four roundhouses beneath it. © Harvey Mills

we had to have rigorous pandemic safeguarding protocols present on site.

One of the elements we included from the start was a major programme of survey, around 40 hectares (99 acres) of it. With license from Historic England to work across the Scheduled Monument, the Wessex Archaeology survey team ran their magnetometers over vast tracts of land to reveal the patterns of fields and enclosures in which the roundhouses sat some 3000 years ago. This was followed by the physical digging of a small area adjacent to the track and field systems in the hope of finding traces of a roundhouse and perhaps even elements of associated midden. Professor Richard Bradley of the University of Reading had noted this some years before in his work on the massively long bank and ditch earthworks known as Bronze Age linear ditches that are a feature of the English downlands and particularly well preserved on Salisbury Plain.

Stripping the thin topsoil off to the underlying chalk revealed the presence of linear scars that tracked across the area, the evidence of ploughing over many years. This might also have been the reason that we were not able to pick up any evidence for the midden, the collection of pot sherds we recovered being far less substantial than recovered in earlier work; perhaps as it had been spread across the field. Fortunately for us it was an altogether different story when it came to postholes; there were a very large number of them, giving the site the look of a Dalmatian dog with dark splodges standing out clearly against the white bedrock.

From above, the postholes of the roundhouse stand out against the chalk and the beautiful location of the Bronze Age farm is equally apparent. © Harvey Mills

The problem was, however, to make sense of any patterns or configurations within the spread of postholes and other dark splodges, just as it had been with Iron Age structures we had seen at Chisenbury Midden. Phil Andrews is nothing if not persistent and was eventually able to tease out a plan of the site based on his observations and the site drawings of Dave Murdie. This plot included fence lines demarcated by rows of smaller stakeholes, and so-called 'four post structures', familiar on Iron Age settlements and traditionally interpreted as storage structures or granaries, raised on poles in much the same method as 'staddles' (the stone mushrooms you see in old villages propping up barns and other farm buildings) were used in the medieval period to keep crops away from the ground and out of the reach of vermin. These structures are now simply four holes in the ground marking the shape of a square with a posthole at each corner; at Dunch Hill they were pretty regularly spaced, 2 m (6½ ft) apart. It was not lost on any of us that one of the governmental health recommendations of the time was that people should try to keep a 2 m distance from each other; it was almost as if this site had been designed with a pandemic in mind.

In addition to fences and granaries, there were a great many other postholes, almost too many to make any sense of. Phil called me one evening to say that, finally, he had been able to identify a circle (of very similar dimension to the houses found around 25 years before at some 7 m/23 ft diameter) among some of the holes we had excavated, many of which had also contained Late Bronze Age pottery around 800–700 BC in date. One of the deepest features on the site, some way to the south of our putative roundhouse, produced a quantity of the gritty and scrappy Bronze Age pottery that we were uncovering across the site. It also held a fired blank rifle round! So, this big feature was in fact one of the many thousands of infantry 'foxholes' cut across Salisbury Plain. Bizarrely, as the soil had slumped into it after use, this had helped preserve an element of 'midden' as the plough skimmed over the top of the hole. This part of the excavation was accomplished by one of our new members, former Fusilier Chris Burdon, who also works as a guide for English

Heritage at the world famous Stonehenge not far from Dunch Hill.

> A few colleagues at work knew I had an interest in archaeology and suggested I should have a look at Op Nightingale to pursue this interest. I found the Facebook page and saw a post asking for volunteers, so I registered my interest. I loved every second of this dig! This was my first excavation (outside of my garden!) and I learnt so much. I felt like part of the team right from day one, something I hadn't felt since I left the army. I also had the find of the dig with my Late Bronze Age disc-headed pin! Since taking part in digs my confidence has soared! This is something I have struggled with since leaving the army. Also being part of a team with other Vets who understand and allow you to be open and honest about issues has massively helped with my anxiety and depression.

So not only pottery and a modern military find, Chris had excavated a star find with his pin. Such discoveries really do help to fire the enthusiasm.

We had long wanted to try an experimental project as this had been so successful at a smaller scale. Dunch Hill gave us just this opportunity as, although we had the postholes, there was still plenty of room for interpretation as to how this building might have looked. This also enabled us to embark on a programme of research that any of our team could do from home on their computer, so vital as further lockdowns occurred and the need for community, friendship and things to do, rose accordingly. Building this house would require many hours of work and such a project was perfect when isolation was bad for everyone, let alone those suffering from underlying issues.

Clockwise from bottom left:

Former household cavalryman Mark Wight cleaning some of the Dunch Hill postholes while a modern artillery crew have a site tour. © Harvey Mills

Getting comfortable. An important consideration on site is how the participants can accomplish their tasks while still considering their ailments. © Harvey Mills

Making sense of the patterns of features at Dunch Hill. Carlos Rocha, in the front of the image, made some of his first finds here. © Harvey Mills

Right: The inimitable Dave Murdie of Wessex Archaeology. His carefully measured, drawn plan at Dunch Hill revealed the configuration of the roundhouse. © Harvey Mills

Below: Not bad for your first find; a Late Bronze Age disc-headed pin in the hands of Chris Burdon. © Harvey Mills

The first step was for our participants to familiarise themselves with the Bronze Age, to research this era in their locality. As we were, by this point, supposed to be staying at home unless deemed to be 'key workers', museum visits were not possible. However, so much research can now be done remotely, many county Historic Environment Records (HERs) are online, as are aerial photographs, images from other experimental works, and publications. We could also share academic papers and data derived from such experts as Dr Rachel Pope whose PhD thesis *Prehistoric Dwelling: circular structures in north and central Britain c 2500 BC–AD 500* was available online for the University of Durham – perfect! Rachel was incredibly generous with both her knowledge and encouragement and this is something we have found throughout from academics, back to the early days of colleagues Phil Abramson and Martin Brown working on a Roman site at Caerwent with Professor Simon James. As we have said, from the start we wished to 'do no harm' to participants, but the same went for the archaeology. One of the veterans, Mark Wight, formerly of the Blues and Royals, produced a really interesting essay on the nature of conflict in the Bronze Age. Were we able to go to pubs I would have loved to discuss his findings over a pint and it really showed, once again, that so many of our team were able to pair their military skills with their new knowledge to produce fresh and thoughtful conclusions.

Armed with the knowledge of Bronze Age matters from all the research we had done, I think we all approached the idea of a house build with thoughts of how we might wish to progress. But this is very much one thing and the practicalities of production another. Step forward the charity Step Together Volunteering. Under Elaine (whom we had first met as a volunteer working on the Spitfire finds but who was now organising veterans to get onto other projects) the group worked with us to consider what elements would work for our house-building project. Not simply the house itself, but all the events, people and choreography that would make such a programme memorable.

I had been chatting with Trevor Creighton about a possible joint endeavour with his employers at Butser Ancient Farm for a while. Butser was a site established by the late Dr Peter Reynolds to run various practical experiments to inform our understanding of the prehistoric past. How much wood was needed to build a roundhouse, and thus how big an area would need to be managed and cleared? How can you store grain in pits and would it last for any length of time? How can you dig ditches with only antler picks and animal shoulder blades? How many people would this take and for how long? These were really interesting questions that I was familiar with from my distant undergraduate days and something I think all students should consider trying, as it really is illuminating. Not only does Butser have lots of reconstructed Iron Age houses, there is a Roman villa, two Saxon longhouses and a very splendid Neolithic house based on one excavated at Horton in Berkshire. There was a noticeable gap in this historic housing estate, namely a Bronze Age element.

Between us all, we drew up plans for our house. Butser found us a suitable part of their land and Step Together gained an Armed Forces Community Covenant grant, which meant that our fortunate participants would be able to immerse themselves in the Bronze Age and its wonders. Looking back on things, it does seem rather ambitious to embark upon such a project with a team that, for the most part, had no experience of this work at all. I am so glad we did though. Butser is located in the most beautiful of landscapes; an oasis of calm and tranquillity where wisps of woodsmoke thread past thatched buildings and cackling woodpeckers flit past or a herd of deer cross the surrounding hills. The embodiment of catharsis and a location that makes you sing; not least when our ability to get out and about was so curtailed. As we could 'socially distance' and were volunteers, we were able to build.

Our first stage, with the Butser expert Claire Walton, was to start making fencing akin to that which was on site at Dunch Hill, with wooden

One of the Butser craftsmen, Darren, explaining the niceties of trimming timber uprights for the roundhouse to the team. © Harvey Mills

Dave discovers the strengths (and weaknesses) of the Bronze Age axe. © Harvey Mills

stakes and interweaving strands to make hurdles so as to demarcate our 'farmstead', all under the watchful eyes of the Manx sheep and English goats that live on the farm. This task was completed remarkably quickly and boded well for the rest of the project. We soon had a track leading to a small open paddock with wonderful views but no roundhouse! In addressing this, we had a couple of main rules. First, the arrangement of posts we were to use had to match the floor plan identified at Dunch Hill precisely. Secondly, every building style we aimed to use at Butser must have been possible at Dunch Hill too. Walls of turf, chalk, 'clunch' (a mixture of earth, animal hair, chalk and water), and wattle could all be permitted. Although there was no direct evidence for this on our dig, all the material was local and probably incredibly sustainable, leaving no trace in the ground. We were starting from a fortunate position that Butser lies on the same chalk spur as Salisbury Plain, so our underlying geology was a decent match. By trying these different walling types we might also get some useful information on what worked best in the Bronze Age, and how often it needed to be repaired; both good questions.

With all the fieldwork it is enjoyable to have a real sense of occasion, especially at the start, and thus it was that Phil Harding, long-standing employee of Wessex Archaeology and veteran of the *Time Team* television series, cut the first turf as we cleared a circle ready to dig postholes in the exact configuration of our Dunch Hill findings. I say the first turf, but Phil stayed to deturf the entire area, teaching the veterans this important art. Many of them had grown up watching *Time Team* and so were quite willing to listen to this lesson.

Something that experimental work gives you is a healthy respect for those that lived before. Once the turf was off, the next stage was to dig out the holes for the posts once we had plotted them on the ground using our Dunch Hill plan. Starting with the best of intentions, huge cow shoulder blades attached to wooden poles were used to scrape away the surface flints while antlers, flint tools and fire-hardened sticks were used to try to dig out the postholes – but what a palaver! The work was both backbreaking and blister inducing, and we eventually finished with some more modern implements. Stage two was initially easier, hardening the bases of the timber uprights using fire, which helps to deter rotting once the post is in the ground. This was after they had been cut to size and shaped with bronze axes, which required constant sharpening, and both of which broke, or at least the bindings holding the metal tools to the hafts did. The timbers with charred ends were then raised into place and we had the beginnings of a house even though it looked very like a Neolithic timber henge at this point.

We had used replica bronze tools of a type found in the Bronze Age to begin shaping the timbers but there is nothing quite like the experience of seeing such objects being made, witnessing genuine 'alchemy' with a transformation of green rock to gleaming bronze metal thanks to fire. We all had a go at making bronze axes at Butser and everyone managed to get some small blobs of copper to begin the process from ore that had been mixed with charcoal and then fired at around 1100°C using extensive bellows work. Copper was then added to tin (in fact the remnants of cut-down tankards inside clay crucibles and heated at a similarly high temperature until molten then poured into fine sand axe moulds. After allowing these to cool, the moulds were opened to reveal

Above: Grinding down malachite to try to extract copper: let the alchemy begin! © Harvey Mill

Below: Former Royal Logistics Corps soldier Kevin (right) pours molten bronze into a mould as we make our first axe under the expert eye of James Clift. © Harvey Mills

First building stage complete as a timber circle is in place ready for the lintels. © Harvey Mills

the finished objects. Most of these had worked incredibly well although one had a series of small holes – casting flaws – with it. The great thing about bronze is that it can be re-melted and poured once more to form a new object and this is why you get collections of scrap bronze in the Bronze Age with smiths being able to recycle lots of material. All the smells and colours and heat of the activity within one of the existing roundhouses seemed so effortlessly timeless and really opened the mind to the work we were doing as well as emphasising the magic, skill and craft involved and just how valuable these items would have been.

While bronze would have been at the forefront of technology 3000 years ago, our walling materials had more of a basic, fundamental quality to them: turf, earth, clunch (which sets almost as hard as concrete), a gabion box of wicker filled with flint, earth and sheep wool, and wattle and daub. All these materials would have been present at Bronze Age Dunch Hill. This was the really valuable element academically as we made one wall of the house from each of these materials and will monitor their effectiveness and durability over time, balanced against ease of material acquisition and availability and perhaps even their traces left in the ground.

The turf we cut from the house footprint was only enough to create one wall, an interesting start, and this led to thoughts of how much bare ground you would be creating in an entire village of houses. This turf, around a year on, has already consolidated and is growing well, or at least it was prior to the summer drought and hosepipe bans in Hampshire in 2022. I suppose this will also give us data on how houses of the past coped with hot summers.

The other walls involved a high degree of getting filthy, incorporating animal dung and hair and generally the sort of things that everyone loves, including the youngsters that came onto site for the family day. These walls rose slowly and dried gradually but soon the structure had the genuine look of a roundhouse with one noteworthy exception: no roof. Although the timbers had been joined to crossbeams around the timber uprights to form a cone above the walls, we still needed to provide a suitable covering; in this case of interwoven reeds. Another conundrum too; on our excavation there was a posthole right in the middle of the house where other reconstructions placed a hearth. We had no evidence for the latter but were not convinced that the central posthole was necessarily part of the house. Nevertheless, we decided to utilise this as a post to lie directly below the pinnacle of the roof and as something that could be used to hold items.

We thought that this would be as straightforward as the experimental walls were ambitious, based on confidence in the ability of the participants. After a day of training with a professional thatcher (what an art form) it was over to the veterans and Butser team members to see if we could complete the build. John Bennett, our finds-magnet from Avon Camp, turned from submariner to master thatcher with uncanny aplomb.

In addition to the fallacy of food being a downright miserable affair in the past (disproved once again from a Bronze Age perspective by Caroline Nicolay here at Butser) another misconception is that everything must have been drab and bland, a life in beige. Art, colour and the aesthetic must surely have been as important 3000 years ago as it is today and this was something we all wanted to emphasise in our house. Cord was made from twisted plant fibres stripped from branches, useful for tying-in roof thatch as well as for internal constructions and you can't beat a session on making pottery, so this also took place. Luckily, the pottery we had found at Dunch Hill was so grotty (and I like prehistoric pot) that our efforts were perfectly acceptable. We discussed the

A circle of turf has been removed and the timbers follow the pattern of the Dunch Hill postholes. At this point it was hard to believe this would look like a house. © Harvey Mills

Wayne Hamlett adds some ties (made from stripped bark) to the rood rafters in readiness for the thatching process. © Harvey Mills

various colours and pigments available to decorate the walls of our house, from ochres through to chalk itself, and drew on all the research elements from lockdown periods to think about designs.

Years ago, my old tutor, the late Professor Andrew Sherratt, somehow persuaded a television channel to let him make a series of programmes called *Sacred Weeds* as he was convinced that some of the art from prehistory was heavily 'influenced' by the taking of limited quantities of narcotics, from henbane through to the famous spotted toadstools (fly agaric). His work was formative and included noticing the resemblance of certain pot types to the centres of poppies before he discovered that the residues within did indeed contain traces of opioids. Andrew was also convinced that hallucinogens may have resulted in some of the spirals and lozenges on sites of the Neolithic and Bronze Age of the British Isles and administered small amounts to willing volunteers to check on the artistic results! We had no need to draw upon this, even if the medication taken by some participants can be pretty strong, and nothing stronger than coffee was required for us to decorate the now chalk-washed walls of the roundhouse.

Rock art was one of our influences, echoing an early Operation Nightingale project run by Phil Abramson at Battlehill in County Durham, laser scanning rock carvings. Spirals were in evidence too as were depictions of the people and animals you find in Scandinavian carvings of the Bronze Age, and there was even our interpretation of the extraordinary Nebra sky disc, some months before the real item was the star of the British Museum

After only an hour or two of teaching, we were all happy to let John Bennett (left) take control of the thatching: he was a natural. © Harvey Mills

John Bennett (age 44)

I asked John which of the projects he had found to be the best. He replied:

I don't really have a favourite as for me they are linked together as a part of my recovery and a new beginning and direction – they were all very awesome!

Getting involved with the Bronze Age roundhouse build at Butser was initially a stepping stone to me being able to work again and having social interaction – social interaction being a big trigger for my Functional Neurological Disorder (FND) associated with Complex PTSD.

It has greatly improved my confidence with other people and myself. I started off really struggling to interact with people and not being triggered by them to having a TV interview with Alice Roberts! Until very recently you wouldn't have got me near a video camera! Having always been fairly shy (I was recently diagnosed with Asperger's too), my participation has really helped to bring me out of my shell.

Butser gave him a few genuine highlights:

Digging turf on the first day of the roundhouse project with Phil Harding was just brilliant! Having grown up watching *Time Team* and then to work alongside him and getting advice was quite surreal.

The camaraderie is one of the biggest and main elements of this. Making me feel like I belong and has done wonders for my self-esteem. It not just about going to the sites, it is also sharing them with new friends and looking forward to catching up with them. I feel much less isolated than I did before. I do still volunteer at Butser and have recently been helping to thatch another roundhouse there.

I had also started a degree in Archaeology at Winchester University as part of a free programme for military veterans who had been medically retired. Unfortunately, only weeks into starting the degree we had the devastating news that my wife was diagnosed with terminal pancreatic cancer and so my degree is on hold for now – I will be going back later. The camaraderie and care from others involved in Op Nightingale and continued volunteering and meet-ups is really helping me in this difficult time. Knowing that there are still more digs and projects to get involved with and looking forward to going back to university to become an archaeologist are all really helpful in giving me a focus and direction and currently a distraction too.

Being with like-minded people who have also gone through traumatic events and come out the other side. Up until getting involved with Op Nightingale I was fairly isolated, and I had no real direction and had been suicidal at times. My FND would flare up so badly that I couldn't really see a future and was especially triggered by people.

It was incredible to see this change in John; he was supervising us all with the techniques of thatching by the end of the build and the quality of the roof is a real testament to his abilities.

John Bennett in his Navy days. © John Bennett

I have no doubts whatsoever that the Late Bronze Age had much by way of decoration and art and the team made sure our roundhouse fitted this. © Harvey Mills

exhibition based around the age of Stonehenge. Yellow, brown, red and white tones gave the house a warm feel and then wooden benches and shelves and dried plants added to the homeliness.

Another army veteran, Wayne Hamlett, showed himself to be incredibly adept at wood-turning, with spoons and bowls forthcoming. These were incredibly useful for our purposes and the sorts of things found in waterlogged conditions on real Bronze Age sites, such as the wondrous Must Farm in Cambridgeshire. Wooden items also found a central role in the house, we decided to have our own attempt at carving figures based on the Roos Carr Warriors (two small, male wooden figures mounted on a simple boat) from East Yorkshire. Were these votive representations from the Late Bronze (or Early Iron) Age, or something more prosaic? Children's toys? Children are often ignored in discussions of the archaeological record and yet there must have been things to play with. The figures, to modern eyes, are perhaps a little disconcerting with their quartz pebble eyes staring from yew faces. They also seem to have very male attributes (detachable), which provided much amusement for our team in their reconstructions. We made our own glue with wax, resin and charcoal for both eyes and phallus and Wayne even fashioned moveable arms. Thankfully his ambition ended there.

During the build, some of us were fortunate enough to sleep out in some of the buildings; the women choosing the Neolithic 'Horton' house, the men opting for the Saxon longhouse; the mead consumed being something to add to the overall experience. This really does enable you to immerse yourself in a feeling of the time and also of tranquillity. Though any romantic notions of the sounds of owls and nature and crackle of fire being all-pervasive was really drowned out by a group of snoring men.

To close our project, in similar fashion to Chisenbury Midden, we decided to place one of the 'Bronze Age' pots as a foundation deposit in the threshold of the roundhouse; unobtrusive and something that visitors will not know is there. This was the archaeology of us, of our project and lived experiences. Who knows, archaeologists of the future may well discover something about us from the items team members chose as their placed offerings to the site; perhaps misinterpreting them just as surely we do the items from millennia ago. Everyone chose something relevant to themselves and the time and they included part of a prosthetic leg, a sherd of pottery from Chisenbury midden – our first ever project – and a lateral flow test kit. Submariner, or rather, Master Thatcher, John offered a Jaguar, badge from a 250 km race he had accomplished in the Amazon where he had seen a live Jaguar, but he also placed a small figure of a phoenix in the pot too, to represent the participants on the project recovering and restoring from their own personal flames. 'One of the two objects to represent myself that I buried at the blessing ceremony for the Bronze

Age roundhouse was a phoenix – coming out the ashes stronger and smarter than before, I felt that it represented most of us there,' said John.

The door posts were now decorated in colourful lozenges, inspired by the gold objects from Bush Barrow, which lies within sight of Stonehenge, that are now in Wiltshire Museum and a hole was dug to hold our pot in readiness for the grand opening at which Phil Harding and Rachel Pope would be in attendance. Alice Roberts had the duty of placing the pot into its resting place (along with the task of cutting our Bronze Age hut cake with a Bronze sword). After having had a look inside the roundhouse she said, 'I've come out as a Bronze Age person. I've experienced what it's like to be inside a Bronze Age house,' and there could be no bigger compliment.

I love reconstruction drawings and art that you see on notice boards and in books but there is nothing quite like the tangible to make things clear to all ages. Walking round the house, along wicker-lined droveways to the sounds of sheep bleating and the smell of woodsmoke as your eyes adjust to the darkened interior, you begin to see the accoutrements, the art, the comfort and you think of those people on Salisbury Plain all those thousands of years ago. It truly is wonderful for the spirit. We see the Bronze Age as it was, in colour, and have the pervasive smell of bonfires in our jumpers that has its own nostalgia. If sitting round a fire ('Hexi TV') is a phenomenon we have encountered on sites as being something so elemental for life and wellbeing, just think on the multiplier when it is sited within a prehistoric house you have created, in a landscape of aching beauty with all the best elements of nature surrounding you.

So, what is the roundhouse like to live in? I'm not sure we'll know this unless there is a much longer-term piece of experimental work but some of the team have now slept in it. During the heatwaves in England in August 2022, three of the

Wayne cleans a deer skin, a useful resource to people in the Bronze Age. He was also an expert wood carver, ideal for kitting out the house. © Harvey Mills

team who are now close friends, Jacqui Hutchings, Jackie Crutchfield and Elaine Corner, escaped the flaming temperatures and the hosepipe bans to stay for a night in the house. There was a dramatic full moon to add to the vibe and Jacqui felt that it was actually the 'perfect temperature, comfy bed, excellent blackout and great ambience'. Elaine concurred with this description: 'it was so exciting to sleep in the house we built. It was nice and cool despite the heat. It was also a fantastic location to wake up in'. Again, location seems simply to add to one's contentment and this will, I think (and hope), always be the human condition. As long as we, as a species, can appreciate the beauty of nature there is hope for us. Jackie felt that it 'always feels calm and welcoming coming to our house. It was lovely and peaceful and a cool temperature to sleep in. I slept so well I didn't see the sunrise, I slept in til 8 am!'. So the house gets a big thumbs up for summer use, perhaps the next test will be the middle of winter. I'll ask for volunteers.

The Dunch Hill team, often in their project T-shirts, meet up regularly, and are now helping with a new Iron Age structure at Butser. They guide visitors around the site and tell them of the whole build project and the excavation work and research that preceded it. They help to organise parking at some of the big event days too, these invariably involve drumming and fire – from the Viking ship burning to the torching of a wicker man. At these occasions, in addition to any duties performed on site, I know we all watch very carefully for any stray sparks dancing over from the flaming centrepiece of the celebration just to make sure our roundhouse does not have an incendiary component to its experimental role.

Our roundhouse and the research beforehand got many of us through lockdown. It also served to emphasise that archaeology is not solely about digging and excavations, there are so many facets to it that really can help people. The long-term investment required at Butser works wonders; the team can continue to meet and to accomplish work. Fences need to be mended, dewponds dug,

Our house in colour, with experimental turf and 'clunch' wall visible. © Harvey Mills

A building opening wouldn't be the same without a suitable cake. Alice Roberts does the honours of cutting, using a bronze sword with frighteningly good technique. © Harvey Mills

thatch repaired, daub and artwork re-applied. The monitoring and assessment of the structure continues as do the endeavours of participants who now have a new safe space to visit and to bring family and friends to, seeing their accomplishments and perhaps joining in.

Chris and John agree that these facets have been important. Chris wrote that:

> I helped with the research for the Bronze Age house build and visited Butser Ancient Farm. I have also researched the military on Salisbury plain to gain a better knowledge of the impact of the army and the landscape in general. Op Nightingale has really helped me become more confident and open about my experiences. It has also helped me realise there is more to life than the army and I now have a new dream of being an archaeologist, something that I never thought was possible for me to do!

John concurred and, when asked what his family thought of it all, told me 'They absolutely love it! – especially seeing the change in me. They like seeing and hearing all about what I have been doing and that I am now going to be an Archaeologist – so cool!'. Whilst the Bronze Age project might well have helped to facilitate a pathway into archaeology for a couple of the team, it is just one of the positive elements we have always looked for. Just as important are the friendships forged around fires of molten rock, for this is the true alchemy.

Opposite: The Dunch Hill farm at Butser from the air, complete with hurdle fences and dewpond. © Harvey Mills

8 HOMES OF THE DEAD

Discoveries at a burial mound on Salisbury Plain

STAND AT STONEHENGE on the edge of Salisbury Plain and consider what you can see. You are surrounded. Mounds of grass like giant anthills are present wherever you gaze, on every ridgeline, encircling the great stone monument. These are round barrows; later than the stones themselves but illustrating that this place in the landscape continued to be of importance from the Neolithic into the Early Bronze Age, over 4000 years ago. Some of the barrows are positioned in rows overlooking the henge, on King Barrow Ridge immediately to the west for example where, in the early morning, their shadows reach out towards this venerated spot. In summer they are a blaze of colour with exotic native orchids, the bursting fireworks of scabius and small butterflies the colour of a perfect blue summer sky. You almost feel watched from these barrows or 'tumuli' as they are often marked on the maps and it is not hard to see how they inspired Tolkien's 'Barrow Wights' in *The Lord of the Rings* – a spectral presence within the ancient tombs. He had also visited nearby Tidworth Pennings close to the Silk Hill barrow cemetery during Officer Training Corps when at school, so perhaps there is a direct local link.

Most of the barrows have been excavated in the past, many in the 18th and 19th centuries, by

Above: Causing trouble. An active badger sett in a barrow at Netheravon unearthed some astonishing items. © Alice Roberts

Opposite: When pieced back together, the collared urn from Netheravon was huge and really rather splendid. © Harvey Mills

so-called 'Antiquaries'; clerics, doctors, gentlemen and the occasional early archaeologist. Some of the discoveries made were extraordinary, not least the collection of exquisite items that were uncovered in the so-called Bush Barrow, which lies within sight of Stonehenge, which includes gold lozenges, daggers, maceheads and enough craft skill and artistic merit to show any sceptic that this was a period of incredible human achievement. But not everything has been recovered; antiquarian excavation shafts dug down to the centre of mounds frequently missed elements of equal importance that lay beneath other parts of the monument – and fashions of retention policy have changed. In the past it was not uncommon simply for the objects, the 'treasure', to be recovered with the human bones put back into the monument. Or for the skulls alone to be retained, leaving a now disarticulated and headless remnant in the ground. This means that there is still important archaeology to be found or, on occasion, to be unearthed by animals burrowing within these homes of the dead. Such was the case in a barrow that Operation Nightingale investigated at Netheravon on Salisbury Plain.

The old air base at Netheravon Camp retains its early 20th-century black and white half-timbered buildings. I think this is the only place in the world with 'Royal Flying Corps wings' above the door to the old officers' mess; the Flying Corps ceased to exist on 1 April 1918 with the formation of the Royal Air Force, towards the end of the First World War. Just outside the gates there is a tiny area of woodland, and in a small glade within it lie three mounds, all prehistoric in origin. These barrows are Early Bronze Age in date and had become covered with scrub and suffered the effects of badger burrowing and the impromptu creation of some off-road bicycle ramps. Rather unsurprisingly the barrows were deemed by Historic England to be 'Heritage at Risk' and thus my attention to them was heightened. I thought of a plan of works to improve the monuments – the first stage being a scrub-cutting programme to, hopefully, encourage recolonisation of chalk grassland, thus creating a pleasant spot outside the military camp. Perhaps this could be followed by placing meshing over the tumuli to keep the animals out.

A contractor was appointed to cut the scrub and this work was supervised by a friend who worked for Landmarc (one of the companies that assists the land management work for the Ministry of Defence), Tom Theed. We didn't expect that such rudimentary work would lead to an Operation Nightingale project but over the next few hours this situation changed dramatically, starting with a series of messages from Tom. These were initially entertaining (and surprising!) and then became increasingly astonishing.

On a Saturday he sent some messages to tell me that workmen had found some 'crockery' (their words) by a badger hole on the monument. As he examined the location, he could see that there were indeed some large sherds of pottery, with decoration, some of them freshly broken. The pieces were from a very large vessel and were not on their own. Soon he had found some antler, some worked bone, a flint artefact (in fact a very fine 'plano-convex' knife) and finally a bronze item that looks a little like the ring pull from a can – though it is around 4000 years old. A photograph of each new discovery made was sent to me in an email, the magnitude of the site's importance increasing with each message. His concluding comment was: 'I am out of my depth and have stopped looking!'

First thing on Monday I visited the site with Tom and a colleague, Sarah Hicks, and we went through the upcast material from the sett. We were rewarded with more pottery, a smooth, cold, rectangular stone archer's wristguard or 'bracer', two stone items with grooves described as being 'arrow straighteners', and a bronze chisel still encased in an antler handle, which had small circular decorations around its base. This latter item was in such good condition it could quite easily have been dropped by one of the workmen – were it not for the fact that it was of an Early

Bronze Age type! In amongst this debris was the remains of a life, cremated human bone, which dusted the top of the barrow that had once sheltered it.

The question was, what to do next? The material that had been cast out of the badger sett was of such importance that we really needed to contextualise it, prior to getting the requisite permissions to add protection measures to the barrow to prevent further damage. All this takes time and money but was an imperative as the monument was already deemed to be 'at risk' even before our discoveries. The manager of our environmental section, Richard Brooks, allocated some of his budget to this task and we were able to put together a team of veterans, volunteers, and archaeologists to investigate a portion of the barrow. First, though, Historic England completed topographic and geophysical surveys to show us the nature of the sett and also the evidence of past human excavation work. Cue the return of Phil Andrews, Dave Murdie and Jackie McKinley of Wessex Archaeology and a dig to establish as much as we could about the nature of the 'crockery'.

Since Barrow Clump, one of the ever-present participants in the Operation Nightingale projects had been our old army tent that provided both shelter and an immediate location for work on finds. Putting up this faithful friend was the first stage of the projects and now all the civilian volunteers are equally adept at putting the frame and canvas together. There was a familiar smell about this tent, of past digs, that was quite comforting and it would be our on-site home as usual. As I write this, we have just finished our first season without it – the tent blew away in a huge gale at Butser – landing hundreds of metres away never to be used again as some of the main supporting poles had bent beyond repair. Having a 'breakout' space is important. We have a nominal routine for hours on site, but it is crucial that people can get away from it all should they need to, for a rest, a place to clear their head of certain thoughts, somewhere just to get a tea or coffee. Our tent provided all

Some of the barrow finds really were rather special: an archer's wristguard, a flint knife, a bronze item we called the 'ring-pull' and still haven't identified, two pieces of a bronze saw, and a bronze chisel in a decorated bone handle. © Harvey Mills

Rob Cummings (1st Battalion, Scots Guards, age 56)

I first got involved with Op Nightingale whilst I was down in Wiltshire at Help for Heroes; my key worker had known that I was interested in archaeology, and knowing that Richard was going to be doing a radio broadcast for BBC Wiltshire, introduced me to Richard, and this was to become a relationship that still goes on today.

The first of my two tours in Northern Ireland was not a great tour for our battalion, as one day whilst we were out doing top-cover sentry, we came under sniper fire and in all the melee, one of my very good friends took two direct hits, one in the neck and one in the chest; we were later to find he died on the way to the hospital. The other incident involved another member in the battalion, when he took his own life due to things that had happened at home. Cookstown in 1990 was a better tour for us as it went by without any major incidents; the Belfast tour was to later be the start of a downward spiral in my mental health.

Op Granby 91 [the codename for the First Gulf War] was full on from the start, as warfare of any type is a theatre where you have to have your wits about you all the time, and although I wasn't aware of it at the time this was the theatre that, in later life, broke the camel's back and led to me being diagnosed as having CPTSD in 2013 some 22 years later.

Amongst other duties, Rob had to deal with the aftermath of the so-called 'Road to Basra', a by-word for the horrors of that conflict and I would defy anyone to experience those sights without consequences.

In many ways Op Nightingale took away the negative thoughts that were ruminating in my head and helped me to refocus them into doing the archaeology, and it became apparent that the more I did the archaeology the more impact it had on my recovery ... as from the beginning it helped me to realise that I wasn't alone with the issues I had to face on a daily basis, which in turn gave me more confidence and some purpose to life again. I was pleased with my involvement, as I got to meet so many great people over the years, along with the sites we did, and I would get involved at a drop of a hat again. The camaraderie was for a lot of people, including myself, one of the great things about doing archaeology, as everyone was able to have a good laugh and joke, which for maybe only a short time took away the pain.

In 2016 I was given the opportunity to do a degree in archaeology at Winchester University and duly, in November 2019, I graduated with a 2:1 in archaeology, and have now been working in commercial archaeology for the past two years, working on major infrastructure projects as part of the HS2 link and currently working on a project for Portsmouth Water, AND I am still getting involved with historical sites, visiting them with my family. From the very beginning I have been supported by my family, who also saw a positive change within me, and are now continuing to help and support me in *my archaeological career.*

Former Scots Guardsman and now professional archaeologist: Rob Cummings worked hard at Netheravon. © Harvey Mills

of these. Certainly, at Netheravon it proved to be crucial when an unexpected Chinook helicopter flight overhead triggered a traumatic response from one of the veterans participating. Our tent was the place of refuge and enabled the situation to be faced appropriately.

Several veterans joined us on this project, including Tyler Christopher, who we met in an earlier chapter, and Rob Cummings. I met Rob on the top of the ridgeline visible from Stonehenge, Beacon Hill, on the edges of Salisbury Plain overlooking the whole military training area. I was chatting with people about the First World War, as Beacon Hill holds some of the best-preserved practice trenches in the area. I needed someone who had served in the army to provide an infantryman's understanding of the features as we explained them to local radio as part of their First World War centenary commemorations, and Rob was that man. Rob had served in the first Gulf War as well as on tours of Northern Ireland with the Scots Guards.

This was one of Rob's earlier ventures with us and he was clearly not put off by the experience! The excavations itself was tricky in that we confirmed that not only had the badgers uncovered items but the barrow had definitely been visited by earlier archaeologists who had not left us with any records. We have no idea who this was but their methods had missed the area with all these incredible finds by only a metre or so.

We concentrated our excavation on the area around the badger hole, making sure we had the correct permissions from Natural England to make sure we were not going to disturb a still active sett. More traces of cremated bone emerged but we also retrieved some unburnt remains which had either been missed by earlier digging or put back as insignificant, even though one of the ribs we found had a cut mark made by a blade in, presumably, the Early Bronze Age. This was early evidence for inter-personal violence. As we have seen, there were weapons injuries found at Avon Camp and we had also dealt with the remains of people killed in conflict. There is an added level of poignancy when encountering such traces when you are working with those wounded in more modern times.

As we traced the line of the animal run we sieved the soil as it was removed in order to collect any further small elements of ash and cremated components. It was important to retrieve as much of this ash as possible as even tiny pieces can be analysed by an osteoarchaeologist. By the end we had recovered precisely 849.8 g of cremated bone; probably the remains of one individual, a young adult 20–23 years of age, which osteoarchaeologist Jackie McKinley thought probably male. The role of specialists is key to providing the story behind most of the excavation work and they come no better than Jackie.

Further items emerged too, including a small rectangle of blue-green bronze with a series of 'teeth' nicked into one edge to form a type of saw blade. Another part of this object had been seen on the surface of the mound before we began work so finding elements inside the barrow was exciting. To me, this looked as though it had been reshaped from an earlier object, like a bronze dagger, but we can't prove it. The excavation continued until it came to the source of the pottery; the rim of a large ceramic vessel still *in situ*. The pot had been turned upside down and placed into an oval-shaped grave some 1.5 m below the surface of the barrow as a 'secondary' deposit after the mound had been built and therefore not the reason for its original construction. The placing of an urn upside down is a common occurrence in Early Bronze Age burials. Although there was ash around it, it was likely that these cremated remains had been in some sort of organic bag, now vanished through decay. We couldn't say for certain that the group of objects found on the surface had definitely been associated with the pot but it would be an incredible coincidence were they not. The pot rim was recovered and, with all the many other sherds, could be seen to be a highly decorated (and huge) 'Collared Urn', the archetypal burial urn of the Early Bronze Age in southern Britain. One of the

Using a grid, Jackie plans the alignment of the badger sett, the location of the urn and the cremated bone. © Crown Copyright

unburned human bones later yielded a calibrated radiocarbon date of 1900–1690 BC, and an antler to 1940–1740 BC.

As with all the other elements of fieldwork, the end of the excavation is when much of the research and hard work begins; conserving the artefacts found, researching them to establish chronologies and parallels and writing up the reports associated with the project so that as many people as possible can learn about the discoveries and use the data for their own subsequent research. For example, although we were unable to determine the name of the excavator who had come before us, the best equivalent for the extraordinary chisel we had found came from a barrow on nearby Snail Down written up and illustrated by one of the most famous of Wiltshire antiquarians, Sir Richard Colt Hoare in his majestic work of 1812, *The History of Ancient Wiltshire*. The archer's wristguard or 'bracer' was possibly made from nephrite jade

Towards the bottom of one of the badger tunnels, the rim of an Early Bronze Age Collared Urn was found. It is around 4000 years old. © Crown Copyright

and the petrologist who studied it for us, told us the stone had certainly come from the European continent: I include it in particular as it is probably my best ever find!

All the finds were put on temporary display at the Wiltshire Museum in Devizes. By this time the pot had been put back together and it was very substantial at around 50 cm in height. To get it to the museum it was covered in bubble-wrap and strapped into the front seat of my car. I think it is probably my most cautious and careful drive since my driving test, many, many years ago. The urn joined 'Kenny's bucket' (see Chapter 6) on display and will ultimately call Devizes its permanent home.

Tom's quick thinking in reporting these finds facilitated this project and enabled us to provide excavation opportunities. Tom is good friends with both archaeologists and veterans involved in Operation Nightingale and this is symptomatic of one of the main benefits of our work: long-term relationships. He erected a cairn on one of the sites to commemorate the work of those involved. Although this was a short piece of fieldwork, it contributed a disproportionately large benefit to both the participants involved and to our understanding of the archaeology. The Netheravon barrows are no longer deemed to be at risk. I keep visiting the site, almost half-expecting to see more finds emerging even though the mound is now meshed over, but am delighted to report it does now seem pretty safe from badger attack.

MINISTRY OF D
PROPE
KEEP OU

9 CONCLUSIONS

Why we dig

SO WHY, YOU MAY ASK, do we do all this? The archaeological benefit is obvious – we have managed to examine lots of different sites and made numerous important discoveries. The work has enabled us to remove some monuments from being deemed 'Heritage at Risk', has resulted in reports that are now used as 'Best practice' guides and have led discussions on new methodologies, and several museums have much better collections. Furthermore, the presence of Operation Nightingale participants has enabled fieldwork to take place that otherwise would not have been possible; collecting thousands of pottery sherds over several weeks at East Chisenbury would have been incredibly expensive for example. We have added to academic knowledge with these results – the first Visigothic brooch from a grave in Britain, a new 'Brother' added to the *Band of Brothers* roll call, confirming final locations of tanks in battle and even the potential construction methods of Bronze Age houses.

Each piece of fieldwork has been designed to enable us to tell a story, as all good archaeology should. It has a report and, hopefully, will

Above: Into the clearing at Netheravon where sunshine now illuminates the barrow. © Alice Roberts

Opposite: The team at Burrow Island after another successful recovery. © Harvey Mills

encourage other people to look at further elements of research, thus enhancing our knowledge still further. But what about the other side of the project equation, the participants?

If we have been consistent in our aims of doing no harm to the archaeology, did we succeed from a human perspective too? There are a large number of anecdotal tales that would suggest this was the case but, from the very first days at East Chisenbury, we have wanted to ensure that this was backed further with some empirical results on the efficacy of the project as a whole.

In the first stages of the assessment of the participants that followed up the fieldwork, the sample and time duration were relatively small; a fortnight for around twenty participants, and we still haven't worked out a way of comparing the participants' well-being to those of similar veterans who did not take part in a project of this kind. Nevertheless, the studies by Dr Wasyl Nimenko (a doctor and psychotherapist attached to the Rifles, the Royal Air Force, and also the Royal Marines) and by Professor Alan Finnegan (a professor of nursing and military mental health) were promising – showing improvements in the lot of those that took part.

Operation Nightingale has now been running for well over a decade and we thus needed someone to acquire and assess data for the longer term. Step forward Dickie Bennett – initially a participant in the project and now the mainstay of the wellbeing component with the company he established: Breaking Ground Heritage (BGH). Dickie, as we have seen, was a former Royal Marine Commando with a large number of operational tours behind him and dug initially with us at Caerwent in Wales, Rat Island and Barrow Clump where he participated alongside his daughter.

> When I left the military I saw myself as worthless and a failure, I intentionally withdrew from my social circle. By coming to the project I was back with the military guys that spoke my language, who laughed at the same sort of things I laughed at. People open up and say 'I'm having a bad day'. Because we have all been there, we can all empathise. It creates a strong bond and a trusting friendship.

Paul Hemingway, Paul Barnsley and James Galvin outside the Crown pub at Aldbourne, forging friendships as the Americans had done 75 years before.
© Harvey Mills

Dickie immediately took to archaeology having enjoyed history but never really considering it before – his career was the Marines. Following a degree at the University of Exeter (First Class Honours no less), and a subsequent Masters degree, Dickie established BGH initially to assist us with recruiting personnel and also the logistics side of operations but, subsequently, to pick up the crucial assessment components, using a range of robust psychological assessment scales to measure the positive outcomes, if indeed there were any, and to examine how this change in the outlook of participants was occurring. Although this work is ongoing, many of the results have been published by Dickie – forming the most comprehensive and accessible corpus for such wellbeing projects. Dickie really examined three main components; the veterans' general wellbeing, their levels of anxiety, and their levels of depression. This was measured before, during and after the fieldwork elements and used standard assessment methodologies such as the Warwick Edinburgh Mental Wellbeing Scale General Anxiety Disorder – 7, and Personal Health Questionnaire – 9. The results were really impressive, showing noteworthy improvements in all categories. Some of the key reasons behind this success were picked out by Dickie and have been really useful in designing the projects; if we know what is promoting a positive increase in the mental health of the participants and the team enjoys doing it, then we can try to build this into our work. After all, although the digging is wonderful, this is only a small part of what I believe we need if each 'Exercise' is to work.

Above: Dickie Bennett (second left) and fellow Royal Marines in Afghanistan. © Richard Bennett

Below: Dickie Bennett checking the ivy for any human burials that might be eroding from the Burrow Island cliff. © Harvey Mills

Right: Standing in a hotel corridor, toasting the memories of the missing. Bullecourt 2017. © Harvey Mills

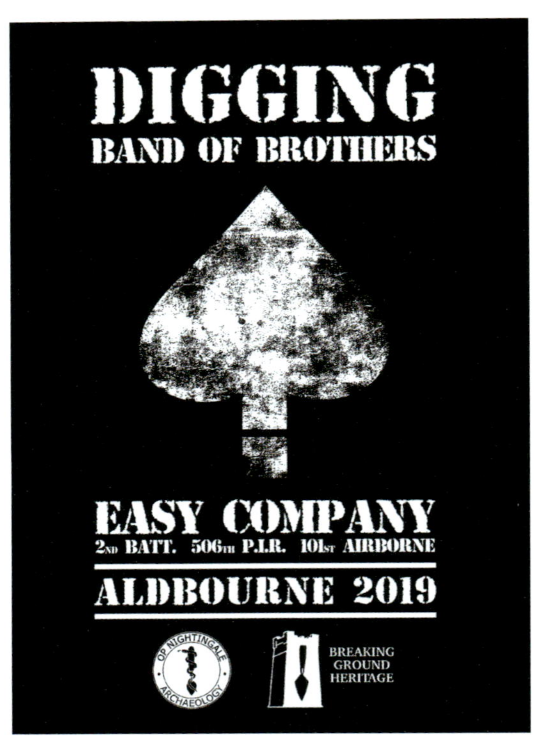

Below: One of our dig T-shirt designs. This is the Mark One Digging Band of Brothers shirt. The spade was the symbol of Easy Company. © Harvey Mills

For example, Dickie's examinations highlighted the importance of interpersonal relationships, something that archaeology really does provide if done well. Respondents to his surveys reported how they really looked forward to doing things in a group, to meeting old friends, and to being part of a team, I suppose to synthesise – having a sense of 'belonging'. This is of course something they would certainly have had in their military roles, with Regiment or Ship's Company being a very close bond, but why not a dig team with a T-shirt showing participation and thus 'belonging' as a civilian equivalent?

Developmental elements were also seen to be critical to results; of doing something meaningful. Both the work undertaken, and the results achieved are genuine. These are sites that for some reason or other, require a degree of intervention and by accomplishing the work, the team members will genuinely be contributing to our shared understanding and ensuring that heritage is not lost. People involved learn as they work, they progress, they find skills they have but were otherwise unaware of, they get jobs and careers and even university places, or hobbies, access to television stars and rugby heroes! By using skills passports, they can highlight their own personal development, from being able to give tours, to showing genuine drawing skills or logistical aptitude. Whilst there is a lot going on on the sites, it is essential that the projects ensure the team members can talk to people, without judgement. Dickie is adamant that we can signpost our new archaeologists to help that might be available to them. Breaking Ground Heritage has been able to develop relationships with other service charities that have the capacity to provide immediate support to those in need. This support might be financial, addressing homelessness, or pastoral but, more often than not, it is psychological. This is an important aspect of the Operation Nightingale project as it provides an additional safety net for those individuals that have somehow fallen through the cracks, for those who aren't aware of what support is available to them, or for those who are just too proud to ask for help. For some of the veterans, the digs are the first time they have felt able to open up about fundamental challenges they are experiencing within their lives. Dickie has said on more than one occasion that it is a badge of honour that Operation Nightingale should wear with pride, to have assisted in all the scenarios mentioned above and more.

Another element that Dickie concluded from his statistical examination was that the responses suggested that there really needs to be continuity.

This suggests that this change in mental health and wellbeing is fast acting and that it diminishes

Veteran Rob Steel contemplates the Canadian memorial at Vimy Ridge in France, lost in his own thoughts. © Harvey Mills

beyond the completion of the project. Participants returning on subsequent projects still have the same uplift in wellbeing and decrease in anxiety and depression, regardless of how many additional projects they attended.

Perhaps this is as good a reason as any why we need to ensure that Operation Nightingale and projects of similar ilk are supported.

I joined Dickie and Giles Woodhouse, former infantry officer, Head of Recovery (South) for Help for Heroes and archaeologist with Wessex Archaeology, at a parliamentary committee in June 2019 on wellbeing and heritage in the House of Lords where we discussed the merits of our programme and how archaeology can assist people. Lots of attempts have been made to improve the lot of servicemen and women on their return from duties that may have had long-term detrimental effects on their wellbeing. Such programmes could include art, gardening, drama and other imaginative projects. As we told the committee, archaeology has all of these (if you include the talks and tours as drama) and more. There is a job for everyone – physical, mental, artistic, practical, whimsical. For mentors and beginners alike. Work varies from day to day and gives the benefit of working outdoors and inside too – with so many other components.

What has also been genuinely heart-warming has been the response from archaeological professionals – from field units through to the statutory bodies, as well as military charities to all this. Throughout the programme, I think both sides have seen the mutual benefit of endeavours. In addition to winning the Ministry of Defence Sanctuary Awards for heritage projects, we have

Award winners at the Ministry of Defence Main Building; Operation Nightingale had won the heritage award. © Crown Copyright

At times we can call upon some pretty spectacular support; here a Royal Air Force Chinook lowers bags of chalk onto the Bulford Chalk kiwi as we restore the Scheduled Monument. © Harvey Mills

been really fortunate to have been presented with a couple of other trophies along the way; The Council for British Archaeology Award for 'Engagement' to the *Exercise Roundhouse* team with Butser, presented by old friend Raksha Dave, a decade after she had joined us with *Time Team* at Barrow Clump.

From a curatorial point of view, I was equally delighted that Operation Nightingale was presented with an Historic England 'Heritage Angel' award by historian and TV presenter Bethany Hughes and Andrew Lloyd Webber for the work we have done to remove monuments from 'At Risk Status'. Although projects like the barrow at Netheravon are part of this aspect, and the more glamorous side of things, just to emphasise that archaeology is not simply about 'digging' the team worked to maintain two other Scheduled Monuments on the Ministry of Defence estate, both altogether younger than the burial mound. The first of these was a scrub-cutting trip to clear the Napoleonic practice fortifications at Napier Lines, now home to King's Troop Royal Horse Artillery, at Woolwich in London, and the second was to re-scour and clean up a famous chalk hill figure in Wiltshire. Figures carved into the chalk hills of southern England are present in a variety of forms and dating from the prehistoric period to the 20th century. You may be familiar with the elegant Bronze Age lines of the Uffington White Horse and the 'earthy' look of the Cerne Abbas Giant but perhaps you have not heard of the Bulford Kiwi? This was carved by New Zealand soldiers at the end of the First World War and is a designated monument. Alongside serving soldiers, local volunteers and the New Zealand High Commission, Operation Nightingale participants clear weeds and scrub from this every year before spreading fresh chalk on it.

The evening of the Heritage Angel awards was also pretty memorable with a few of us able to attend an event in London. Amongst the veterans, as part of this delegation, was Tyler Christopher. The ceremony took place at the Palace Theatre in London and we were all in suits – unusual enough for archaeologists – but Tyler looked especially resplendent. In addition to his suit, he was using two particularly space-age looking prosthetic legs, really visible with his shorter trousers. The phenomenon of the new West End production of 'Harry Potter and the Cursed Child' was the new hot ticket in London and was being staged here at the Palace Theatre. Crowds were still held back and there was a red carpet outside. We were also told, in no uncertain terms, not to take photographs of the stage set – so the overall enclave was still surrounded by some showbiz magic. As we walked out of the theatre at night, along the carpet, there were still lots of tourists hoping to glimpse actors or celebrities and Tyler really fitted the bill – looking like a cross between Robocop and one of the fantastic components of the Hogwarts world. He was the subject of quite a few excited photographs and, dare I say, performed the part frighteningly well. The affirmation of these events is important as it emphasises that the archaeology work has been well done. From the start we were insistent that the digs we did were ones that had a genuine justification for undertaking; they would inform curation and management, recover deposits under threat, set standards and report findings.

If the goals for the archaeological worth of Operation Nightingale were clear, what design components work best for the participants? It will vary from dig to dig and I know that Alex, Guy and Phil in my team will have their own take on this but, for what it's worth, I believe these elements to be pretty important.

First: the chance of discovery; be it feature or object. Finding 'stuff', or at least the prospect of doing so, is really beneficial. I firmly believe that the thrill of being the first person to see/touch said object in X thousand years is one of those very human things that unites us. It all helps if this work takes place in a landscape of beauty, be it the Cotswolds, Salisbury Plain, Otterburn or Lulworth. If you are camping, having this as your 'window' is uplifting as you wake up each morning or watch the sun set before you go to the campfire. Big skies, big views, nature at its finest. This also draws in the thoughts on accommodation – camping or hotels? For some work the latter is the only option, having shared rooms helps too so that people can chat and look out for one another. The former, however, draws in the chance to have those chats around a campfire and to sleep by the site itself (always a special moment). It also saves the budget, and this is not to be taken lightly when putting together lots of projects. It can also assist if you want to take people to other local sites and museums, to contextualise their work and also to set their site in a regional context.

Staying on the site also helps to facilitate lots of other vignettes that all help to immerse the team in heritage: smithing, pottery making, re-enactors, field tutorials from experts such as zooarchaeologists, archaeobotanists, osteologists, photographers. The team gets to learn, gain new skills, increase their confidence. By dint of this they will also have the space to consider whether they want to do more work after the dig itself: to do research, volunteer for a museum or field unit or indeed even to go on to university to study archaeology as quite a number have now done. Several participants now work as professional archaeologists too.

The key is that they can make these choices and at the same time know who to ask for advice and assistance. All our diggers can choose whether they dig, or draw or survey – they set their own parameters. We also have only nominal work hours; while some like the routine of set timings,

Clockwise from top left:

The Bullecourt dig team stand in front of the most famous tank excavated, the Deborah. © Harvey Mills

The *Exercise Roundhouse* dig T-shirt ensured we could never forget the posthole configuration. © Harvey Mills

Our team at Butser Ancient Farm. © Harvey Mills

Pleased with one's handiwork. Veterans Richard Thompson and Elaine Corner look at the now complete Bronze Age roundhouse at Butser. © Harvey Mills

others like to pace themselves and it is sensible that all of them are aware that if they need a break, to take themselves to a quiet spot, that they can do this without fear of criticism.

We put a lot of the dig findings onto social media so people can see images of the finds made, can read the reports of results, see the post-excavations models made, learn about exhibitions and talks. By so doing, you can bring in a whole new audience and perhaps reach others for whom accessibility is otherwise a problem. Media outlets like *Time Team*, History Hit and *Digging for Britain* add exponentially to this reach and it is always enjoyable to read the 'banter' between team-mates as they spot themselves on the various productions.

Team compositions provide the dynamic that enables these sorts of projects to succeed. You need good, caring professional archaeologists (and also local volunteers that can ensure that the work will continue even if every veteran is having the sort of day that prevents their participation on site). This being said, if you allocate a feature of interest to a veteran, woe betide you giving it to somebody else in their absence – people invest emotionally in their work and this is a good thing. It is important they are able to see it through and it is poor form to take anything for a 'professional' to complete if it looks interesting or tricky. There must always be a way to facilitate continued involvement of the veteran even if extra input is required from the archaeologist. After all, access to many of these deposits is not only a privilege, it can also be incredibly relevant to the ethos of those participating and this really is empowering; if they build model kits, they can use soil from the actual site for the diorama, or bring in knowledge from their excavation work to really personalise their displays. Such an opportunity is unique.

By doing this you build teams, you create the desire to display digging 'battle honours' with the Dig T-shirt. You enthuse people to accomplish their own 'outreach', giving tours or mentoring newer participants. Participants can feel they are making progress not only in their fieldwork skills but also emotionally as they make important, and often lifelong, friendships.

The sites can draw families together; not only by providing respite for both the soldier or sailor doing the digging but also for their families. You can provide a safety net on site too by enabling family members such as a partner or their children to be with them in a cathartic, inclusive environment. Children are an interesting dynamic on such projects; whilst this builds in extra complications with safeguarding and risk assessments, there can be very valuable outputs whereby the veterans can become more of the carer than recipient. We have worked with the Jon Egging Trust – a charity established in memory of flight lieutenant Jon Egging, a pilot in the RAF display team the 'Red Arrows' who was killed in a crash in 2011 – to support vulnerable and under-confident young people to help mentor some of their students on our excavation projects and there does seem to be a bond of respect from the young people towards the veterans, which is an interesting dynamic.

Archaeology is a social activity. Kinship is forged on the digs, friends are reunited, people smile. There have been marriages resulting from Operation Nightingale projects between veterans and archaeologists, and the first Nightingale baby has been born!

It all began in an attempt to enable Corporal Winterton, 'Winno', to do some archaeology. For him 'just being around people and things like that. It slowly and surely builds you back up again'. You can face your demons but realise there is hope. Archaeology is about the study of people and it is a social activity *by* people. When, in preparation for this book, I asked the veterans what they had found valuable in the projects, the common denominator in all their answers was friendship. If archaeology is about people, then one of the key things that makes us human – friendship – is what makes this work.

Opposite: Why we dig. The faces of some of our incredible veterans that you have met in this book. Archaeology is something extraordinary, and so are they. Both represent the human spirit and indomitability. Courtesy of the Veterans

RHSW R 11
STRIKE FACE
FWD
01/07/

The sites and further reading

This section highlights where you can read more about the various Operation Nightingale excavations mentioned in the book. Some of the sites have published reports, others less formal accounts and all have what is known as a 'grey literature' report: a technical report of findings which has been submitted to the relevant local Historic Environment Record (HER) as a permanent, publicly accessible, record of the work undertaken.

Some sites are accessible to the public and this is noted below, though there may be little or nothing to see! Many are situated within the Salisbury Plain Training Area in Wiltshire and are not necessarily accessible (or not on a regular basis). Though there are many public rights of way, this is an active military training zone and all visitors must both stick to designated footpaths and bridleways and obey signs, especially red flags. Further information about access and routeways can be found at https://assets.publishing.service.gov.uk.

For a general introduction to the archaeology of Salisbury Plain see:

McOmish, D., Field, D. and Brown, G. 2002. *The Field Archaeology of the Salisbury Plain Training Area*. Published by English Heritage

CHAPTER 1

Chisenbury Midden

East Chisenbury Midden is a site that dates from the Late Bronze Age/Early Iron Age, around 700 BC. A large enclosure with deep ditch surrounded a settlement of roundhouses. The 'rubbish' pile of the midden itself is probably much more than just that: reflecting repeated episodes of celebration, bonding and expressions of power. The detritus in this area: pottery, animal bone, burnt flint and other objects, also includes chalk platforms where structures had been placed. Human remains were also found but the bones, when dated, seemed to be hundreds of years older than the settlement associated with the midden where they were found, suggesting curation and indicating importance of the ancestors in the lives of the living. Scientific assessment of the animal bone considered where they were raised before slaughter through study of the stable isotopic elements in the bones.

Opposite: The road to recovery – a chalk track leads to the excavations at Barrow Clump. © Harvey Mills

The Midden has incredible panoramic views and such big skies too. © Harvey Mills

The site of the midden was discovered in the middle of the 20th century by members of the Royal Air Force. Although it is not protected as a Scheduled Monument, the Ministry of Defence has it marked very clearly as an 'Important and Fragile Site', its top level of protection. It is marked on every map given to soldiers on military training, shaded blue to make it clear and also demarcated on the ground with palisades holding signs saying 'no digging'. The site lies on Salisbury Plain between East Chisenbury and Eversleigh. There are public footpaths in the general area but the midden site and enclosure are not obvious on the ground.

Andrews, P. 2021. East Chisenbury Midden 2015–17: further investigations of the late prehistoric midden deposits, enclosure and associated settlement. *Wiltshire Archaeological and Natural History Magazine*, 114, 84–121

McOmish, D., Field, D. and Brown G. 2010. The Bronze Age and Early Iron Age Midden Site at East Chisenbury, Wiltshire. *Wiltshire Archaeological & Natural History Magazine* 103, 35–101

Walshe, D., Osgood, R. and Brown, M. 2012. Archaeology as rehabilitation. *British Archaeology* 122 (January–February), 38–43

CHAPTER 2

Hessian Camp

The Hessian Camp, situated to the north of Winchester in Hampshire, was 'home' to thousands of mercenaries from Hesse, in what is now Germany. These men were employed at the outset of the Seven Years War with France (1756–1763) to help garrison southern Britain and were later employed within the Crown forces fighting in the American Wars of Independence. The location was well known, but it was only when the site was excavated in advance of housing development that the level of its preservation and association with Hampshire Regiment kitchens became clear. Nothing survived above ground before excavation and the site is now under a housing estate.

Osgood, R. and McCulloch, P. 2018. The Hessians of Barton Farm: when a German army defended Britain. *Current Archaeology* 345 (December), 20–25. Available at https://archaeology.co.uk/articles/features/the-hessians-of-barton-farm-uncovering-when-a-german-army-defended-britain.htm

Television

BBC *Digging for Britain*. Series 07 Episode 02 West (2018) https://www.bbc.co.uk/programmes/b0btc333/episodes/guide

Aldbourne

During the latter part of the Second World War that most famous of US military companies 'Easy Company' of the 101st Airborne Division, was stationed in the pretty Wiltshire village of Aldbourne during the build-up preparations for D-Day. Most of the men were housed either at Hightown Stables or in temporary huts and tents in the area of the village sports field, with officers billeted among local families and

Left: Trowelling around the field kitchen at Barton Farm. © Harvey Mills

Right: 'Hearts and Minds'. A Brylcream bottle emerges from the earth. © Harvey Mills

houses. The project undertaken by Operation Nightingale set out to establish if any traces of the Quonset huts (similar to Nissen huts) and other elements of the camp survived and to seek any memorabilia and personal/family remembrances of the American 'invasion' of this usually sleepy rural village. Ultimately the aim was to provide valuable information to inform both protection elements for the village and also for future planning considerations.

'Easy Company' has been made famous by the *Band of Brothers* TV series and Aldbourne attracts international visitors on a 'Band of Brothers' pilgrimage. The area of the camp, off Farm Lane, has been extensively levelled for football pitches and tennis courts but the original cookhouse is still standing. The stables at Hightown were demolished and shipped to the Currahee Military Museum ('Home of the Band of Brothers' in Toccoa, GA in 2004: https://www.toccoahistory.com/). The Aldbourne Heritage Centre in the village has displays relating to the village's wartime experience and includes objects recovered in the excavation. A short history of the Easy Company stay in Aldbourne can be found at https://aldbourneheritage.org.uk/village-history/.

Osgood, R. 2019. Overpaid, oversexed, and Under Aldbourne? Digging D-Day's '*Band of Brothers*'. *Current Archaeology*, 354 (September), 36-41 https://archaeology.co.uk/articles/features/overpaid-oversexed-and-under-aldbourne-digging-d-days-band-of-brothers.htm

Television

BBC *Digging for Britain*. Series 08 Episode 04 WWII Special (2019) https://www.bbc.co.uk/programmes/m000c5yk

History Hit TV *Uncovering the Band of Brothers* (2022) https://access.historyhit.com/uncovering-the-band-of-brothers

CHAPTER 3

Rat Island

Rat Island, properly known as Burrow Island, is the tip of a small peninsula of land extending into the west side of Portsmouth Harbour, almost directly opposite Nelson's flagship HMS *Victory* in the Historic Naval Base. Today it is little more than an unprepossessing tree and scrub covered sand and gravel hummock amidst the moorings of small boats, framed by the urban sprawls of Gosport and Portsmouth on either side of the harbour. The low cliffs along its shore have seen increased storm erosion over the last decades, leading to the discovery of the human remains that precipitated the Operation Nightingale investigation here. It was thought most likely that the remains represented burials of prisoners from convict 'hulk' ships that were moored in the harbour during various conflicts from the Napoleonic Wars into the 19th century. Radiocarbon dates from the site, coupled with limited historical documentation, show the probability that the burials were made from the mid-18th through until the earlier 19th century.

The 'island' is MOD property and strictly out of bounds to the public.

Osgood, R. 2018. A Wicked Noah's Ark: Exercise Magwitch and the prisoners of Rat Island. *Current Archaeology* 339 (June), 34–40

Osgood, R., Daniell, C., Márquez-Grant, N. and Bennett, R. 2017. *A Wicked Noah's Ark: Exercise Magwitch, Rat Island 2017* Available at: https://breakinggroundheritage.org.uk/onewebmedia/Ex%20Magwich%20report.pdf

Right: Viewed from Royal Clarence Yard, Burrow Island lies adjacent to a marina with the Spinnaker Tower on Portsmouth's seafront and HMS *Warrior* within the Historic Dockyard in the background. © Harvey Mills

Television

BBC *Digging for Britain*. Series 06 Episode 01 West (2017) https://www.bbc.co.uk/programmes/b09gfx7g/episodes/guide

Channel 4 *Britain's Most Historic Towns*. Series 3 Episode 3: Portsmouth (2020) https://www.channel4.com/programmes/britains-most-historic-towns/on-demand/70449-003

CHAPTER 4

Bullecourt

Bullecourt lies just south-east of Arras in the Pas-de-Calais, northern France. By 1917 it had been heavily fortified by the Germans as part of the Hindenburg line and saw two important, but not very well known, battles on 11 April and 3 May as part of the wider battle for Arras and its hinterland. There were many casualties, especially among the Australian and British infantry and the loss of much ordnance, including numerous tanks.

This area of northern France, of course, abounds with battle sites, cemeteries, museums and other sites of remembrance from the two World Wars but often with little to show on the ground. There is an excellent small museum in Bullecourt itself (https://www.arraspaysdartois.com/en/remembrance/visit-bullecourt-1917-museum/) and a walking trail. A good account of the battles can be found at https://sjmc.gov.au/first-second-battles-bullecourt/.

Osgood, R. 2017. *Mud, Blood, and green fields beyond: Exercise Joan of Arc, Bullecourt 2017.* Unpublished interim report Available at: https://breakinggroundheritage.org.uk/about-1/ex-joan-of-arc-1.html

Osgood, R. 2018. *Mud, Blood, and green fields beyond: Exercise Joan of Arc, Bullecourt 2018.* Unpublished interim report Available at: https://breakinggroundheritage.org.uk/onewebmedia/Bullecourt%202018.pdf

Osgood, R. 2019. Under the track: the Battle of Bullecourt. *Iron Cross* 1, 62–65

Osgood, R. 2019. Mud, blood, and green fields: an archaeology of the First World War at Bullecourt. *Current World Archaeology* 94 (April/May), 28–33

Military history

Coombs, D. 2017. *The Battles of Bullecourt 1917*. Published by Big Sky Publishing.

Kendall, P. 2017. *Bullecourt 1917: Breaching the Hindenberg Line*. Published by History Press

Television

BBC *Digging for Britain*. Series 07 Episode 03 East (2018) https://www.bbc.co.uk/programmes/m0001jg7

Mametz Wood

Mametz Wood played a strategic role in the first few days of the Battle of the Somme, which began on 1 July 1916. It was heavily defended by experienced German troops, blocking the advance of the British who had already suffered horrific casualties. Leading the attack were soldiers from the 38th Welsh Division who were charged, on 7 July, with making a frontal attack in daylight and were mowed down by machine guns. It wasn't until 12 June that the woods were taken, with the loss of about one-fifth of the Welsh infantry, many to brutal hand-to-hand combat in the infamous sea of mud. Close to the surviving woodland, down a narrow country lane, is a memorial to the 38th Welsh, topped with a splendid red dragon.

Former Royal Marine Ric Coulson excavates the remains of fallen soldiers. © Harvey Mills

Osgood, R. 2015. *A certain cure for lust of blood: archaeological excavation report Mametz Wood, Somme. 2015*. Unpublished interim report. Available at: https://breakinggroundheritage.org.uk/onewebmedia/Mametz%20Archaeological%20Excavation%20%20Report.pdf

Military history

Hicks, J. 2016. *The Welsh at Mametz Wood. The Somme 1916*. Published by Y Lolfa Cyf

Television

BBC Wales and the Somme: Gareth Thomas and the Battle of Mametz Wood (2016) https://www.bbc.co.uk/programmes/b07jj41w

Perham Down

A complex of full-size practice trenches, known as the 'Bedlam Trenches', was dug during the First World War on Perham Down, near Tidworth on the edge of Salisbury Plain. These replicated German trench systems in the Somme region, enabling soldiers to learn trench warfare tactics by practising attacking the enemy lines, as well as learning how to construct trenches. No earthworks survive above ground, but there is a lane in the village called *Somme Road*!

Perham Down World War 1 Practice Trenches, Salisbury Plain, Hampshire. January 2017. Archaeological Evaluation Report. Salisbury: Wessex Archaeology Ref: 113940. Available at: https://breakinggroundheritage.org.uk/onewebmedia/Perham%20Down%20Evaluation%20Report%20v1.pdf

Television

BBC *Digging for Britain*. Series 05 Episode 01 West (2017) https://www.bbc.co.uk/programmes/b084xym3

CHAPTER 5

Every year a few applications are received by the Ministry of Defence under the terms of the *Protection of Military Remains Act* (1986) to excavate the remains of crashed aircraft; but most have already been explored in some way. In the majority of cases there is nothing to show on the ground surface that any wreckage might be present and most are found by accident or as a result of often very detailed examination of historic records made by enthusiasts. The crash sites discussed here, of a Spitfire and a Hurricane from the Battle of Britain of 1940, were identified through a combination of literature and air photographic searches combined with local knowledge, followed by non-intrusive survey work and, finally, excavation.

British veteran Mark Mortiboys with two of the Polish team members, Emil Maluk and Łukasz Zub. Such multinational team composition is a valuable dynamic of the project. © Harvey Mills

Spitfire

The pilot of this aircraft, Paul Baillon, was a pupil at Ratcliffe School, Leicester. A school project was initiated alongside the excavation to research Baillon's war career and his loss. It can be found at: https://ratcliffespitfire.com/paul-baillon/.

Osgood, R. 2014. Recovering Spitfire P9503: Exercise Tally Ho! *British Archaeology* 136, 30–35

Osgood, R. 2014. Exercise Tally Ho! Archaeological Project Report for the Recovery of Spitfire P9503 at Lidbury, near Upavon Wiltshire under the Protection of Military Remains Act (1986). Report for English Heritage. Available at: https://historicengland.org.uk/images-books/publications/exercise-tally-ho/diospitfirep9503-final-report/

Hurricane

Television

BBC *Digging for Britain*. Series 04 Episode 03 East (2016) https://www.bbc.co.uk/programmes/b073mr9r

CHAPTER 6

Barrow Clump

Barrow Clump is a small area of woodland on a west facing slope overlooking the River Avon at Figheldean on Salisbury Plain. As the name suggests, an upstanding burial mound survived within it. This was the last survivor of a group of barrows comprising a Bronze Age cemetery that had otherwise been ploughed flat in the surrounding fields. Operation Nightingale's project here resulted from the need to assess and control damage to the barrow made by badgers and resulted, in addition to excavation of the Bronze Age barrow, in the discovery of archaeology dating from the Neolithic period, with an Anglo-Saxon cemetery focused on the earlier Bronze Age mound(s). The imposition of Saxon burials on or into prehistoric burial sites is not an unusual occurrence in this area.

Barrow Clump is on farmland in an area of managed access within the Salisbury Plain Training Area. A public footpath runs close beside it on the south-eastern side. Finds from the excavation are now in the Wiltshire Museum, Devizes, with some pieces on display (https://wiltshiremuseum.org.uk).

Andrews, P., Last, J., Osgood, R. and Stoodley, N. 2019. *A Prehistoric Burial Mound and Anglo-Saxon Cemetery at Barrow Clump, Salisbury Plain, Wiltshire: English Heritage and Operation Nightingale excavations 2003–14*. Salisbury: Wessex Archaeology Monograph 40 (available from Oxbow Books)

Andrews, P., Last, J., Osgood, R. and Stoodley, N. 2020. Warriors ancient and modern: digging Barrow Clump. *British Archaeology* 172 (May/June), 20–27

Osgood. R. 2018. Bearing arms on Salisbury Plain: Anglo-Saxon sword burials at Barrow Clump. *Current Archaeology* 343 (October), 14–15

Osgood, R. and Andrews, P. 2015. Excavating Barrow Clump: soldier archaeologists and warrior graves. *Current Archaeology* 306 (September), 28–35

Television

Channel 4 *Time Team*. Series 20 Episode 05 Warriors (2012) https://www.tvguide.com/tvshows/time-team/episodes-season-20/1000185730/

BBC *Digging for Britain*. Series 03 Episode 02 West (2015) https://www.bbc.co.uk/programmes/b052775b

BBC *Digging for Britain*. Series 07 Episode 02 West (2018) https://www.bbc.co.uk/programmes/b0btx2zs

Cherington

The Gloucestershire village of Cherington lies in the Cotswolds near Shipston-on-Stour. The Operation Nightingale project came about as the result of reporting of metal detector finds of

Matt Smith excavating one of several Early Bronze Age burials in further investigations at the Clump. © Harvey Mills

Anglo-Saxon objects, which proved to have been ploughed out from a small cemetery. Indications of the presence of a small, rural Roman villa were also encountered.

Marsden, K., Nichol, M. and Osgood, R. 2019. *Current Archaeology* 356 (November), 26–31.

Television

BBC *Digging for Britain*. Series 08 Episode 01 West (2019) https://www.bbc.co.uk/programmes/m000bn2l

Avon Camp

Avon Camp lies on MOD-owned land in the Avon Valley just north of Figheldean, on the opposite side of the river and within sight of Barrow Clump. Proposals for a new Artillery Museum required archaeological work to be carried out on the site to identify any significant archaeological remains. Although the project was abandoned, the discovery of Anglo-Saxon burials soon leaked out and the site was in danger of looting, so excavation was undertaken as an Operation Nightingale project. A ring-ditch and well-furnished Saxon graves were excavated.

Sean uncovers the grave of a child at Avon Camp, an inhumation that expressed so much reverence. © Harvey Mills

Television

BBC *Digging for Britain*. Series 09 Episode 05 West (2022) https://www.bbc.co.uk/programmes/m0013f61

CHAPTER 7

Dunch Hill

Dunch Hill is a ridge of mixed arable, managed grazed downland and woodland overlooking the River Bourne within the Salisbury Plain Training area on its eastern boundary. It is crossed by a complex of earthworks including a later Bronze Age 'linear ditch' – one of numerous such bank and ditch monuments that stretch for miles across the chalk downs of southern England. The ridge is also largely covered by extensive prehistoric field systems and dotted with burial monuments. The laying of a stone track across the military area here in the 2000s required archaeological investigation along its route and a Bronze Age settlement, comprising roundhouses and other structures, was discovered. A plan to remove ploughing consent from the area of the settlement led to the instigation of the Operation Nightingale project to further examine the layout of its buildings and associated features.

Dunch Hill lies right on the edge of the 'Danger Zone' of Salisbury Plain and is criss-crossed by numerous public footpaths, bridleways and by-ways. The earthworks, barrows and parts of the field systems are clearly visible.

Volunteer Janine Peck teaches former Royal Logistics Corps soldier Jesse Swanson how to draw his feature. © Harvey Mills

Andrews, P. 2006. A Middle to Late Bronze Age Settlement at Dunch Hill, Tidworth. *Wiltshire Archaeology and Natural History Magazine* 99, 51–78

Creighton, T., Osgood, R. and Pope, R. 2022. An experiment in earthen walls. Operation Nightingale, Butser Ancient Farm, and the Dunch Hill Roundhouse. *Current Archaeology* 383 (February), 28–35

Dunch Hill Salisbury Plain Wiltshire, Archaeological Excavation Report. March 2021. Wessex Archaeology Report Accession Number DZSWS:25-2020. Ref: 233640.04

Butser

Set in a green downland valley near Chalton, Hampshire, Butser Ancient Farm was founded in the 1970s by landscape archaeologist Peter Reynolds, initially to learn about and demonstrate how to build an Iron Age roundhouse using ancient technology. Peter's experimental approach has been hugely influential in British archaeology and Butser quickly expanded to become a leading educational centre for experimental archaeology, ancient building and farming techniques and a host of other activities based around archaeological knowledge and experimentation. It is also a genuine 'ancient' farm growing crops from prehistory and keeping rare breeds of animals. It is open to the public and for school visits at weekends and holidays during the summer and holds many special events and workshops: https://www.butserancientfarm.co.uk/.

Janine and Jesse taking the turves from the site stripping to form one of the experimental roundhouse walls. The entire footprint of the building only produced enough turf for one wall. © Harvey Mills

Operation Nightingale was responsible for adding a new, Bronze Age, roundhouse to the farm's collection of ancient buildings, based on the plans of buildings excavated at Dunch Hill.

Creighton, T., Osgood, R. and Pope, R. 2022 (February). An experiment in earthen walls. Operation Nightingale, Butser Ancient Farm, and the Dunch Hill Roundhouse. *Current Archaeology* 383, 28–35

Television

BBC *Digging for Britain* Series 09 Episode 02 South (2022) https://www.bbc.co.uk/programmes/m001363k

CHAPTER 8

Netheravon barrow

Netheravon barrow sits between two other burial mounds in a woodland clearing by the entrance to the old Royal Flying Corps base at Netheravon in the Avon Valley north of Salisbury, Wiltshire. As with the mound at Barrow Clump, this barrow was being badly damaged by badgers who had brought Bronze Age pottery and other finds to the surface. Excavation by Operation Nightingale recovered the cremated remains of a young adult and some important artefacts dating to the Early Bronze Age. A public footpath runs through the woods.

Andrews, P. and McKinley, J. 2019. A Remarkable Discovery – an Early Bronze Age cremation burial at Figheldean, Wilshire. *Wiltshire Archaeological and Natural History Magazine* 112, 37–73. Available at: https://www.academia.edu/59258696/The_Collared_Urn_in_A_remarkable_discovery_an_Early_Bronze_Age_cremation_burial_at_Figheldean_Wiltshire

The team decide upon locations to excavate around the disused badger sett.

CHAPTER 9

A key element of the Operation Nightingale ethos is the assessment and monitoring of the, sometimes intangible, beneficial effects of the projects on the lives and wellbeing of the participants. It is important that the findings are publicised, not only to demonstrate the efficacy of the programme itself, but to inform a much wider audience of professional bodies and the public alike of some, perhaps not very obvious, opportunities for therapeutic activities that may be able assist in the alleviation of a variety of medical and mental health conditions such as PTSD. Such conditions are not, of course, confined to members of the armed forces.

Bennett, R. 2022. How do interventions using heritage-based activities, impact on mental health and wellbeing? An analysis of Breaking Ground Heritage and Operation Nightingale outcomes. In Everill, P. and Burnell, K. (eds) *Archaeology, Heritage, and Wellbeing: authentic, powerful, and therapeutic engagement with the past*, 197–207. Published by Routledge

Everill, P., Bennett, R. and Burnell, K. 2020. Dig in: an evaluation of the role of archaeological fieldwork for the improved wellbeing of military veterans. *Antiquity* 94 (373), 212–227 https://breakinggroundheritage.org.uk/onewebmedia/dig_in_an_evaluation_of_the_role_of_archaeological_fieldwork_for_the_improved_wellbeing_of_military_veterans.pdf

Finnegan, A. 2016. The biopsychosocial benefits and shortfalls for armed forces veterans engaged in archaeological activities. *Nurse Education Today* 47, 15–22. DOI:10.1016/j.nedt.2016.03.009

Nimenko, W. and Simpson, R.G. 2014. Rear Operations Group medicine: a pilot study of psychological decompression in a Rear Operations Group during Operation HERRICK 14. *Journal of the Royal Army Medical Corps* 160, 295–297. https://www.researchgate.net/publication/259386012_Rear_Operations_Group_medicine_a_pilot_study_of_psychological_decompression_in_a_Rear_Operations_Group_during_Operation_HERRICK_14

Osgood, R. 2018. Marching on: the latest manoeuvres of Operation Nightingale. *Current Archaeology* 338 (May), 41–47 https://archaeology.co.uk/issues/current-archaeology-338-now-on-sale.htm

Paul Hemingway and Paul Barnsley at Littlecote House, home of HQ Company of the 506th Airborne in 1944. © Harvey Mills

Index

Numbers in *italic* denote pages with figures. Place names are in Wiltshire, unless otherwise stated.